THE TRUTH ABOUT
HARVARD

A Behind-the-Scenes Look
at Admissions and Life
on Campus

THE TRUTH ABOUT HARVARD

A Behind-the-Scenes Look at Admissions and Life on Campus

BY

DOV FOX

Random House, Inc.
New York
www.PrincetonReview.com

Princeton Review Publishing, L. L. C.
2315 Broadway
New York, NY 10024
E-mail: bookeditor@review.com

ISBN 0-375-76435-6

Editorial Director: Robert Franek
Editor: David Daniel
Designer: Scott Harris
Production Editor: Vivian Gomez
Production Coordinator: Scott Harris

Manufactured in the United States of America

9 8 7 6 5 4 3 2 1

First Edition

ACKNOWLEDGMENTS

In memory of
my grandparents.

I'd like to thank the Judith and Karl Thomas Foundation for making it possible for me to attend Harvard; Professor Michael J. Sandel for providing inspiration and mentorship during my time in Cambridge; Professor Bob Whitman for having confidence in me to write a book about undergraduate life; *The Harvard Crimson* for providing groundwork for my research; the students, staff, faculty, and administrators of Harvard College for their willingness to share with me their thoughts and experiences; John Weber for giving me lodging accommodations while I wrote; Brett Leghorn for encouraging me throughout the writing process; my brothers for being my greatest friends; and, most of all, my mom for loving and supporting me always.

CONTENTS

Preface 1

Chapter One: Reputation and Admissions 7

Chapter Two: The Student Body 33

Chapter Three: Academic Life 59

Chapter Four: Dormitory Life 105

Chapter Five: Extracurricular Life 127

Chapter Six: Social Life 145

Chapter Seven: Life Beyond Campus 159

Chapter Eight: Campus Discipline 173

Chapter Nine: Campus Health Care 181

Conclusion 191

Internet Resources 197

Appendix 201

Endnotes 207

PREFACE

My time at Harvard has been pretty eventful. I've had classmates like Tatyana Ali ('02), Natalie Portman ('03), and Jonathan Taylor Thomas ('04). I've learned from professors like Alan Dershowitz, Sam Huntington, and Stephen Jay Gould. And I've seen guest speakers on campus from Maya Angelou, Will Ferrell, Connie Chung, Chevy Chase, and Larry Flynt to Pakistani President Pervez Musharraf, Serbian Prime Minister Zoran Djindjic, Japanese Prime Minister Junichiro Koizumi, and Bill Clinton.

I've twice watched Pedro Martinez and Roger Clemens face off at Fenway Park, witnessed the Celtics' 2002 26-point fourth-quarter playoff comeback at the Fleet Center, and rushed the field in New Haven when Harvard football in 2001 capped its first undefeated season since 1913 with a victory over Yale. I've been evacuated from campus buildings when my roof collapsed fall semester of my freshmen year, when my basement caught fire spring semester of my sophomore year, and when a man walked into our 2000 final exam for "Images of Alexander the Great" and threatened to blow up the building. I've listened to the Boston Symphony Orchestra perform Mozart at Symphony Hall, watched whales off Boston Harbor, and observed closing arguments for the Federal District Court case legalizing same-sex marriages in the Common-wealth of Massachusetts. I've sledded down the steps of Widener Library on a cafeteria tray, caught sunrises while rowing a one-man skull on the Charles River, and run laps—along with hundreds of other naked undergraduates— around Harvard Yard in below freezing temperatures on the night before final exams.

I couldn't anticipate any of this when I was a junior or senior in high school. I had no idea what life at Harvard—or any other college—would be like.

I was thrilled to be accepted to Harvard in 2000, but I had no idea whether I'd like going there. I looked all over for information about student life at Harvard. I'd scrutinized rankings by *U.S. News & World Report*, pored over blurbs by *Barrons* and *Yale Daily News,* examined the university's websites for "Undergraduate Admissions" and "College Student Life," went on Pre-Frosh Weekend and freshman orientation programs, visited the Cambridge campus, followed guided tours, attended class lectures, corresponded with faculty, wandered around Boston, and stayed overnight with undergraduates. But after tapping every available resource, all I'd figured out was that most admissions officers, tour guides, and blurbs were either shallow or uninformed and that I was kidding myself thinking I could get a good sense of what it was like to go to Harvard simply by talking to a few kids, sitting in on a few classes, and going to a few parties. When I finally committed to Harvard, I still didn't have a sense of what life was like as a student at Harvard or how an undergraduate experience there would be different than it would be anywhere else I'd applied.

Students accepted at Harvard are usually choosing among five types of schools.

(1) Top large liberal arts schools like Princeton, Yale, Stanford, and Duke

(2) Top small liberal arts schools like Williams, Amherst, Wellesley, and Swarthmore

(3) Top math/science schools like California Institute of Technology (Caltech) and Massachusetts Institute of Technology (MIT)

(4) Top state schools like the University of Virginia, the University of California—Berkeley, the University of North Carolina (UNC)—Chapel Hill, the University of Wisconsin—Madison, and the University of Michigan—Ann Arbor

(5) Top pre-professional schools like Julliard (music), Wharton (business), and the UNC School of Journalism and Mass Communication (journalism).

Each offers distinctive advantages over Harvard, such as lower costs, smaller classes, more school spirit, or a narrower focus on intellectual interests or professional studies. Harvard students say that the most important reasons they choose to attend Harvard instead of other schools are: (1) prestige/name recognition, (2) academic programs, (3) geographical location, (4) graduate school preparation, (5) financial assistance, (6) social atmosphere, (7) student diversity, and (8) family pressure.[1] But prospective Harvard undergrads have no idea whether or not they'll be happy at college for the next four years if they choose Harvard or anywhere else. They may know why they chose Harvard, but they don't know how accurate their perceptions were or whether they'll be happy with their reasons for choosing it, four years down the line.

As a high school senior, I wanted to know exactly how Harvard decided who to accept, what the students were like, how much of an advantage the Harvard name actually provided in landing big name opportunities during summer and after graduation, what the social life on campus was like, whether professors took the time to get to know students, how hard the classes were, and what my chances were with the ladies.

This book answers all the really tough questions about life at Harvard. Based on interviews with more than 3,000 Harvard College students, surveys polling more than 5,000 Harvard undergraduates, and four years of personal experience as a student in the Harvard College ('04), this book presents a candid and comprehensive take on every aspect of life at Harvard—from the admissions process to post-graduation career prospects; from one-on-one tutorials to 1,000-student lectures; from food, dorms, facilities, and safety on campus to cheating, date rape, depression, and suicide; from drugs, alcohol, and sex within the student body to grade inflation, race relations, and dining hall conversations.

This is what it's really like to go to Harvard.

CHAPTER ONE
REPUTATION AND ADMISSIONS

THE HARVARD NAME

"Gather 'round, children of Crimson, and pay homage to the name. It is the name that brought you here and, often, it is the name that keeps you here. The name will open doors for you. From internships to consulting jobs to admission to the best retirement homes, the name of Harvard takes care of its own."[2]

It's no secret why Harvard attracts the best and brightest undergraduates in the world. Students believe that their affiliation with Harvard's reputation will carry lifelong professional advantages. Forty-two percent of Harvard undergraduates say that prestige/name recognition is the most important reason they chose to go to Harvard.[3] Prospective students are lured to Harvard foremost by the prospect of reaping personal gain from the institution's illustrious educational renown and the high-powered infrastructure of 270,000 living alums, among which number vats of CEOs, doctors, lawyers, entrepreneurs, and entertainers. As one student explains: "When people ask why I chose Harvard over other schools in my senior year of high school, I always try to give an objective answer: interesting courses, a diverse student body, great reputation, and all of the other familiar factors. Few of us openly admit which card really trumped our decision. For almost too many of us, it was certainly the mystical and romantic fascination our society has with the institution."[4]

Harvard's consummate name recognition reflects the superior scope of its libraries, museums, and laboratories; the extraordinary contributions of its students, faculty, and alums; and "its access to the money that made it all possible."[5] *The Boston Globe* agrees: "By nearly every measure, Harvard stands at a pinnacle of power and prestige. It boasts an unmatched 90 libraries, 35 Nobel Prize-winners, 12 museums, 41 varsity teams, and dozens of think tanks that help shape national policy and rebuild faltering economies from Latin America to the Pacific Rim."[6]

Regardless of what you do with your Harvard education—whether your major undergraduate achievement is discovering a new chemical element or taking first place in your suite's *Zelda* contest—your acceptance to Harvard in itself constitutes among the most stately status-symbols that money can't buy, what author Melanie Thernstrom ('87) calls an "irrevocable stamp of approval" that "connotes not so much intelligence as chosenness—a destiny to do significant, lucrative work, a kind of good luck charm, whose spell is always new."[7] It is this everlasting talisman that entices 20,000 students to apply each year and, for the magical chosen few, to enroll.

But how much advantage does going to Harvard *really* provide in the pursuit of fellowships, grad school admissions, and well-paying job offers after college? The advantage, according to Bill Wright-Swadel, Director of Career Services at Harvard College, is an "issue of perception." Harvard's reputation for academic excellence gives Harvard College grads a distinct edge against grads from less prestigious institutions, but means no more to fellowship, grad school, and employment entrance committees in the United States than similarly reputable colleges and universities like Princeton, Yale, Stanford, Duke, MIT, Caltech, Williams, Amherst, and Swarthmore. Almost 200 firms and corporations, including high-profile financial consulting and investment banking companies, like Goldman Sachs, Smith Barney, and McKinsey and Company, recruit Harvard undergraduates at the on-campus career fair each year. Sixty percent of Harvard College students find immediate employment after graduation, and 30 percent are accepted to enroll at graduate schools. These statistics on recruiting, employment, and admissions for Harvard students far exceed national averages but are nearly identical to those at other top colleges and universities.[8]

There are, however, three broad post-collegiate pursuits where Harvard graduates stand out against those at even the foremost institutions. Harvard undergrads enjoy disproportionate rates of success in national fellowship award competitions, in Harvard's graduate and professional school admissions, and in opportunities outside of the United States. Paul Bohlmann, Director of Fellowships at the Office of Career Services, reports that one of every fifteen fellowship applications submitted by Harvard undergraduates, and one of every eight Harvard applicants overall, wins a fellowship award each year, higher proportions than at any other college or university in the United States.

That Harvard consistently tallies so many Marshall, Fulbright, Goldwater, and Rhodes scholars is most tellingly attributable not to name recognition and prestige, but rather to the extraordinary caliber of advising available at the college's Fellowship Office, far and away the most extensive in the country. Harvard's highly regarded law, business, and medical schools, which accept fewer than 10 percent of all applicants, always take an excessively higher percentage of undergrads from Harvard than from other top schools. Harvard Law School, for example, accepted just 555 out of 5,900 applicants (nine percent) for its overall Class of 2004, but admitted 70 out of 169 applicants (41 percent) that year from Harvard College.[9] Although Harvard undergrads tend to score well on graduate and professional school entrance exams, the large numbers with which they are accepted to the university's post-collegiate degree programs follows in part from a special brand of confidence that admissions office reserve for the graduates of Harvard College.

The influence of the Harvard name is most strikingly reflected in the professional advantage that Harvard undergrads encounter among international enterprises. Unique among every other institution of higher learning, Harvard implies excellence in education to people all around the globe. None among Princeton, Yale, Stanford, MIT, Oxford, and Cambridge command universal prominence as does Harvard. "Harvard is the key to … opening up whatever you want in Japan," says one former undergraduate now working for JP Morgan in Tokyo. "If you went to Harvard," she says, "you are automatically elevated to some kind of 'super-human' status."[10] Harvard College graduates report experiencing similar professional advantages in countries across North America, South America, Central America, the Caribbean, Europe, Africa, Asia, the Middle East, and Australia. In general, former Harvard students report, "the further you get away from Boston, the more famous [the Harvard name] becomes."[11] The one glaring exception is the American South, where the Harvard name carries less weight and where there are comparably few Harvard alums to provide professional connections.[12]

The Harvard name also carries social meaning for undergraduates. When you leave the gates of Harvard Yard, almost everyone you encounter has opinions about what your Harvard affiliation says about you as a person. There's no shortage of material on which opinions about Harvard can be formed. Harvard is mentioned every week in the media on account of a recent faculty appointment, academic accomplishment, or alumni donation. "It's easy to make a story out of Harvard," says Ethan Bronner, former education correspondent and current editorial page editor at *The New York Times*. "[I]t's kind of like endless sex appeal."[13] Cultural references are dropped in dozens of novels, movies, and TV shows. Harvard College is given prominent attention even in landmark opinions of the United States Supreme Court, such as the 1978 affirmative action case of *Regents of the University of California v. Bakke*.[14]

People tend to label Harvard undergraduates as smart, talented, hard-working, rich, privileged, preppy, and, most of all, conceited. When they say that they go to Harvard, students hear the same replies again and again: "Oh, Hahvad!", or "What'd you get on your SATs?", or "So you want to be president of the United States, huh?" Hesitant to incur a stereotype of intellectual elitism, most students attempt to avoid telling people they go to Harvard by saying they go to college in "the Northeast," "New England," "Massachusetts," "Boston," or "Cambridge." But people always manage to narrow it down to Harvard, such that you are left exuding an image ranging from snotty prick to geography twit.

The Harvard typecast for narcissism and pomposity is perpetuated by pop culture, on-campus frills, and Harvard itself, which Victor S. Thomas Professor of Government and Sociology Theda Skocpol calls "the most arrogant university in the western world."[15] Harvard students are portrayed as self-important snobs in movies like *Love Story* (1970), *The Paper Chase* (1973), *A Small Circle of Friends* (1980), *Soul Man* (1986), *With Honors* (1994), *Good Will Hunting* (1999), *Harvard Man* (2001), *Prozac Nation* (2001), *Legally Blonde* (2001), *How High* (2002), *Stealing Harvard* (2002), and *Homeless to Harvard* (2003).

Campus luxuries reinforce the cinemagraphic depictions of toffee-nosed Harvard students: undergraduates live in lavish dorm rooms housed by flowery Georgian architecture; they eat in majestic dining halls enclosed by stained-glass windows, where oil paintings and marble sculptures line the walls, and chandeliers hang from palatial ceilings; they take classes and attend forums with world leaders and academic superstars; they have unlimited access to the greatest museums, libraries, and laboratories in the world; they regularly don tuxes and formal dresses for black-tie dances, dinners, and Masters' teas; and they are set apart from the surrounding city by massive cast-iron fences that radiate an imposing exclusivity.

Besides pigeonholing motion pictures and on-campus trimmings, Harvard's reputation for superciliousness grows out of its all-consuming fixation with itself.[16] History concentrators study the institution of Harvard during the junior year tutorial. Other students enroll in Religion 1513, "Harvard: Five Centuries and Eight Presidents," taught by Pusey Minister and Plummer Professor of Christian Morals Peter J. Gomes, who since 1974 has drawn generations of university members and resident Bostonians to the sermons on life, religion, and Harvard he delivers each Sunday at The Memorial Church and to the open teas he hosts every Wednesday at his home just outside Harvard Yard.[17] Widener Library maintains an entire division devoted to Harvard archives and another to "Harvardania." This book probably doesn't help much either. Nor does the standard roll-call of Harvard College alumni that admissions officers so relish reeling off: Ralph Waldo Emerson (Class of 1821), John Quincy Adams (Class of 1822), Henry David Thoreau (Class of 1839), Oliver Wendall Holmes (Class of 1861), Franklin Delano Roosevelt (Class of 1904), John Fitzgerald Kennedy (Class of 1949), and other dead white guys with three names.

The impression that your Harvard affiliation has on potential romantic interests depends largely on your personality. The Harvard name is an asset in attracting significant others to the degree that you're associated more with the intellectual component of the Harvard reputation than with the elitist or nerdy components. "If you're a borderline dork, then Harvard seals you as a dork," one undergraduate reports. "[But] [i]f you're kind of smooth, then the name can only help."[18] As long as you're socially capable, potential romances tend to associate your status as a Harvard student with success and intelligence, qualities that usually aren't too bad to have in your back pocket when you're on the prowl. "I think I'm more charming [to girls] because I go to Harvard," says one student. "I would say 60 percent of it is my personality and 40 is definitely because I go to Harvard. [T]hey assume that you're going to be rich and successful. They think that you're a more worldly, amazing person because you go to Harvard."[19]

The Admissions Process

Harvard College maintains the lowest acceptance rate and highest yield rate of any school in the country.[20] About 20,000 students apply to Harvard each year. The vast majority of applicants have course curriculums, grade point averages (GPAs), and standardized test scores that suggest they could handle Harvard academics without a problem. Dean of Admissions and Financial Aid William R. Fitzsimmons affirms that, 80 to 90 percent of applicants are qualified to be [at Harvard]."[21] But the college offers admission to fewer than ten percent of those who apply.[22] Harvard is the most selective among the seven other undergraduate Ivy League schools, which traditionally rank, in order of selectivity: Princeton, Yale, Brown, Dartmouth, Columbia, University of Pennsylvania, and Cornell. Eighty percent of those who are accepted at Harvard choose to enroll, by far the highest yield of any college in the country.[23]

Harvard accepted 2,056 of the 20,986 applicants in 2002 in order to fill the 1,650 spots in the Class of 2007.[24] "No one wants to be turning down 15,000 people," Dean Fitzsimmons said in 1998. "But if you want to build that great class you have to do that."[25] As a result, each year the overwhelming majority of applicants get online letters from the admissions office email account with subject headings that read: "Re: jection." Not really. But that might add a little zing to the admissions process.

Harvard uses only the common application; it doesn't have a separate institutional application, although it does require a supplement to the common application. After you complete the common application for Harvard, you can use copies of that same application to apply to other colleges that also accept it, among which the most selective are Amherst, Bowdoin, Cornell, Dartmouth, Duke, Rice, and Williams. All of the forms can be completed either on paper or online. As for the application fee, make sure you request a fee waiver from your high school counselor if you qualify for one.

In fashioning each incoming class, the Harvard Admissions Committee carefully reviews each student's admissions materials. Those materials include: (1) the common application, including essays, and the required parts of the Harvard Supplement (2) the high school transcript, school report, and mid-year school report—all submitted by a student's guidance counselor, (3) standardized test scores—submitted by the College Board, (4) teacher and guidance counselor recommendations, (5) optional on-campus and/or off-campus interviewer evaluation, (6) optional personal statements (found on the Harvard Supplement) in addition to the required essays, and (7) optional music tapes, artwork slides, or samples of academic work.[26] As your admissions materials are received at the admissions office, they are stamped, dated, sorted, and organized in a folder, called your "file," along with a scorecard, called your "reading sheet," that is used to evaluate your eligibility for admission.[27]

Here's how the admissions office reads your file. Each Harvard admissions officer is assigned to geographic regions of the world, called "dockets," where they travel each year to recruit prospective applicants and become familiar with local high schools in the area. The first admissions officer who reads your file is the officer assigned to your docket. After the docket reader has looked through and graded your file on the reading sheet, the folder is passed on to two more readers, who examine and evaluate all materials on separate reading sheets. The information from your three reading sheets is compiled onto a single sheet of paper. Once a final reading sheet has been prepared for all applicants, the admissions committee convenes to discuss the eligibility of all applicants from your docket. Finally, there are 10 days of committee sessions, called "rerun," during which your file is reviewed once more, taking into account any late-breaking admissions information you've submitted. After rerun, a final decision is made either to accept, reject, wait-list, or (twenty cases each year) offer one-year deferred admission.[28]

If you are admitted and decide to accept Harvard's offer of admission, chances are you'll finish there: 96 percent of undergrads graduate with a Harvard degree within five years, the second-highest retention rate in the country. However, graduation is not necessarily the clearest path to success. Just ask Harvard drop-out, Bill Gates.

What happens when applicants are wait-listed? Early Action applicants who are placed on the waiting list have their files reviewed again when regular decision applications are read in the spring. Regular decision wait-lists are reviewed again in May after the admissions office has received students' updated class grades, test scores, and achievements. Fewer than five percent of those placed on the waiting list are ultimately accepted. Those students offered one-year deferred admission comprise the college's "Z-list." Though independent research by *The Harvard Crimson* suggests that the Z-list is reserved for students whose parents went to Harvard and whose high school credentials are insufficient for immediate acceptance, Director of Admissions Marlyn McGrath Lewis points out that "there's not much in common" among one-year deferred admits and, more directly, that the Z-list is "not a legacy list."[29]

Students who are accepted for immediate enrollment are allowed to defer admission for a year if they want, as long as they don't enroll in any other degree-granting institutional program. Typically, 20–60 admitted students in each incoming class take a year off from school before enrolling at Harvard.[30] Harvard reserves the right to withdraw acceptances from students who have been admitted for academic or disciplinary reasons, such as dropped classes, poor grades, academic dishonesty, suspension, expulsion, or police arrest. Typically, Harvard rescinds acceptances for only one or two students each year. The most sensational take-back in recent years was that of Gina Grant, whose acceptance was revoked in 1995 after Harvard learned that she'd been convicted of manslaughter four years earlier for bludgeoning her mother to death with a candlestick.

Harvard offers need-blind admission to all applicants, including international and transfer students. Harvard's need-blind admissions policy states that the admissions committee decides whether or not a student will be accepted without considering whether a student has applied for aid, whether a student qualifies for aid, or for how much aid a student qualifies. Harvard offers both Early Action and regular decision programs for admission. Under regular admission, applicants send in their application materials by January 1 and hear back by early April about whether or not they've been admitted. Under the Early Action program, applicants send in all their application materials by November 1 and get word by mid-December. Harvard uses the same methodology and resources to calculate financial award packages for all students, regardless of when they apply, so students accepted under the Early Action program receive the exact same financial aid award as they would have if they'd been accepted regular decision.

Harvard typically fields about 16,000 regular decision applications and about 4,000 Early Action applications.[31] Unlike Early Decision procedures at some highly selective colleges, Harvard's nonbinding Early Action procedure allows applicants to reject Harvard's offer of admission and to wait until May 1 to decide whether to attend.[32] Early applicants to Harvard may not, however, apply to other colleges under early admission.[33] Harvard usually accepts about 20 to 25 percent of Early Action applicants, who then take about half of the seats for each incoming class. Although Early Action applicants are accepted to Harvard at almost twice the rate of regular decision applicants, applying early to Harvard does not typically give students any better chance of admission.[34] Higher Early Action acceptance rates "reflect the remarkable strength of Early Action applicant pools—not less rigorous admissions standards," says Dean of Admissions and Financial Aid Fitzsimmons. "Early Action applicants have, on average, stronger admissions credentials than regular applicants."[35]

How does Harvard decide whom to accept? The admissions committee evaluates each applicant's file on the basis of two broad categories: academics and extracurricular/personal qualities. Academics are weighed about three times more heavily in the admissions evaluation than are extracurricular/personal qualities. About three-quarters of your evaluation hinges on the academic rating, which is based principally on the high school transcript and standardized test scores. The remaining quarter of the evaluation rests on your extracurricular/personal ranking, consisting of: (1) extracurricular/athletic involvement, indicated primarily on the activities chart in the common application, and (2) personal qualities, like integrity, honesty, and altruism, indicated primarily in teacher recommendations, the alumni/ae interview assessment, and essay responses to prompts given in the common application and Harvard supplement.

You will be given "special preference" in the admissions process if you are a legacy, recruited athlete, or racial, ethnic, or geographic minority. Applicants with these valued statuses get an unspecified extra advantage in the admissions evaluation that reduces emphasis on academic and extracurricular/personal categories accordingly.[36]

Harvard's academic rating—on a scale of one (high) to six (low)—consists primarily of three parts: (1) the average of your highest SAT I math and verbal test scores (or converted ACT test scores), (2) the average of your three highest SAT II subject test scores (this average is bumped higher or lower by Advanced Placement (AP) and international baccalaureate (IB) exam scores in the same areas as your SAT II tests), and (3) a standardized determination of high school class rank in terms of high school class size, according to either actual class rank, percentile rank, or grade point average weighted for honors and AP courses, (depending on what your high school uses). Academic initiative outside of the classroom, demonstrated by participation in summer programs, special projects, research papers, or independent studies, can also help your academic rating. The honors/awards chart on the common application helps to confirm admissions judgments about your academic ability and achievement.

Class rank is weighted most heavily among all academic factors, approximately twice as much as SAT I scores, and about three times as much as SAT II (+AP/IB) scores. The admissions committee determines class rank by weighing: (1) the difficulty of the classes you took out of those available at your high school, (2) the grades you got in those classes, and (3) how your grades, weighted for honors, AP, IB, and college classes, compared to those of other students in your high school class. "We look first at grades in college-bound courses," says Senior Admissions Officer David Evans because "[t]he best indication of future excellence is past excellence." Harvard receives applications from roughly 3,000 high school valedictorians each year. Three-quarters of the applicant pool graduates in the top 10 percent of their high school classes; most applicants who are accepted at Harvard have overall grade averages of A- or above. "A student with a B+ average," Evans says, "only gets in if there is much more to the student. It must be the case that the B+ doesn't represent the student."[37]

Although admissions officers allege that "four years of high school are more telling than four hours on a Saturday morning," SAT I and SAT II (+AP/IB) standardized test scores, *all combined,* count for just as much in the admissions evaluation as extracurriculars, recommendations, essays, and interviews combined, and almost as much as class rank. There are no cut-off scores for the standardized tests, but averages tend to be extremely high. More than 56 percent of applicants to the Class of 2008 averaged 1400 or higher on their combined SATs, with 2,700 students scoring a perfect 800 on the SAT Math test and 2,000 scoring an 800 on the SAT Verbal test. 2,500 applicants scored a perfect 800 on the SAT II Math test and 2,000 scored 800 on the SAT II Writing test.[37] Harvard rejects 3 out of 5 applicants with perfect SAT scores.[38]

The highest academic rating of one is reserved for students who rank first or second in their high school class, score over 700 on at least five SAT tests, score 4 or 5 on at least three AP tests or 6 or 7 on three IB tests, and show academic initiative outside the classroom. Applicants with successively lesser ranks and scores are given a two, three, four, five, or six for the academic rating. Roughly 10 percent of applicants to Harvard are given academic ratings of one, about half have academic ratings of two or three, and approximately forty percent have academic ratings of four, five, or six. Academic ones are virtual locks for admission.[39]

Harvard's extracurricular/personal rating, much more subjective than the academic rating, comprises the admissions committee's determination of the depth of your extracurricular commitment, leadership, and achievement as well as personal qualities, like concern for others and demonstrated ability to overcome socioeconomic/educational disadvantage or physical/mental disability. Like the academic rating, the extracurricular/personal rating is ranked on a scale of one to six for each applicant. The admissions committee evaluates your extracurricular merit according to the employment and activities charts that you fill out on the common application. These charts ask for years of participation for each extracurricular commitment, hours of participation per week, and any special leadership positions held or honors earned.

In addition to the common application charts, many applicants attach an additional resume or written explanation of extracurricular involvement. If you're good enough at sports to participate at the collegiate level, a Harvard coach of the appropriate team will judge your athletic ability by coming to high school games, checking out your stats, and talking with high school coaches.[40] Essays and recommendations may also shed light on your commitment to extracurriculars.

Admissions officers use required essays and recommendations to evaluate your personal qualities. The common application asks you to respond in 250 to 500 words to one of five essay prompts.

(1) Evaluate a significant experience, achievement, risk you have taken, or ethical dilemma you have faced and it's impact on you.

(2) Discuss some issue of personal, local, national, or international concern and it's importance to you.

(3) Indicate a person who has had a significant influence on you, and describe that influence.

(4) Describe a character in fiction, an historical figure, or a creative work (as in art, music, science, etc.) that has had an influence on you, and describe that influence.

(5) Topic of your choice.

The essay gives you an opportunity to elaborate on your background, interests, and values, and perhaps most importantly of all, demonstrate your writing ability. Michele A. Hernandez, former Assistant Director of Admissions at Dartmouth College and author of *A is for Admission*, says that the best kinds of admissions essays are "slice-of-life" essays, which concentrate on one "small, seemingly insignificant incident...that sheds light on your personality...or any factors in your background that have influenced what kind of person you are."[41] In *The Guide to Getting In*, Harvard Student Agencies notes that the key is to convey an "honest and genuine interest or love for your [essay] topic ... [by] pepper[ing] the essay with interesting and relevant details and anecdotes."[42] (I included the essays I wrote for Harvard in the appendix. Two essays were required when I applied in 1999–2000.)

Teacher and guidance counselor recommendations bear insights on your personal character, classroom personality, and commitment to learning. For the two teacher recommendations, you should ask teachers who know you well both personally and academically, who write exceptionally well, and who will take the time to write a thoughtful, original letter.

Interviews, personal statements, and music/art/academic samples can also influence the admissions committee's evaluation of your personal qualities. All three are optional. The admissions office recommends that you have an interview if possible, but discourages you from sending personal statements and work samples unless they reveal something truly exceptional about you that isn't already demonstrated elsewhere in the application. You can choose to have an on-campus interview with an admissions officer, an off-campus interview with alumni/ae, both, or neither. After your application is received at the admissions office, an alum will contact you to set up a time and place to meet for an off-campus interview. Interviews are available in all 50 states and in 46 countries, but international students have the extra burden of initiating contact with an interviewer, although the admissions office will provide the names and contact information.

Interviews clarify the admissions committee's impression of you as a person and give you a chance to explain any special personal circumstances like travel, learning disabilities, or a death in the family.[43] Interviewers typically ask about your personal interests, influences, and strengths and weaknesses. On average, those who have both on-campus and off-campus interviews do slightly better in the admissions process than those who have only one, and those who have one interview do slightly better than those who have neither. However, there isn't necessarily a causal relationship between interview and acceptance, since those applicants who have more interviews tend to have stronger admissions credentials in the first place.[44]

Possible personal statement topics are listed in the Harvard Supplement to the common application. They include: unusual circumstances in your life, travel or living experiences in other countries, books that have affected you the most, an academic experience that has meant the most to you, or a list of books you have read in the past twelve months. Music tapes, artwork slides, or samples of academic work are evaluated by Harvard faculty members, who then inform the admissions committee of their assessment.

On Harvard's six-point scale for the extracurricular/personal rating, the highest rating of one is reserved for applicants with stellar essays and recommendations, as well as "national recognition"[45] for extracurricular achievement, such as writing a book, patenting a product, founding a community service organization, competing in the Olympics, performing at Carnegie Hall, or winning the Siemens Westinghouse and Intel® math and science competitions. The next highest rating of two indicates slightly less exceptional essays and recommendations and recognition at the state or regional level. The average applicant to Harvard has an extracurricular/personal rating of three, which denotes solid essays and recommendations, and substantial commitment/leadership at the high school or local level, such as student government president, editor-in-chief of the school newspaper, captain of a couple of varsity sports, Eagle Scout, or working 20 hours a week at the local supermarket.[46] Or you could costar with Ralph Macchio in *The Karate Kid*, like Elisabeth Shue ('86) did before she came to Harvard.

Harvard gives special preference in the admissions process to minorities, legacies, and recruited athletes. Legacies are applicants whose parents went to Harvard. Recruited athletes are identified and ranked by Harvard sports coaches. Harvard's affirmative action policy determines which applicants will be counted as minorities. Harvard uses a "diversity-discretion" model of affirmative action, whereby it selectively de-emphasizes its four admissions categories in favor of "diversifying" factors, such as race, ethnicity, and geography, in order to increase the number of minorities in the applicant pool and student body. For affirmative action purposes, African American, Native American, and Hispanic (but not Asian American) applicants count as racial/ethnic minorities. Geographic minorities are international applicants and American applicants from the Midwest, the South, and the northernmost states in New England (Vermont, New Hampshire, and Maine).[47] For the record, only since the 1970s has Harvard used its long-standing "diversity-discretion" policy to encourage minority enrollment; Harvard used an unprincipled model of affirmative action in the 1920s for the express purpose of keeping Jewish students *out* of the college.[48]

Although Harvard claims that special status weighs only negligibly into the admissions process, statistics from the Harvard Admissions Office suggest that it counts for much more. Harvard administrators assert that the college weighs minority and legacy birth statuses only as a tie-breaker when all other factors are equal. And a fall 2000 letter from the Ivy League Deans and Directors of Admission and Directors of Athletics affirms that Harvard "admits all . . . athletes on the basis of their . . . potential as students." But admitted minorities, legacies, and recruited athletes have, on average, much lower standardized test scores than the average nonminority/nonrecruit/nonlegacy Harvard undergraduate, and between two and four times higher acceptance rates than the general applicant pool.[49] Admitting a large number of legacies and recruited athletes is necessary, explains Director of Admissions Marlyn McGrath Lewis

('70–'73, in order to "command the loyalty of our alumni."[50] Relaxed admissions standards for minorities are warranted, argues former University President Rudenstine, because diversity stands as a fundamental aspect of a good education: "[T]he opportunity to live and learn among peers whose perspectives and experiences differ from their own," he affirms, "challenges students to explore ideas and arguments at a deeper level."[51]

The future of affirmative action at Harvard may be greatly impacted by the U.S. Supreme Court's decisions in the University of Michigan cases of *Grutter v. Bollinger* and *Gratz v. Bollinger*, which challenged the constitutionality of University of Michigan policies that consider race/ethnicity as one factor among others in university admissions decisions. In a friend-of-the-court brief signed by seven other universities, Harvard asked the Supreme Court to uphold the principle of affirmative action in *Grutter* and *Gratz*, which was decided in the summer of 2003.[52] While the Supreme Court held that affirmative action is a worthy (and legal) goal, it struck down a system in which a predetermined number of points were automatically awarded to students from identified minority groups. How this decision may impact admissions decisions at Harvard is yet to be seen.

Transfer admissions rates have dropped consistently from 1998 to 2002 as fewer Harvard undergraduates have chosen to live off campus or take leaves of absence. Harvard admitted 35 out of 1,100, or three percent of all transfer applicants in the 2002–2003 academic year.[53] The number of transfer acceptances has been as high as 55 students, but it varies. Admissions Director McGrath Lewis ('70–'73) explains that the number of "anticipated spaces available in the housing system" accounts for the variable acceptance rates.[54] Not all students at other colleges are eligible to transfer to Harvard. To be considered for transfer admission, you must have satisfactorily completed a minimum of one and maximum of two continuous academic years of full-time college study within a liberal arts curriculum that is similar to Harvard's.

Transfer applicants follow a slightly different admissions procedure than first-year applicants. Like freshman applicants, transfer students fill out the common application, but they check off the "transfer student" box on page one of the application and then include information from their current college in the "Educational Data" section on page two. Instead of filling out the freshman supplement to the common application, transfer students submit a complete college transcript, two faculty recommendations, a Dean's report on good standing, and a transfer application supplement, which is available each year in October and can be downloaded online. There is no Early Action policy for transfer students, who are considered for either September or February enrollment. The Committee on Transfer Admissions meets in May to evaluate the files of both fall and spring term applicants, all of whom must submit admissions materials to Byerly Hall by the same February 15 admissions deadline.

EXPENSES AND FINANCIAL AID

Including room, board and other expenses, a Harvard College education in 2003–2004 is about $40,000 per year, which almost helps you empathize with the two Harvard undergraduates who pled guilty to embezzling $100,000 from Harvard's Hasty Pudding Theatricals in 2002.[55] At $27,000 for tuition, $9,000 for room and board, and $3,000 for health and student fees, plus $800 mandatory health insurance if you're not covered under your family's health plan, plus another $2,500 or so for books and supplies, you could practically start up your own small college for the $39,880 costs to go to Harvard for a year.

Given that 20 percent of admitted students reject Harvard's offer of admission each year, it's a good bet that many of those 20 percent turn Harvard down in favor of full merit-based scholarships at highly regarded public universities. The cost of a Harvard education rose by 5 percent 2003–2004 and 2004–2005, its largest tuition hikes in seven years before that, highest among all Ivy League schools, and once again far outstripping the national inflation rate.[56] Still, the cost of attending Harvard is just about the same as attending other Ivies.

Is Harvard worth the money? Most students justify the high price of a Harvard education by the quality of life on campus and the economic returns they expect to gain from a Harvard degree. Sixty-four percent of Harvard undergraduates believe that they get "extremely high" or "very good" value for money spent on tuition, and 51 percent believe they get "extremely high" or "very good" value for money spent on room and board—at least 10 percent more than students at any other of the 17 top Ivy League and private universities except for Williams, according to a 1996 Target Management survey of over 4,000 undergraduates at those schools. Harvard undergraduates believe that the future value of their college education is most substantially due to the general credibility and respect of a Harvard degree, but also mention educational experience, advantage in graduate school admission, career connections, broadened intellectual perspectives, social connections, friendships, and personal confidence.[57]

Harvard requires that you pay tuition and fees before you register each semester. Fall term bills are sent out in July and due back by mid-August. Spring term bills are sent out in December and due back by mid-January. On top of Harvard's term bill each semester, there are also personal expenses like required course books, entertainment, shopping, laundry, non-Harvard food, and dues for social organizations. Required course books cost $300–$1,000 per semester at the Harvard Cooperative Society (the COOP) in Harvard Square. While books for most courses are available on reserve free for three-hour sign-outs at one or more of Harvard's libraries, library reserves are not readily available during paper crunches or exam period, which is inconvenience enough for most students to buy their books outright.

Fortunately, the college's deep pockets usually lower the cost for a student considerably. As long as you remain an undergraduate at Harvard, the college will meet 100 percent of your calculated family need with some form of aid. The college awards financial aid only to students who need financial assistance in order to attend, giving no aid on the basis of academic, extracurricular, or athletic merit. Harvard's need-based financial aid awards include grants (money that's conferred toward Harvard expenses outright and doesn't need to be paid back), loans (money that you need to pay back with interest after you graduate), and jobs (money you earn during the academic year at $8–$10 per hour). Financial aid awards range from under $500 to over $33,000, with an average annual award of over $27,000, almost 70 percent of a student's total costs.[58] Twenty-four percent of undergrads report that financial assistance/scholarships is an "extremely important" reason for their classes to attend Harvard.[59]

In the 2004–2005 academic year, Harvard will dish out $80 million in scholarship grants to almost half of all undergraduates. Harvard provides some form of aid to 70 percent of the student body, with 46 percent of undergraduates receiving some amount of scholarships grants, 44 percent receiving student loans, and 55 percent receiving term-time jobs on campus. The average student receiving aid in 2002–2003 funded their education with $20,500 in scholarship grants, $10,700 parent contribution, $2,600 student contribution, $1,300 in outside scholarships, $1,100 in student loans, and $750 earned through work-study.[60] Per a $2 million financial aid initiative beginning in 2004–2005, parents of students with family incomes of $40,000 or less no longer need contribute to the cost of their children's education.[61]

Harvard's Committee on Financial Aid (CFA) makes the final determination of your family's need. The CFA calculates need on the basis of financial information provided in your and your parents' tax returns and in two other forms: the Profile Form and Free Application for Federal Student Aid (FAFSA), available from your high school counselor and online. International students requesting aid don't fill out the FAFSA and Profile Form. Instead, students applying from outside the United States submit Harvard's Financial Statement for Students from Foreign Countries, also available online. All financial aid forms for prospective incoming freshmen are due to Harvard by the first of February.

You have to file a new application each year to renew financial aid, and your aid award is adjusted if there's a significant change in your or your parents' financial resources. The CFA calculates your total financial aid award package (a combination of scholarship, loan, and job) by taking the total annual cost of attending Harvard (including travel) and subtracting the amount of financial support that you and your parents can be expected to provide. The difference is defined as your "need" and should equal the amount of your financial aid package at Harvard. Sally Donahue, Director of Financial Aid and Senior Admissions Officer, says that the college's standardized process for calculating how much you and your parents should contribute "considers a number of factors, such as the size of a student's family, the number of members in college, family income and assets, and any unusual circumstances or expenses" like family medical bills or students' children.[62] The expected student and parent contributions typically come out to approximately 30 percent of what families have but vary depending on the amounts and sources of income, assets, and expenses in each case. Forty percent of students receiving need-based scholarships from Harvard come from families with incomes less than $60,000. Twenty percent from families with incomes between $60,000 and $85,000. Forty percent with incomes more than $85,000.[63]

After the CFA calculates your financial need/aid, it subtracts from that figure a certain amount of "self-help" that you are expected to contribute. The self-help level for all students receiving financial aid for the 2002–2003 academic year was $3,250. You can meet this amount in full either by working 10–12 hours per week during the academic year, by taking out a $3,250 student loan, or by any combination of term-time work and student loans. If you choose to work to help meet the self-help expectation, you're guaranteed an on-campus job through the Student Employment Office (SEO). If you decide to meet the self-help portion of their financial aid package entirely with loans, you'll have about $13,000 to pay back after you graduate. The average overall debt of a graduating student in the Class of 2003 was $8,800.[64]

Although Princeton University in 2001 replaced all loans with scholarship grants, guaranteeing that no Princeton undergraduates would have to borrow money to attend college,[65] Donahue defends Harvard's inclusion of mandatory jobs and loans in financial aid packages: "We encourage students to work in order to keep their indebtedness at a reasonable level. Our graduates have excellent prospects for jobs and a very low default rate on their loans."

Any outside scholarships you earn are first used to replace the self-help portion of your financial aid package. If an outside scholarship amount exceeds your self-help contribution, then the remainder will offset the financial aid award offered by Harvard. In addition to term-time jobs and loans, students receiving financial aid from Harvard are also expected to make $2,000 each summer to be contributed toward educational expenses for the following year. This requirement limits some students' ability to accept low-paying internships during their college summers.

What's more, Harvard's financial aid system doesn't meet all students' needs. While attending Harvard incurs nominal financial burden for really poor students (who get full scholarships) or really rich students (who don't need any scholarships), it encumbers to varying degrees those middle-class students whose families lie in between the economic extremes. The cost of a Harvard education proves particularly oppressive for students whose parents provide no financial support. The CFA bases financial aid decisions only on ability and not on willingness to pay, taking "no account," as one student learned first-hand, "for the fact that some parents just will not contribute" to funding their child's education, due to conflicts ranging from divorce to pregnancy to sexual orientation.[66] The CFA expects your parents to provide as much assistance from both income and assets as is feasible for the duration of your time as an undergraduate at Harvard. If your parents don't cough up, then you're required to pay whatever portion of the expected parental contribution your parents withhold. Most students in this situation are forced to take out exorbitant student loans. One undergraduate says that she "will be approximately $100,000 in debt … [b]y the time [she] get[s] out of Harvard."[67] The FAO is currently in the process, however, of drafting much-needed reforms under which students can be freed from the burden of making up their estranged parent(s)' expected contribution by submitting third-party documentation verifying their financial independence from one or more parents.[68]

To help you figure out how to meet the cost of college, Harvard's Financial Aid Office (FAO) provides extensive financial information online, over the phone, or in person through one-on-one consultations with the financial aid officer assigned to your graduating class.[69]

VISITING THE CAMPUS

The college's 380-acre campus, in the middle of the University's 4,750-acre campus, is dappled with Georgian architecture and towering oaks amidst vast pastoral lawns. There's lots of green grass, lots of big trees, and lots of impressive-looking buildings. In the words of Margaret Floyd Henderson, author of *Harvard: An Architectural History*, "Harvard architecture is unparalleled for its sense of place as an extended urban design: a contextual campus in intimate dialogue with the City of Cambridge."[70]

If you want to see the campus for yourself, you can get there by any mode of transportation. By car, get on the I-90 Massachussets Turnpike and take the Cambridge/Allston exit 18. At the end of the ramp, turn left onto Soldiers Field

Road. Then, take the Harvard Square exit, bear right across Anderson Bridge, and drive straight into Harvard Square. From Harvard Square, the Admissions Office is a three-block walk down Garden Street; parking is tough around Harvard. Your best bet is to check out the meters along Quincy Street, bordering Harvard Yard on the opposite side of the main Johnston Gate entrance. If there aren't any open meters along Quincy Street, you've got to shell out the bucks for a space in the public Church Street lot, located in Harvard Square right across from Johnston Gate.

By plane, travel to Logan Airport in Boston and take the free shuttle bus to the "Airport" subway stop on the "Blue Line." From there, either take a 30-minute, $25 taxi ride or a 45-minute, $1 subway ride to Harvard. By subway, take the Blue Line "inbound" four stops, and get off at "Government Center." Buy a soft pretzel from Stu the subway vendor. Then switch to the "Green Line." Take the Green Line one stop inbound and get off at "Park Street." Check out the guy breakdancing in the subway, and drop some change in his hat. Switch again to the "Red Line." Take the Red Line four stops "outbound," and get off at "Harvard." Walk up the stairs, and you'll be standing directly between Harvard Yard and Harvard Square.

By bus or train, travel to South Station in Boston, get on the subway, and take the Red Line six stops outbound to Harvard.

Hour-long campus tours are given year-round with no appointment necessary. Guided tours start at 3:00 P.M. on weekdays and at 11:00 A.M. on Saturdays, with an extra tour running at 11:00 A.M. on weekdays from April through November. Campus tours are administered by the admissions office and delivered by undergrads. The tour is aimed more to impress than to educate and consists mostly of useless facts about the history behind different buildings on campus. For example, Widener Library, tour guides proclaim, was named after someone who died in the Titanic. Armed with that knowledge, you can certainly decide if Harvard is the right college for you.

A more valuable way to check out the campus is to roam around on your own, asking students for directions along the way. Key things to check out on campus are the grill and gaming area at Loker Commons; the classrooms at Memorial, Sever, Emerson, Robinson, and Harvard Halls; and the computer and science labs at the Science Center. Unfortunately, a student ID is required to gain access to the most worthwhile sites for prospective students to see—the book stacks at Widener Library, the study rooms at Lamont Library, the serving and dining areas at Annenberg Hall and House dining halls, and the athletic facilities at the Malkin Athletic Center. High school seniors can pick up one free meal ticket and a list of class times at the Admissions Office on Garden Street. As far as checking out Harvard suites, resourceful prospective students will play on the sympathies of ID-wielding undergraduates to swipe them into the dorms, and let them look at the layout of a couple of rooms.

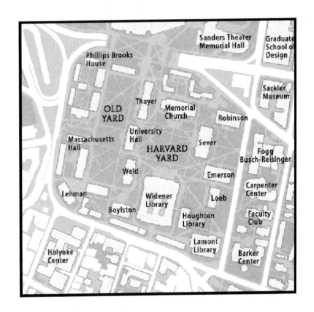

Spend the night at Harvard if you can. Contact the admissions office three weeks in advance, and they'll set you up to stay overnight with an undergraduate on Monday through Thursday, from mid-October to mid-March. They'll let you come only if you're a high school senior, though, and only for one night. Of course, if you know undergraduates at Harvard, you can just arrange to stay with one of them. On-campus interviews are offered six months during the year. Contact the admissions office in mid-May if you want a 30-minute on-campus interview anytime in between June and August or contact them in mid-July if you want an on-campus interview September through November. If you want to interview with a faculty member or athletics coach, you have to make arrangements with the specific concentration department or sports team.

BOSTON WEATHER

The extreme variability of weather at Harvard keeps things from being dull, but you'll definitely find more sunshine at colleges elsewhere. Temperatures can vary literally 40 degrees from one day to the next, requiring that students wear shorts one day and snow pants the next. *The Harvard Crimson* sensibly recommends that students take every opportunity to get outside and "sit, run, or make out by the Charles River" in the warmer months of September, early October, late April, and May. While the autumn foliage and springtime wildflowers are gorgeous, temperamental Boston weather can at times lower students' spirits. "For a great many people," says Dr. Randolph Catlin, former chief of Mental Health at University Health Services (UHS), "the reduced daylight and [exercise] restrictions [in the wintertime] is a cause of depression."[71] It's not rare for Boston snow to fall well into April. Winter gives students snow fights in Harvard Yard and ice skating in Boston Common, but it also gives them dark skies at four in the afternoon, frostbite-inducing windchills, and the kind of superpower sludge that decomposes your underpants.

CHAPTER TWO
THE STUDENT BODY

The best thing about going to Harvard is your fellow students. They come from interesting places, have interesting experiences, do interesting things, and hold interesting opinions. "The dynamic of bright and talented individuals," says one former Harvard counselor, "makes for an environment that is socially and intellectually challenging, engaging, and fun."[72] In other words, the students you meet at Harvard make for a pretty awesome college experience.

"The main source of Harvard's fame and success," *The Harvard Independent* aptly affirms "is its student body"[73] Harvard undergraduates consistently lead the nation in prestigious Marshall, Fulbright, Goldwater, and Truman fellowship award winners. The student body comprises a wide range of racial, ethnic, religious, sexual, political, and geographic diversity. Undergraduates are evenly split among men and women, one-third are ethnic and racial minorities, two-thirds hail from public schools, and at least a few come from each state and over 100 countries.

With 6,600 undergraduates amidst a larger university backdrop, the student body is not intimate. While you're sure to bump into at least a few people you know while walking to class or eating in the dining hall, there'll be lots more you've never seen before. It's virtually impossible to know everyone on campus, so there are always new people to meet.

HOMOGENY

Although the college maintains that "[t]here is no typical Harvard student," when you assemble the world's finest high school graduates, they're going to have a lot in common. In fact, Harvard's student body is nearly as diverse ethnically, racially, religiously, and geographically as it is alike in other areas, like socioeconomic background, political ideology, attitudes about education, and experiences with academic/extracurricular success. Every Harvard student was president of something in high school, earned top grades, and got near-perfect scores on their standardized tests. Every student placed a special value on learning in the classroom and exhibited a high degree of self-motivation to work hard. And the vast majority of students reaped the special advantages of privileged educational resources at home, at school, or in the community. These shared experiences and attributes among the student body render undergraduates more homogeneous than the college admits.

Harvard students aptly describe their classmates as unique, bright, talented, motivated, friendly, and, above all, ambitious and independent.[74] Undergrads are overwhelmingly polite and caring, the kind of people who mind their pleases and thank you's and make a point to smile and say hello. The vast majority is also extroverted, down-to-earth, and easy to get along with, the kind of people who are eager to meet other students for fabulous meal-time conversation. Many, too, are artificial, concealing their personal insecurities in an effort to create outward impressions of personal confidence, social comfort, and general put-togetherness. There are also small pockets of students at Harvard, particularly among math, pre-med, and computer science concentrators, who lack in modesty and/or interpersonal skills. They spend most of their time studying on their own, though, so you don't see them around campus too much. The only way you really know they're there is when you see, every once in a while, an algorithmic sonnet extolling the author's latest Cisco certification scrawled in the science library bathroom stall.

Pervasive ambition and independence among the student body enrich college life in tangible ways. Undergrads' self-directed push toward success propels them to take on a number of out-of-class commitments and leadership positions, making for a remarkably active extracurricular life, with over 250 student organizations on campus. Exhibiting astonishing levels of achievement, Harvard students zealously pursue an eclectic mix of activities and issues. You'll meet people on campus who win Olympic gold medals, run their own businesses, and find international peacemaking organizations. Whether students throw themselves into politics, performance, or public service only at a few other colleges in the country are students as passionate about and good at what they do. And Harvard undergrads are rarely shy about sharing their thoughts. In the words of one student, "We speak well, we have profound things to say, and we love to hear ourselves talk."[75] Graduating seniors often report that their best teachers at Harvard were their classmates and the most meaningful and memorable learning took place outside the classroom.[76]

But the determined drive that brought them to Cambridge also contributes to negative aspects of student life at Harvard, such as the stressful environment, lackluster social scene, and ineffective support system. Most students rank

GPA above "the college experience" on their list of personal priorities. While dogged initiative thrusts students toward extraordinary accomplishments, there is a fine line between ambition and obsession, and between independence and isolation. Students doggedly pursuing individual excellence often neglect community beyond narrow academic and extracurricular interests. A 2001 UHS survey revealed that over 35 percent of undergraduates felt "overwhelmed" 11 times or more in the past academic year.[77] BSC Director of Mental Health Dr. Charles Ducey explains that "perfectionistic" Harvard students "have an internal critic that pushes them to do too much." The majority cram their schedules with multiple out-of-class commitments, maintaining the frenzied high school lifestyles that helped them get into Harvard. Undergrads on campus are, asserts *The Harvard Crimson*, the "product of an achievement-oriented culture that pressures young people to … sacrific[e] happiness for the sake of success . . . regard[ing] sleep, leisure and other hallmarks of a healthy lifestyle as bargaining chips in the war against their limited time."[78]

Harvard students work hard and get a whole lot done. Most are textbook Type-A personalities with high expectations for themselves and instinctual tendencies toward perfection. "It's not that Harvard expects so much from us," says one undergraduate. "It's us."[79] Other students concur that "pressure here is entirely self-inflicted."[80] Students are driven to constant self-improvement and feel guilty if time and energy are spent on something other than "getting ahead." Expressing the attitude of many of his classmates, one student says, "Inactivity bores me, so I always feel like I have to be doing something."[81] Harvard students hate wasting time, so they've mastered the art of time management efficiency, which often means hard-core multitasking: reading while you eat, making cell phone calls while you walk to class, making social and professional connections while you participate in extracurriculars. If you go to the cardiovascular room on the second floor of the Malkin Athletic Center any time of day, you'll find sweat-soaked, highlighter-wielding students turning textbook pages as fast as exercise machine wheels and pedals. At the same time, you'll also find laid-back students watching bad movies in their dorm rooms and hanging out in the dining halls for hours after they've finished eating. But there are a whole lot more ellipticizers than *Waterworld* fans.

While some kids study purely for the sake of learning, the two most common reasons for studying so hard at Harvard are peer pressure and future success. Harvard is not cutthroat. Students don't compare grades or sabotage each others' work; in fact, students frequently help each other out working together in small collaborative study groups amidst a general atmosphere of academic cooperation.[82] While overt competition among Harvard students is negligible, the atmosphere of unyielding student industry creates a powerful unspoken competition. Undergraduates at Harvard feel compelled to throw themselves into their books because everybody else is doing it. "You'll feel driven to pull all-nighters and lock yourself up in libraries," one student explains, "because of the relentless workaholic atmosphere that prevails."[83]

The more fundamental reason Harvard students work so hard is their unwavering gaze to career prospects. Earmarked for greatness and provided with the resources and reputation to help them achieve it, the majority of students at Harvard are highly motivated by prospects of future wealth, fame, success, and social contribution. Acutely aware of graduate school admissions and professional prospects, the typical Harvard student has rigidly defined designs for his or her own future. With nudging from Harvard fellowship tutors, grad school advisors, and on-campus company recruits, the majority of undergrads are guided along traditional career paths and conventional definitions of success without ever asking themselves whether or why they want to get there. Harvard administrators report that many former students admit realizing only too late that they "missed their youth entirely, never living in the present, always pursuing some ill-defined future goal."[84]

Some students use their time at Harvard doing things that are genuinely meaningful to them; but a greater number expend their energies doing things they hope "other people might find impressive someday."[85] When 19 percent of Harvard students identify graduate school preparation as an "extremely important" reason for coming to Harvard,[86] it is not surprising that so many approach their undergraduate education not as an experience in itself but as a means to subsequent career advancement. Because these students' principal immediate objective is to climb extracurricular hierarchies and pad their resumes, "papers and essays, once ends in themselves, become 'writing samples,' teachers become 'recommendations,' acquaintances become 'contacts' and…realized dreams become 'stepping stones' to bigger-and-better things."[87] Grades matter more to most students than scholarship for its own sake, a point that is not lost on professors. According to Loeb Professor of Classical Art and Archaeology David G. Mitten, Harvard students "are less concerned about learning … [than] about getting straight As to get into medical school or law school." And Associate Linguistics Professor Bert Vaux remarks, "I have never seen such grade-grubbing students as one encounters here."[88]

Most undergrads carry this "stepping stone" mindset into their planning for summer breaks. In the pursuit of meaningful or prestigious summertime research and employment, Harvard students benefit from tremendous on-campus resources, including the Office of Career Services, the Fellowships Office, the Institute of Politics, and the University's online search page of MonsterTrak.com.[89] One Harvard student reenacts the typical reply she gets when asking a classmate about his or her summer plans: "This summer I'm going to travel to Tanzania and help the new government plan a capitalist economy, while faxing my weekly column in to *Newsweek*. Then I start my gig with Greenpeace in August and I hope to have saved the humpback whales by September."[90] College students don't do this stuff for fun. Harvard undergrads view the summertime as one more crucial opportunity to get a leg up on the competition, rather than as a chance to unwind and have fun. Far more Harvard students spend their summers wearing suits and shuffling papers at I-banking and consulting internships inside New York offices than landscaping, lifeguarding, or beach-going outside, near the water, with friends.[91]

Ambitious and independent Harvard students also tend toward high levels of anxiety and self-absorption. Former Harvard College student counselor Howard Greene explains that undergrads "live with the stress of competing against other star students to achieve the necessary GPAs to accomplish the next step of their goals."[92] Harvard students describe the "anal-retentive," "sleep-deprived" "panic-culture" they create for themselves on campus. For highly motivated students constantly mulling over their balance academics versus extracurriculars versus employment versus summer plans versus social life versus sleep, it is little wonder that mealtime conversations among students sometimes degenerate into laundry lists of upcoming responsibilities and complaints about how much work they have. "Self-improvement becomes the routine of our lives," one student explains. "[W]e spend our days writing papers and practicing instruments and memorizing foreign languages and working out on elliptical machines. Sometimes self-reliance easily becomes self-absorption instead."[93] Many students are so engrossed with their personal studies and activities that they don't make time for social interaction, what kids on campus call "too-busy-for-other-people" syndrome. One undergraduate says, "[W]e don't want to hang out unless there's a productive sense of accomplishment in doing so."[94] Every weekend, you'll find some students chilling out, letting loose, and partying wild, but you'll find just as many cooped up, cramming hard, and working toward the next stepping stone.

DIVERSITY

Harvard prides itself on being the ultimate salad bowl of higher education. Harvard students report that attending college with classmates unlike themselves has a distinctly positive impact on their undergraduate education. One reason that diversity at Harvard works so well is that virtually all admitted students share common attitudes about the importance of education. Interacting with people who come from different backgrounds but share similar basic values about learning helps to dispel stereotypes and cultivate intercultural understanding. Another reason that diversity at Harvard works is that the administration does a good job of encouraging students to appreciate that their time at Harvard is a unique opportunity to experience a range of people and ideas wider than any they will ever have again.[95]

During the summer before their first year, incoming freshman receive a booklet in the mail containing several essays about diversity. These essays include one by Henry David Thoreau on self-reliance, identity, and integrity; one by Anne Fadiman on maintaining an open mind about different perspectives; one by Henry Louis Gates, Jr. on feeling conflicting pressures from different groups on a college campus; one by former university president Rudenstine on how civility makes living together a positive learning experience; and several by undergraduate ethnic organization members on the challenges and rewards of finding common ground at college. Faculty volunteers meet with all freshmen in groups of 20–30 students to discuss students' thoughts on diversity before first-semester classes start. Students report gaining a great deal from the opportunity to discuss how they might deal with the differences among themselves. During the academic year, the Harvard Foundation for Intercultural and Race Relations works with race relations advisers and student liasons to organize annual campus-wide activities designed to promote awareness and appreciation of Harvard's cultural richness. Events include an annual culture festival, a science conference for minorities and women, an intercultural film festival, and a series of panel discussions on diversity. The college also promotes a positive experience from the diversity on campus by enforcing a comprehensive nondiscrimination policy. This policy prohibits discrimination on the basis of race, color, ethnic or national origin, age, sex, sexual orientation, gender identity and expression, handicap, religion, political belief, source of income, marital or prenatal status, or veteran status in admission to, access to, treatment in, or employment in the college's programs and activities.[96]

The broad scope of student identity groups on campus reflects the diversity of the undergraduate student body. More than 50 ethnic, racial, religious, geographical, and gender-based undergraduate organizations give minorities a place to meet, hang out, and celebrate their respective cultures with the larger campus. In accordance with Harvard's nondiscrimination policy, these groups are open to all members of the undergraduate student body. Sometimes these groups promote diversity by fostering deeper intercultural understanding though discussion panels and culture shows, and other times they serve primarily as intra-group social clubs which target social events primarily at members of their own group. Identity groups also publish *The Women's Guide to Harvard*, *The Guide to Black Life at Harvard*, *The Guide to Jewish Life at Harvard*, *The Harvard Asian American Association's Guide*, *La Vida at Harvard: The Latino Guide,* and *The Guide to Bisexual, Gay, Lesbian, and Transgendered Life at Harvard*. These guidebooks for Harvard undergraduates narrate the history of identity groups at Harvard, explore current opportunities and resources for these groups on and off campus, and examine diversity issues in the academic, extracurricular, and social lives of students.

Gender

Women make up 48 percent of Harvard's student body. The female undergraduate population rarely joins together as a cohesive community. But Harvard offers some special academic and social opportunities that are aimed at (although not restricted to) women on campus. Harvard has a small Women's Studies program, with 35–45 undergraduate concentrators, 5 seven course offerings per semester, and faculty who are mostly borrowed from other larger academic departments in the FAS. The Radcliffe Institute for Advanced Study (formerly Radcliffe College) hosts prominent female lecturers from around the world and gives out annual cash awards to female undergraduates on the basis of leadership and professional achievement at Harvard. In 2000 the Radcliffe Union of Students (RUS), which promotes women's issues on campus, hosted a three-day symposium on women's representation and experiences in academia at Harvard.[97]

Undergraduate student groups devoted to women include career-oriented groups like Harvard Women in Business, Computer Science, Economics, Government, Philosophy, and Science; racial, ethnic, and religious groups like the Association of Black Harvard Women, Latinas Unidas for Latina Women, and the Hillel Women's Group for Jewish Women; a cappella groups like the Radcliffe Pitches, the Radcliffe Choral Society, Kuumba Sisters; the Tampoon, a female humor magazine; and the Athena Theatre Company, which produces the *Vagina Monologues*. Social organizations on campus aimed especially at women include two sororities and three social clubs. These organizations host meetings, parties, and community service projects that provide opportunities to bond, relax, and dance for the 60 "sisters" in each group, but—unlike male social organizations—none have a space of their own. Harvard is also the only Ivy League university without a women's center.[98]

Geography

Harvard students come from every state and more than 100 countries. Approximately 28 percent of all students come from the Mid-Atlantic United States, 20 percent from New England, 16 percent from the Pacific Coast, 16 percent from the South, and 12 percent from the Midwest.[99] Compared to the U.S. population, a higher percentage of students at Harvard come from the Northeast, a lower percentage come from the South, and about 30 percent of the overall student body come from Massachusetts, New York, or California. Geographical residence within the United States hardly ever forms the basis of social interaction at Harvard. You'll meet other incoming Harvard students from your area at an alumni dinner that is held the spring before your freshman year, but once you get to campus, regional community doesn't exist. The only student groups devoted to American states are Holoimua of Hawaii, Harvard Lovers of the Garden State, the Texas Club, and the Minnesota Club of Harvard.[100]

International students make up approximately eight percent of Harvard's student body. Unlike most schools, Harvard has no international students' house. Instead, The Harvard International Office (HIO) assigns each international student to a host family and a foreign student advisor. Foreign students report that their assigned advisor and host family typically provide nominal support. During college breaks in November, December, January, and April, international students can choose either to go home, to remain in Harvard dorms, to make arrangements with American friends, or to stay with a host family assigned by the HIO. The HIO hosts a reception each fall for incoming international students and provides them with general orientation services, printed materials on living in the Boston area, and advice counseling on immigration regulations, financial issues, and social and cultural differences. In addition to student groups devoted to specific countries and cultures, the Woodbridge Society is an all-encompassing international student group with about 200 undergraduate members. The Woodbridge Society organizes faculty dinners, open houses, and a mentoring program that matches freshmen with upperclassmen from their home countries. Most but not all international students report feeling well-adapted to Harvard life in the states.[101]

Education

Two-thirds of Harvard's student body come from public high schools, one-third come from private schools, a handful are home-schooled, and about two-and-a-half percent (about 165 students) transfer from other colleges before coming to Cambridge. Private, public, and home-schooled students report feeling equally prepared for the demands of Harvard academics and social life.[102] But transfer students say they often have difficulty getting used to Harvard's academic system and breaking into tight-knit social groups.

Transfer Links, an organization made up of former transfer students, organizes dinners, parties, and outings into Boston for recent transfers, but some transfer students complain the organization suffers from poor student leadership and lack of continuity.[103] Some transfer students remain heavily involved in the transfer social network throughout their Harvard career while others branch out into other social settings.[104]

Economics

Harvard's student body is made up predominantly of rich kids. Although the college's need-blind admissions policy and need-based financial aid policy render a Harvard education accessible to even the most destitute students, and although Harvard recruits high-performing students from low-income backgrounds, who are then given slight preferences in the admissions process, very few needy students are actually admitted to Harvard.[105] Out of Harvard's 6,600 undergraduates in 2001–2002,[106] four percent came from families with annual incomes less than $20,000, 10 percent came from families with incomes less than $40,000, 18 percent came from families with incomes less than $60,000, 25 percent came from families with incomes less than $80,000, and 33 percent came from families with annual incomes less than $100,000.[107] So while the median annual income of American families was $51,751, according to the 2000 U.S. Census, two-thirds of Harvard students' families are pulling in more than a hundred grand a year. While only Cornell and Columbia among the Ivies admit significantly more low income students, Newsweek writes that Harvard is more a "recycler of privilege" than an "engine of upward mobility."[108]

Harvard's affirmative action policy does not forge socioeconomic diversity. Racial and ethnic minorities accepted under Harvard's affirmative action policy are rarely culturally disadvantaged students from inner cities or midwestern farms. More often, students of color at Harvard have benefited from the same socioeconomic advantages—from professional parents to academic summer programs to SAT prep classes—as other privileged Harvard students. Because such a staggering proportion of the student body grew up in a cultured, financially comfortable environment, undergrads rarely have the opportunity to interact with classmates who have experienced a wide range of socioeconomic issues—from urban education to environmental policies, from minimum wage to farm subsidies.[109]

Although poor undergrads form a clear minority within the student body, there are no campus groups devoted to economically disadvantaged students at Harvard. Many poor students report that the identities wrapped up in their modest upbringings are easily lost in Harvard's "bourgeois liberal consensus." "If you come from a poor family, you are expected to adopt the mannerisms, body image, clothing, and speech patterns of the privileged," says one undergraduate. "I don't know how many times I have been told that I am no longer a poor person because I am a Harvard student."[110] If you're an economically disadvantaged student coming to Harvard, prepare to blend into the culture of affluence or to fight hard to retain your economic identity.

Religion

There is a strong religious presence on campus. Fifty-two percent of students describe themselves as religious, and 60 percent say they believe in God.[111] Of the one-half of each incoming Harvard class that declares a religious affiliation, about 29 percent are Protestant Christian, 27 percent are Jewish, 24 percent are Catholic, seven percent are Hindu, six percent are Buddhist, five percent are Muslim, and two percent are Baha'i, Mormon, Zoroastrian, or other faiths.[112] Most religious students at Harvard reject fundamentalist religious convictions in favor of either liberal elements of their respective faiths or broader notions of spirituality. Atheists and agnostics constitute a large minority of the student body.[113]

Religious diversity on campus is valuable, explains Richard Light, Harvard Professor of Education and Statistics and author of *Making the Most Out of College*, because it enables undergraduates to reaffirm their religious commitments, to understand and respect other religions, to explore their individual beliefs, to create bonds between religious students, and to make connections between class discussions and their personal lives.[114] The rich plurality of beliefs at Harvard may in fact render students' religious experiences in Cambridge more meaningful than at a college that is more religiously uniform. One religious student praises Harvard's "campus context of competing interests, diversity, and secularism [for] forc[ing] [him] to articulate what [he] believe[s] more clearly than might be necessary in a less challenging culture."[115]

Students of all religions report feeling welcome at Harvard. The United Ministry, an interfaith coalition of chaplains, serves as an umbrella group for all religions at Harvard, offering spiritual programs, worship events, and confidential counsel to Harvard students on a wide range of spiritual and personal issues. Of the 22 student organizations on campus devoted to issues of religion, the five largest student groups are: Harvard-Radcliffe Hillel (for Jewish life), the Catholic Students Association (CSA), the Harvard Islamic Society (HIS), the Harvard Buddhist Community (HBC), and Dharma (for Hindu life). Religious student groups on campus offer regular spiritual services for students of all denominations within each faith.

There are about 900 Protestant Christian students at the college. Approximately 350 Protestant undergraduates regularly attend Sunday services at Memorial Church in Harvard Yard or at local churches in Cambridge, about 60 sing in the Memorial Church University Choir, and 40 teach Sunday school classes. Student groups for Protestant undergrads include: the Harvard-Radcliffe Christian Fellowship and the Asian American Christian Fellowship, which have about 80 members each, as well as the Reformed Christian Fellowship, the Orthodox Christian Fellowship, and the Asian Baptist Student Koinonia, which have about 20 members each.[116]

Catholic undergraduates at Harvard number about 700. About 300 Catholic students at the college regularly attend Sunday mass and over 500 claim membership in the Catholic Students Association (CSA). The CSA holds regular prayer groups, community service projects, and guest lecture events addressing issues facing Catholics on campus and across the world. The CSA also organizes several "spaghetti suppers," two or three barbecues, and one dance each year.[117] About 15 Harvard students are closely affiliated with Opus Dei, a controversial Catholic sect that maintains a center of permanent residence outside of Harvard Square and recruits among Catholics on the Harvard campus.[118] Reverend Thomas E. Brennan of Harvard's Catholic chaplaincy believes that Opus Dei is especially attractive to ambitious Harvard students. "It's all about getting the ultimate 'A,' salvation," Father Brennan explains. "They want very focused people, and who's more focused than an Ivy League student?"[119]

Approximately 500 of the 800 Jewish undergrads participate in Harvard-Radcliffe Hillel, which has its own building in Harvard Square. Besides regular and special religious services, Hillel holds weekly classes, text-study sessions, and panel discussions on Jewish life on and off campus. Hillel also hosts regular social events like dances, outdoors activities, "*Simpsons* and Smoothies" night, and trips to professional sports events.[120]

There are roughly 230 Hindus in Harvard's undergraduate student body, approximately 100 of which are members of Dharma, the student group devoted to Hindu life on campus. Although "most Hindus [at Harvard] aren't very religious," according to one undergraduate member of Dharma, the organization holds weekly religious observation, devotional singing programs, and regular Sunday brunches. In addition to organizing trips to local temples in Cambridge, Dharma also hosts opportunities for undergraduates to study, discuss, and celebrate Hindu life on campus. "The hardest part for practicing Hindus [on campus]," says one Harvard student, "is finding a good variety of vegetarian options."[121]

About 150 of the 200 Buddhist undergrads in the student body belong to the Harvard Buddhist Community (HBC). The HBC organizes meditation instruction classes and trips to local meditation centers. The organization also holds weekly meditation sessions and discussions on Buddhist life, as well as monthly dinners and holiday celebrations. Regular meditations typically draw between three and seven students.[122]

Approximately 80 of the 165 Muslim undergraduates on campus participate in the Harvard Islamic Society (HIS). Although HIS has no official religious center or religious leader, Muslim students come together to take the five daily prayers at the Islamic prayer room in Harvard Yard, and they congregate around campus for weekly discussion groups and congregational prayers. During the month of Ramadan, HIS members gather every evening to break the fast and pray.[123] HIS also organizes social activities several times a semester, including cookouts, movies, and formal dinners featuring Muslim art, music, and poetry.[124]

Sexual Orientation

Four percent of Harvard undergraduates, the vast majority of them men, identify themselves as homosexual.[125] The largest student group is the Bisexual, Gay, Lesbian, and Transgendered Supporters Alliance (BGLTSA), which holds social, political, community, and awareness-raising events on campus. There were 389 undergrads, alums, grad students, and House tutors on the 2002 BGLTSA email list, although there are many people at Harvard who are not involved with BGLTSA. The BGLTSA holds three dances a year, which draw between 100–400 students each, including students from other area colleges. The BGLTSA also holds public, on-campus observances of National Coming Out Day and the National Day of Silence, as well as a month of events and awareness in the spring call "Gaypril." Other student groups on campus include: Girlspot, a discussion group for women and their friends; Beyond Our Normal Differences (BOND), a social group that holds small parties in dorm rooms on campus; Cornerstone, a group for Christians; BAGELS, a group for Jews, and SPECTRUM, a group for students of color. Harvard's student groups often co-sponsor events with each other and with other student groups on campus.[126]

Queer social life revolves around the Boston nightclub scene. The BGLTSA organizes monthly club nights, but most students just go clubbing independently with groups of friends. There are lots of dance clubs in Boston with events geared toward gay people. Some Harvard students also attend big events hosted by queer student groups at other Boston area colleges. The Wellesley College "Dyke Ball" and Brown University "Sex, Power, God" dance always attract a number of Harvard students. The Yale University Co-op also sponsors Harvard-attended parties when Yale hosts the annual Harvard-Yale football game every other year in October.[127]

The college offers a variety of support services for students. The BGLTSA Resource Center in Harvard Yard provides books, magazines, videos, and a place for students to feel at home. Queer graduate student tutors are assigned to every upperclass House to serve as a general resource for queer students and also to host monthly events like the Queer Tea in Eliot House and the Queer Film Series in Mather House. Contact, a peer-counseling group, fields anonymous students' phone calls and drop-ins on issues of sexuality and sexual orientation. The First-Year Sexual Orientation Discussion Group and Quest (the equivalent upperclass sexual orientation discussion group) hold weekly meetings to discuss queer issues on campus.[128]

Despite the general open-mindedness of Harvard's student body, heterosexual undergraduates are very seldom curious about, appreciative of, or hospitable to the queer community at Harvard. "While students certainly don't talk derisively about the homosexual community on campus," reports one member of BGLTSA, "people don't readily show support to the community," by, for example, wearing rainbow stickers during Coming Out Week.[129]

"There's a lot of opportunity available, and there's a great deal of tolerance on campus," says another undergraduate member of BGLTSA. "But in terms of administrative outreach to students or a feeling of really being welcomed by the administration, I think a lot of other schools beat us in that area."[130] While most at Harvard are tolerant of students and issues, latent bigotry persists among a small minority on campus. Anti-gay graffiti was scrawled on walls of Dunster House during "Queer Month" in 1997, and BGLTSA advisor K. Kyriell Muhammad's Mather House room was targeted in 1999 by repeated acts of homophobic vandalism.[131]

Disability

About 200 Harvard students in 2002 were registered with physical and mental disabilities through the Student Disability Resource Center (SDRC). The SDRC evaluates each student's situation on a case-by-case basis and provides temporarily or permanently disabled undergraduates with personalized services to accommodate their specific handicaps. In accordance with Section 504 of the Rehabilitation Act of 1973 and the Americans With Disabilities Act (ADA) of 1990, the college must provide free reasonable accommodations to all students with documented physical and mental disabilities. Students with physical disabilities are guaranteed compatible housing arrangements, campus-wide building access, and special on- and off-campus transportation. A number of dorm rooms on campus are equipped with special resources like handicap-accessible bathrooms and automatic door openers. Additional in-room services are granted on the basis of "approvals," according to Katherine Callaghan of the SDRC. So if you've got allergies, for example, and you want an air conditioner in your room, the SDRC would approve your request as soon as you show the SDRC proper medical documentation.

Approximately 50–100 students at Harvard suffer from Repeated Stress Injury (RSI) as a result of excessive typing. RSI needs to be documented every term in order for students to receive accommodations, such as the voice recognition software available at the Adaptive Technology Laboratory (ATL) in the Science Center. RSI students have to find their own typists, but the college will pay for them. The college also finds and pays for scribes for final exams, but not for midterm exams, when RSI students have to find and pay for their own scribes. Learning-disabled undergrads at Harvard may get recorded textbooks, laptop computers for note taking, or additional time on exams, depending on their specific disability.

Although there are a few hearing- and sight-impaired undergraduates at Harvard each year, there's no community of blindness or deafness on campus. There aren't any disability-based student groups at Harvard, and no FAS courses are offered in either Braille or American Sign Language (ASL). The SDRC usually, but not always, provides blind and deaf students with the resources they need to be successful at Harvard. Visually-impaired students can have materials read or recorded for them at the Lamont Library Reader Service and can access large print monitors and Braille computers at the ATL, but they complain of inadequate assistant reader services through the SDCR.[132] Special in-room accommodations for blind students include bed-shaking fire alarms and doorbells. Hearing-impaired students praise the quality and accessibility of Harvard's interpretation services, carried out in ASL, signed English, Computer Aided Real-Time (CART) reporters, and cued speech transliteration. In-room accommodations for deaf students include flashing fire alarms and vibrating alarm clocks.[133]

Political Ideology

Most students care more about whether their midterm is curved than about the latest happenings in Washington. But when students do think about politics, the dominant perspective is distinctly liberal. According to a 2000 survey by *The Harvard Crimson*, more than one-half of undergraduates identify themselves as liberal, one-third identify themselves as moderate, and only one-sixth as conservative. Most Harvard students believe that government is an effective body for solving social problems and few feel that big government is a threat to America's future. The majority of students favor legalizing gay marriage, legalizing marijuana, banning race-based affirmative action, banning the death penalty, and bringing Reserve Officers Training Corps (ROTC) back to campus.[134]

What accounts for the overwhelmingly left-leaning political perspective of the student body? Morton and Phyllis Keller argue in their book *Making Harvard Modern: The Rise of America's University*: "Harvard's admissions standards—high board scores, preternatural extracurricular talent and/or community engagement—foster … a certain sameness of social outlook."[135] I'm not quite sure what elevated SAT scores have to do with political ideology, but the fact remains that the liberal presence on campus, while neither oppressive nor stifling,[136] is clearly huge.

For conservative and Republican students on campus, "Harvard is a constant test of one's ability to defend and advance his views."[137] One conservative undergraduate cogently argues that "[c]onservatives get a better education [at Harvard] than liberals do"[138] because conservatives are constantly forced to overcome greater intellectual resistance. The educational gains reaped by minority conservatism at Harvard are made possible by the atmosphere of free and uninhibited dialogue on campus. Former President Rudenstine, author of *Pointing Our Thoughts: Reflections on Harvard and Higher Education 1999–2001*, rightly deems Harvard's institutional "commitment to the protection of free speech" and the concurrent "willingness of students and faculty to express their views openly" the single greatest strength of the modern university, even though it requires administrators to reject periodic attempts to enact campus speech codes, the most recent of which sought to remove *Playboy Magazine* from the Widener Library collection.[139]

Race and Ethnicity

The racial and ethnic makeup of the student body is approximately 55 percent non-Hispanic white, 17 percent Asian American, 8 percent African American, 9 percent Hispanic, 1 percent Native American, and 10 percent students of mixed, other, or unreported races and ethnicities. Nine percent of undergrads say that racial/ethnic diversity on campus is an "extremely important" reason they decided to come to Harvard.[140]

Student groups on campus represent every racial and ethnic group the student body has to offer. Predominantly White ethnic student groups include the Central and Eastern European Club, the Irish Cultural Society, and the Hungarian Society; Asian American student groups include the Asian American Association (AAA), the Asian American Brotherhood (AAB), the Asian American Political Action Coalition; African American student groups include the Black Students Association (BSA), the Black Men's Forum (BMF), the Association of Black Harvard Women; Hispanic groups include RAZA, Fuerza Latina, and Concilio Latino; and Native American student groups include Native Americans at Harvard College (NAHC) and the Harvard University Native American Program (HUNAP).

Of the 14 student groups representing 1,120 Asian American undergraduates at Harvard, the largest is the 350-member Asian American Association (AAA). The AAA hosts weekly study groups, monthly events, and guest speakers on educational and political issues facing Asian Americans such as affirmative action, gender and sexuality, Asian American involvement in politics, anti-Asian American violence, and interracial dating. The AAA also sponsors social events like techno dances, movie nights, and Asian cuisine study breaks. Cultural events organized by the AAA include Asian American-themed performances, films, artwork, poetry, literature, and music.[141]

There are approximately 540 African Americans among the Harvard College student body. Increasing competition among top colleges and universities for the recruitment of African American students has led to steadily declining African American enrollment in successive years, reports Director of Admissions Marlyn McGrath Lewis ('70–'73). About 148 African Americans enrolled in the Class of 1997, compared to just 112 in the Class of 2006, when 61.2 percent of African Americans accepted the college's offer of admission. Harvard failed to lead the nation in the percentage of African American yield for the first time in 20 years, according to a study published in the *Journal of Blacks in Higher Education*.[142]

Of the nine African American student groups, the largest is the Black Students Association (BSA), with 300 undergraduate members. Each September, the BSA hosts an incoming freshman class reception, an African American community meeting, and a big sibling/little sibling night out, which pairs freshmen together with upperclassmen mentors. In October the BSA organizes the highly popular Apollo Night, which showcases singing, dancing, and comedy by African American undergraduates. Also in October, the BSA holds a career forum to help African American undergraduates get in touch with the BSA's alum network of close to 3,000 members. The BSA also holds lecture series' throughout the year as well as monthly House activities like study breaks and movie nights.[143] Academically, Harvard has one of the foremost African American studies departments in the country, and in a 1998 study conducted by *Black Enterprise* magazine, Harvard ranked twenty-eighth out of all American colleges "where African Americans are most likely to succeed," higher than any other Ivy League school except for Columbia.[144]

Hispanic undergrads number approximately 590 at Harvard. Among the eight Hispanic student groups on campus, RAZA is the largest, with an undergraduate membership of 200 students. RAZA members describe a "tight-knit Latino community at Harvard." RAZA holds weekly Mesa dinner meetings, after which group members often hang out, watch movies, or go clubbing. RAZA also hosts an annual Cinco de Mayo celebration, East Coast Chicano Student Forum, and a variety of events for Hispanic students staying on campus over the Thanksgiving break.[145]

There are about 65 Native American undergraduates at the college, and about 120 Native Americans within the larger University community, representing over 50 different tribes. The undergraduate Native American student group, called Native Americans at Harvard College (NAHC), is a part of the larger university-wide Harvard University Native American Program (HUNAP). About one-third of the Native American students usually participate in monthly HUNAP-sponsored events, including town meetings, dinners, and study breaks. HUNAP members also recruit prospective undergraduate Native American students at annual off-campus events called College Horizons and Upward Bounds.[146]

Very few students of color perceive unfair treatment on campus on account of race or ethnicity. About 7.6 percent of Harvard undergraduates report having experienced racism on campus—a smaller percentage than at any of the other top 17 private American universities except for Princeton, according to a 1996 Target Management survey.[147] Asked to rate the general spirit of openness and civility of race relations at Harvard, undergraduates gave the campus a B+ overall and the college administration a B-minus, according to the 1998 Race Survey jointly conducted by *The Harvard Crimson* and Harvard's Institute of Politics.[148]

Those dissatisfied with race relations at Harvard complain of tension associated with affirmative action, self-segregation, and the scarcity of minority faculty and of curricular programs dedicated to the study of minority cultures.[149] In order to enhance the diversity of viewpoints on campus, the admissions committee de-emphasizes to some extent academic, extracurricular, and personal measures in favor of minority race and ethnicity as independent criteria in the admissions process. Although minorities accepted under the college's affirmative action policy are, on average, slightly less prepared academically than non-minorities, admitted students of color are overwhelmingly qualified for every aspect of life in Cambridge. Nevertheless, African American and Hispanic students on campus are sometimes offhandedly typecast as affirmative action admits who owe their Harvard acceptance less to personal merit than to skin color. These groundless classifications give many Harvard students of color cause to question their abilities and to carry the burden of "proving" that they belong at Harvard.[150]

Harvard undergrads also correlate tense race relations with deficient public interaction among students of different races. According to a 2002 poll conducted by *The Harvard Crimson,* more than fifty percent of undergraduates believe that social clusters at Harvard self-segregate to a "great degree," particularly with regard to race and ethnicity.[151] Undergraduate social segregation happens every time Harvard students sit down for a meal. Look around any Harvard dining hall, and you'll see separate tables devoted to classifiable student groupings based on athletics, extracurriculars, academic interests, or, most noticeably, race. Many students believe that the extent of social segregation on campus damages the quality of undergraduate experience by undercutting the diversity of the student body. While it is true that undergrads often choose to congregate with those who have similar appearances, experiences, interests, or tastes in music, most Harvard students do a good job of balancing identity-preservation with intergroup contact. Harvard undergraduates interact with students unlike themselves all the time—within courses, extracurriculars, and randomized upperclass Houses, for example. The vast majority of students report having close interracial friendships at Harvard.[152] While most undergrads would prefer that there be less self-segregation among them, only the active extension of individual students—sitting at the "other" table in the dining hall or attending different racial/ethnic group meetings—can substantively improve the quality of interracial interaction on campus.[153]

The lack of faculty diversity also concerns many undergraduates. Harvard tenures fewer women and minority faculty than other top colleges. As of fall 2001, the FAS employed 33 percent women junior faculty, 17 percent women senior faculty, 15 percent minority junior faculty, and 14 percent minority senior faculty.[154] As of spring 2002, there was only one tenured African American woman in all of the FAS: Professor of African American Studies Evelyn Brooks Higginbotham. There is only one minority dean at the highest levels of any of the University's 10 schools: Division of Engineering and Applied Sciences Dean Venkatesh Narayanamurti. Some students report that the overwhelmingly white and male makeup of the FAS faculty and administration deprives them of diverse faculty perspectives and diverse academic role models. African American undergraduates, for example, have a much tougher time finding academic mentors at Harvard than they would at predominantly African American colleges like Howard, Hampton, Spelman, or Fisk.[155]

Former University President Rudenstine affirms that the shortage of women and minority faculty is not the result of discriminatory hiring practices or of any lack of institutional commitment to diversity. Rudenstine attributes the low numbers instead to the dearth of women PhDs in the 1970s and 1980s and to the nation-wide "pipeline problem," whereby high concentrations of qualified minority PhDs in a certain few departmental fields causes them to be in short supply in many other fields.[156] But Narayanamurti, like many undergraduates, believes that Harvard doesn't do enough to recruit women and minority faculty members.[157]

Harvard is in fact undertaking substantial efforts to increase the number of women and minority professors in its ranks. Throughout the 1990s, former Dean of the FAS Jeremy R. Knowles created several administrative bodies to promote the recruitment and retention of female and minority faculty. The recently established Office for Faculty Development, for instance, now works with other departments to identify qualified women and minority candidates for tenure, while the Task Force on Faculty Diversity focuses on advancing diverse faculty in both the natural/engineering sciences and the humanities/ social sciences.[158] The results of these efforts have been promising: Harvard's faculty employment rates far exceed the availability rates of women and minority faculty—the number of women and minority PhD recipients in the fields in which the FAS seeks to appoint new faculty members.[159] Harvard's 2002 Affirmative Action Plan Summary showed that the percentage of women faculty increased by 7 percent from 1993 to 2002, while the number of minority faculty in the FAS grew by almost 20 percent in that same time.[160]

Diversity in the Curriculum

A final issue that compromises the temper of diversity on campus is the lack of academic departments devoted to the studies of group identity. Undergraduates have undertaken substantial efforts to diversify Harvard's identity-based curriculum, agitating for the creation of new academic departments in queer studies, ethnic studies, Latino studies, Native American studies, and Asian American studies, in addition to the two existing identity-based departments, Women's studies, and African American studies. The 2002–2003 *Cultural Studies Handbook* explains that these fields typically combine the humanities and social sciences in order to address "the role of cultural forms in shaping the situations of marginal groups." Administrators resisting the creation of new identity-based curricular departments argue either that such interests can be pursued by existing departments in the FAS or that they don't merit their own academic departments on scholastic grounds.[161] Undergraduates currently interested in ethnic studies at Harvard can either apply to pursue an independent track of study or settle for a tangentially-related academic field. A few FAS courses that focus on the study of identity include "Government 1208, The Politics of Islamic Resurgence;" "Comparative Literature 166, The Comic Tradition in Jewish Culture;" and "Women's Studies 163: Nations, Genders, and Sexualities in Comparative Perspective."[162]

Several of these diversity issues came to a head after a 2002 conflict between University President Lawrence H. Summers and highly popular

Fletcher University Professor of African American Studies Cornel West ('74). Citing undisclosed senior faculty members, *The Boston Globe* reported on December 22, 2001 that during an October meeting between Summers and West, Summers criticized West for inflating grades in his introductory African American Studies class, for recording a rap CD during his medical leave of absence, for leading a political committee for the Reverend Al Sharpton, and for writing books that were "more likely to be reviewed in *The New York Times* than in academic journals." West left the meeting feeling "disrespected" by Summers, and, even after thousands of undergraduates petitioned him to stay at Harvard, he resigned from his professorship and left for Princeton, citing "fundamental differences with Summers about the purpose of education."[163]

After West resigned, several undergraduate groups on campus joined together in 2002 to form a "diversity coalition," consisting of the Black Students Association (BSA), Black Men's Forum (BMF), Association of Black Harvard Women, Asian American Association (AAA), RAZA, Bisexual, Gay, Lesbian and Transgendered Alliance (BGLTSA), Girlspot, Diversity and Distinction, and the Progressive Student Labor Movement (PSLM). Student protesters were inspired by Summers's involvement with West's resignation, the concurrent resignation of Carswell Professor of African American Studies and Philosophy K. Anthony Appiah, and Summers's perceived "inactivity and indifference" regarding diversity in the FAS faculty and curriculum. The diversity coalition first staged a silent protest, during which they donned white masks to symbolize faculty demographics and later organized a campus-wide diversity rally.[164]

Following the 2002 diversity protests on campus, students from the Harvard Foundation for Intercultural and Race Relations submitted to all upper-level Harvard College administrators a comprehensive proposal for an annual diversity progress report. The proposal included recommendations for the immediate creation of a Center for the Study of Race and Ethnicity, a race and ethnic studies concentration, a House-based race-relations initiative, and four professorial chairs—one each in Native American, Asian American, Latino, and Comparative Race and Ethnic Studies. It remains to be seen what institutional changes, if any, will result from recent student efforts to amplify Harvard's commitment to diversity.[165]

CHAPTER THREE
ACADEMIC LIFE

Harvard College boasts among the most brilliant students, the most expansive resources, and the most renowned professors in the world. Harvard is an institution "devoted to the highest reaches of scholarship and research, where ideas and ideals, theories and postulates, problems and solutions are the basis of daily existence; where *summas* beckon [and] Nobel Laureates are a dime a dozen."[166] Nevertheless, there remain considerable weak spots in the academic environment at Harvard. The Faculty of Arts and Sciences (FAS) instituted reform measures in 2002 for glaring problems with grade inflation and study abroad and are currently undergoing reviews of the core curriculum, faculty hiring, and ethnic studies. But the biggest failing of an otherwise stellar Harvard education is insufficient student-faculty interaction.

DEGREE REQUIREMENTS

To graduate from Harvard with a degree in the bachelor of arts (BA) or the bachelor of science (BS), you typically have to pass 32 semester-long courses and receive letter grades of C-minus or higher in at least 22 of them. So your average Harvard undergrad takes four courses per semester over eight semesters and four years for a total of 32 semester-long courses. Advanced Standing and sophomore transfer students, granted a year's worth of credits, have to pass 24 semester-long Harvard courses and get a C-minus or higher in at least 15 of them. Junior transfer students, granted two years' worth of credits, have to pass 16 semester-long Harvard courses and get a C-minus or higher in at least 10 of them. In order to receive a BA or BS degree, all undergraduates have to complete requirements in writing, foreign language, the core curriculum, and a field of concentration. Bachelor of Science degrees are awarded only to the 10–20 students in each graduating class who focus their studies in the more rigorous engineering sciences. Ninety-six percent of Harvard undergrads get a degree within five years; the other four percent either drop out, transfer, get dismissed, or take an extended leave of absence.[167]

Of the 32 courses you take, just about half must be in your chosen field of concentration. You need to take seven courses in those areas of the core curriculum most distant from your concentration. And you have to take one course in expository writing during your freshman year. If you haven't fulfilled the foreign language requirement with test scores or a placement exam, you also have to take two courses in a foreign language. Of your remaining "elective" courses, usually about nine or so, you can study abroad at a foreign university, fulfill pre-med requirements, pursue citations and certificates, cross-enroll at Harvard professional schools or Massachusetts Institute of Technology, or take graduate courses, general education classes, freshman and House Seminars, or any other classes that interest you. If you're a transfer student, the foreign language requirement is the same, the writing requirement may or may not be waived depending on how you do on a writing test, and the core curriculum requirement is modified so as to comprise about a quarter of the courses you take at Harvard.

The magnitude and rigidity of Harvard's degree requirements stems from the college's commitment to providing undergraduates with a broad liberal arts education. While students have varying degrees of choice in every academic course they take at Harvard, at least two-thirds of those courses need to comply with specific requirements. The FAS' conception of a liberal arts education issues, first, from former University President Abbott Lawrence Lowell's conviction that properly educated adults "should know a little of everything and something well," and, second, from the understanding that college students need faculty direction to take the classes that will enable them to attain the desired scope of knowledge by the time they graduate. "In defining the requirements for the bachelor of arts and bachelor of science degrees," the *Handbook for Students* says, "the faculty has sought to…establish a framework for study in the college that ensures involvement with important areas of general knowledge (the core requirement) and in-depth study of one specific area (the concentration requirement)." The *Handbook* justifies the writing and foreign language requirements by reasoning that competence in these skills is essential for meeting the "complex demands of modern society." The FAS helps students meet other "complex demands" with courses like Psychology 1204, "Hormones and Behavior;" Literature 105, "The Theory of Sexuality;" and Science B-29, "Evolution of Human Nature," more commonly called "Sex," which one student describes as "more explicit than anything I have found online."[168]

Courses

The 800+ page *FAS Courses of Instruction* tome, available online at www.registrar.fas.harvard.edu/Courses/, infuses in students "the thrill of realizing that…even if you attended Harvard five times you could never exhaust the possibilities."[169] The *Handbook for Students*, available online at www.registrar.fas.harvard.edu/handbooks/student/, outlines academic requirements and special academic cases, such as taking more than four courses, taking courses at the Harvard graduate schools, or cross-registering for courses at other Boston-area colleges. The *Committee on Undergraduate Education* (CUE) *Guide*, available online at www.fas.harvard.edu/~cueguide with a Harvard student ID and Personal Identification Number (PIN) number, provides information on course content, requirements, and assigned reading, as well as quantitative and qualitative student opinions on course workload, difficulty, professor approachability/availability, and quality of lectures and assignments. In the 2000–2001 *Cue Guide*, students gave high overall ratings for courses throughout the FAS. Courses in the humanities got the highest overall ratings, at 4.4 out of 5.0. Students rated courses in the social sciences a 4.2 out of 5.0 and courses in the natural sciences a 4.0 out of 5.0.

Academic Calendar

Harvard starts and ends each year at least a week after just about every other college in America. This means that you don't have spring break when your high school friends do, that some summer programs start before you get out of school, and that by the end of August, while you're still on summer vacation, "everyone's gone but your old high school teachers and your bridge-playing great uncle."[170]

Harvard's freshman orientation programs take place in late August. Incoming freshmen receive applications in the mail for orientation programs like dorm crew, the First-Year Outdoor Program (FOP), the First-Year Urban Program (FUP), the First-Year Arts Program (FAP), and the First-Year International Program (FIP). Orientation programs select participants on the basis of eagerness and enthusiasm rather than ability or experience, and turn away a majority of applicants each summer. During these orientation programs, pre-freshman meet classmates while scrubbing toilets for pay (dorm crew); hiking and canoeing across New England (FOP); building houses for nonprofit community organizations in Cambridge and Boston (FUP); singing, dancing, and acting with upperclass artists on campus (FAP); and getting acclimated to the states alongside other incoming foreign students (FIP). Students report having lots of fun at Harvard's orientation programs, but say that FOP and FAP cost too much and that few undergrads actually keep in touch with the friends they meet during orientation.

The rest of the freshman class arrives on campus in the beginning of September, a week before upperclassmen get to school. The freshman-only first week of school is known to students as "Camp Harvard". That week is pretty much the only time when students have nothing school-related (except for a couple of placement tests) to worry about—no classes, no extracurriculars, no jobs, no summer applications. Just 1,600+ kids, all in their first week at Harvard, with lots of time to meet people, check out the campus, and head into Boston. The Crimson Key Society of upperclassmen also hosts a variety of optional social mixers for freshmen, such as a dance, movie night, and ice cream bash. When Camp Harvard ends in mid-September, freshmen grieve, upperclassmen arrive, and classes begin.

Registration at Harvard just means making sure your tuition is all paid up, checking over your personal information as listed in Harvard's records, and receiving a study card for course-enrollment. After Registration Day, the fall term kicks in with 12 consecutive weeks of classes (speckled with a few days off), followed by two weeks of winter break, two weeks of "Reading Period," ten days of exam period, and then one week of "intersession" before spring semester finally begins. Harvard's fall semester lasts about 19 weeks in total, running later than most other colleges, from start to finish.

But students appreciate Harvard's struggles with punctuality. Most colleges require students to register for courses before the term begins, forcing them to choose their courses based solely on the three-line blurbs in the course catalogue. Harvard, by contrast, doesn't make students register for courses until seven days into the semester, after they've had a full week of "Shopping Period," when they can sit in on as many courses as they like in order to get as much information as they can on syllabi, class sizes, and professor teaching styles. Undergrads use Shopping Period "mainly to weed out classes they dislike or trim their lists of classes down to four."[171] Degree requirements, faculty sabbaticals, course lotteries, and limited enrollment takes care of a good deal of trimming for you. But because they have so much information about the courses available to them and so much time to choose which courses they will take, Harvard students are much happier with their final course decisions than they would've been without the freedom that Shopping Period affords them. Students are responsible for all work assigned during Shopping Period, but most professors give shortened or repeated lectures during the first two weeks of the semester. Official course enrollments, submitted on the study card, aren't due until two weeks into the term. And up until the fifth Monday after you hand in your study card you can add courses, drop courses, or change them to pass/fail grading with the permission of the instructor.

Besides the late start, late registration, and late-running terms, Harvard's schedule is also unique in that fall semester exams come after winter break, with a "Reading Period" in between. It might seem like having exams hanging over your head would keep you from fully enjoying your break or reconnecting with high school friends back home. But during winter break, which falls in the last couple weeks of December, you take comfort in knowing that exams are weeks away, and that you'll have at least 12 days of Reading Period when you get back from break to catch up on work, organize study groups, make review sheets, and cram for exams. Unlike students at most colleges, Harvard undergrads don't face a three-week hell between Thanksgiving and Winter Break, during which they've got to rush to complete term papers, final projects, and final exams. Having exams after break means that you have between two and four times as many days to study for final exams than students at any other Ivy (except Princeton, which also has exams after break). Despite the shortened winter break and longer study period, many Harvard students choose to bring their books home with them over break to write final papers, work on final projects, or study for final exams. Because they're just so much fun.

When winter break ends just after New Year's, you're supposed to be back on campus for a two-week Reading Period. The *Handbook for Students* maintains, "students are expected to remain in the immediate vicinity of Cambridge during the Examination Periods, Reading Periods, and term time" and "may not be absent from the area for extended periods of time during the term without the permission of their Allston Burr Senior Tutor or the Dean of Freshmen." In truth, senior tutors and freshman deans have no idea when students come back from break and don't discipline them in any way for returning late to campus. Accordingly, students willing to miss out on whatever review sessions are offered during Reading Period can come back to Harvard just in time to take their final exams and extend their winter break by up to two weeks. The vast majority of students, however, get back to campus for the start of Reading Period.

Reading Period, according to the *Handbook*, provides time for students to "work independently, explor[e] special topics or integrat[e] the material covered in … course[s]." No classes meet during Reading Period, except for scattered optional review sessions and mandatory language courses, which meet regularly. Dean of Freshmen Elizabeth Studley Nathans says that Reading Period gives freshmen "the chance to review and consolidate material not fully assimilated from the early weeks of the term, when first-year students may still have been adjusting to the quantity of work assigned in university courses and to the qualitative expectations of their instructors."[172] Translation: most students, freshmen and upperclassmen alike, use Reading Period to catch up on reading and other work they didn't do during the semester.

Although Reading Period incurs heavier workloads if your professors assign a term paper or other project due before exams start, the full two weeks of Reading Period usually provides more time than is necessary to complete final projects and prepare for exams. Many students find that the extra time on campus is an ideal opportunity to invite friends from other schools to visit them at Harvard. Reading Period ends in mid-January when the two-week fall examination period begins.

Exam period is more stressful for some students than for others. Regardless of how prepared they are, some Harvard undergrads always go nuts under the pressure of exams, while others remain more monotonously mellow than Al Gore ('69) doing a hookah. But the level of stress that most students feel during exam period simply depends on how many exams they have and how closely together those exams are scheduled to take place. There are two exam sessions a day, each three hours long. Morning exams begin at 9:15 A.M. and afternoon exams at 2:15 P.M. Old final exams for most courses are available online at www.fas.harvard.edu/~exams/. During the two-week exam period, you'll have anywhere between zero and five finals, depending on how many courses you're taking and how many of them require a final exam (some don't). Your exams may be spread out evenly across exam period or come one right after another. The Registrar's Office posts exam schedules during Reading Period. The earlier your exams end, the sooner you get a start on your second winter break, called "intersession." Intersession, which lasts for about a week until the start of spring term, is more relaxing than winter break. With a fresh semester ahead of you and no lingering work or exams to do when you get back to school, you can truly kick back and relax. Some students go home, some students stay at Harvard, and rich students go someplace warm.

Spring semester starts with another week of Shopping Period and then eight total weeks of classes before a week-long spring break, followed by another five weeks of classes, two weeks of Reading Period, and ten days of final exams. You're done for the year when your last exam is over in the spring. The last day of exams usually comes at the end of the third week of May, after which all undergraduates, except for graduating seniors, are booted out of the dormitories. Graduating seniors stay on campus for pre-commencement "Senior Week," when they party hard at Six Flags New England, the senior barbecue, the "Booze Cruise," and the "Last Chance Dance," notorious for Ivy League baby-making. Senior Class Day, held in early June, has drawn comedian speakers such as Rodney Dangerfield, Conan O'Brian ('85), Al Franken ('73), and Will Ferrell.[173] Harvard's commencement is held in Harvard Yard, where the grass is reseeded, a massive tent is pitched, and red silk flags are strewn across the treetops. Commencement speakers in recent years have included Chairman of the Federal Reserve Bank Alan Greenspan, U.S. Secretary of State Colin Powell, and Czech Republic President Václav Havel.

Class Size and Student-Faculty Interaction

Fully 70 percent of Harvard's courses number fewer than 20 students, including most foreign language classes and all expository writing classes, freshman seminars, sophomore tutorials, junior seminars, and one-on-one senior thesis supervision. These small classes make high levels of in-class student-faculty interaction possible. As one student explains, "The relationship you have with your professor [in a tutorial or seminar] is much more fulfilling academically than anything you could have in a lecture."[174]

Undergraduates have large lecture-style classes for 25 percent to 60 percent of the courses they take at Harvard, depending on their concentration and personal preferences. Seventeen percent of classes at Harvard enroll between 20 and 50 students, and 13 percent of classes have more than 50 students, higher percentages than at any of the other 12 highest-rated schools in the country, except for Stanford and MIT, according to *U.S. News & World Report's* 2003 edition of "America's Best Colleges." Part of the reason why there are so many big courses in the FAS is that Harvard has fewer faculty positions than other top colleges with a comparable undergraduate enrollment. At eight undergraduates per faculty member, Harvard has a higher student-faculty ratio than any of *U.S. News and World Report's* other 12 highest-rated schools, except for Duke and Dartmouth.

The largest classes at Harvard consist of core curriculum requirements and introductory courses required of large concentrations. These courses consistently draw more than 100 students. Five of them enroll over 400. These behemoths are held in either Sanders Theater or Science Center Lecture Hall C, both located just outside the gates of Harvard Yard. Professors report that teaching in these cavernous halls minimizes contact with students and turns lectures into performances.[175] The sheer size and physical distance between professors and students in these classes makes it unlikely that a professor will be able to get to know students. Professor of the History of Science Everett I. Mendelsohn admits, "Someone will walk through the Yard and smile at me, and I'll have no idea that they are in my class." Large lecture courses also make it easy for students to skip, sleep, and distract themselves during class without anyone noticing.[176]

But large class size doesn't necessarily make a course unengaging, and low level of student-faculty interaction doesn't necessarily diminish the quality of undergraduate education. Students choose to take the largest lecture classes expecting that they'll be enormous and noninteractive. And most of the time, students give these courses just as high overall ratings as all other classes in biannual *CUE Guide* surveys.[177]

Bass Professor of Government Michael J. Sandel (a dead ringer for *The Simpsons'* Mr. Burns, on whom his former students, now comedy writers, based the character) typically attracts more than 1,000 students to his core course "Moral Reasoning 22: Justice," taught every other year in Sanders Theater. Sandel intersperses lectures on Rawles' "right" and Bentham's "good" with class surveys, movie clips, personal anecdotes, and frenzied student participation, during which he power-walks around Sander's Theater auditorium, passing the microphone among quarrelling students, setting them up against each other Jerry Springer-style. Faced with a choice between a leviathan taught by a legendary scholar or celebrated lecturer and a small seminar taught by an unknown faculty member, students often opt for Springer. Harvard could create smaller classes by instituting strict limitations on class sizes, like they do at other Ivy League colleges, but such cut-offs would greatly restrict the range of courses from which students could choose.

Every lecture course in the FAS is supplemented by weekly labs or discussion sections of 10–15 students each. Fifteen percent to forty percent of undergraduates' total in-class instruction at Harvard is conducted in these complementary labs and sections. Sections are led by teaching fellows (TFs), two-thirds of whom are students at Harvard graduate or professional schools and one-quarter of whom are visiting affiliates from other universities.[178]

Although "teaching fellows serve as the go-between for students and faculty members where no middleman should exist," *The Harvard Crimson* argues, TF-directed discussion sections "enhance undergraduate education by providing an opportunity to deal with the material in a hands-on way," according to Associate Dean of the FAS for Undergraduate Education Jeffrey Wolcowitz. Sections engage course material through casual interactive discussion, including games, simulations, related current events, and question-and-answer sessions designed to tackle the material in a less theoretical and more concrete way than lectures do. There is no back row in these discussion sections, but the one or two aggressive participants in every section enables inhibited students to lay low if they don't want to contribute.

A shortage of graduate students in some math, computer, and natural science departments also makes it necessary to hire 50–100 undergraduates each year to serve as teaching assistants (TAs) in those classes.[179] Undergraduate teaching assistants undergo a two-day training program at the Bok Center for Teaching and Learning before getting in front of a class to teach. While sections are supposed to be assembled so that undergraduate TAs don't know any of the students in their section, in a few upper-level computer science courses, TAs report knowing almost everyone in the class, making it impossible to avoid grading their friends' work. But grading math, computer, and natural science problem sets is a fairly objective process, much more so than grading papers in the humanities and social sciences (where no TAs are used). Although some students object on principle to "paying $35,000 a year to be taught by [their] blockmate[s],"[180] Professor of Computer Science Henry H. Leitner says that undergraduates make even better teachers than graduate students because undergrads have fresher memories of course materials and better English skills than some first year grad students. Undergraduate teaching assistants "have generally done excellent jobs," Leitner says, "and in fact have won more Bok Center teaching awards than the grad student TFs."[181]

Very few Harvard faculty members have regular out-of-class conversations with their students or take the time to learn about students' interests. Seventeen percent of Harvard seniors in 2001 reported that no faculty members in their courses had gotten to know them during the past academic year, and another 16 percent said that just one faculty member had done so.[182] Harvard undergrads can interact with professors either during office hours or meals, but in both cases, students bear the burden of seeking out contact. Even the most prominent Harvard professors are required to hold open office hours each week, an ideal time for students to hash out ideas about class, college, and life in general with some of the world's greatest minds. Curiously, few students attend their professors' office hours. Meals are another option for out-of-class student-faculty interaction. While Harvard University Dining Services (HUDS) allows faculty members to eat in dining halls free, professors hardly ever volunteer themselves for mealtime discussions or even let it be known that they are willing to have meals with students who ask them. Organized student-faculty dinners take place just once each semester.

TEACHING QUALITY

Harvard's FAS faculty of about 600 professors features an unparalleled number of Pulitzer and Nobel Prize winners. Distinguished faculty members teach every undergraduate course at Harvard. Although Harvard professors are recruited and hired primarily on the basis of research and scholarship, with little regard for their teaching ability, most professors are dedicated and engaging lecturers, particularly in the humanities. Students recognize the faculty's effective teaching with high ratings in biannual *CUE Guide* surveys, published by the Committee on Undergraduate Education, used in 90 percent of FAS courses enrolling more than 20 students as well as a small number of seminars, tutorials, and conference courses, and distributed to undergraduates each fall.[183] In the 2000–2001 *CUE Guide*, students gave professors teaching courses in the humanities an average rating of 4.5 out of 5.0, gave professors teaching in the social sciences an average of 4.3 out of 5.0, and gave professors in the natural sciences a 4.1 out of 5.0.[184]

The Committee on Undergraduate Education doesn't calculate average overall ratings for teaching fellows. While most teaching fellows fall somewhere between mediocre and good, undergraduates are certain to get at least a few of the best and worst TFs in their time at Harvard. The best TFs are teaching professionals and specialists in the course materials, having had extensive experience teaching in the classroom and prior study in the specific subject area. They come to sections early, well-prepared, and sociable, and make themselves available for extra help outside of section by email or phone and during office hours or meetings by appointment. The worst TFs are marked by inadequate teaching ability, excessive graduate commitments, or general apathy for teaching responsibilities. They are weak at facilitating discussion and uncomfortable with talking in front of students or even with the English language. They come to class late, don't hold office hours or respond to student emails, have little background in the course materials, and are insufficiently prepared each week for the course's assigned reading or problem sets. These are the ones who turn an otherwise excellent Harvard course into a bad experience and make a mediocre course insufferable. Students have little or no say in the teaching fellows they get assigned. While it is possible to switch sections early on in the term, students are discouraged from switching unless they have legitimate schedule conflicts. Attempting to switch sections in order to get a more dedicated or less demanding TF is usually not possible, anyhow, because "[b]y the time you get far enough into the course to figure out if the TF is any good, it's too late to switch."[185]

The persistence of weak section leaders stems in part from Harvard's in-semester course registration. Ideally, professors would be able to carefully scrutinize and select prospective teaching fellows from a large pool of applicants and would have ample time to prime them in the specific course materials and general teaching duties before they were responsible for explaining the information to undergraduates. But because of Harvard's Shopping Period, which extends official course registration until after classes have already started, many professors don't know until two weeks into the term exactly how many students will be in their course or how many teaching fellows they should hire to lead discussion sections. "There are surprises every year," explains William G. Witt, copyright officer in the Office of Sourcebook Publications. "One year a class may have had 200 students, and this term it has 500 students."[186] When many more undergraduates enroll in a course than the professor anticipated, professors are resigned to hiring unscreened, untrained, or unqualified teaching fellows to meet the unexpected student demand for class sections. "[I]f you take a young grad student who's never taught before," one student points out, "and throw him or her into a class on a subject about which he or she is even vaguely uncertain, it's a recipe for disaster."[187] In order to promote more capable section leaders in the FAS, Dean of the Faculty William C. Kirby is currently pursuing a program of pre-registration that would retain the Shopping Period, but would require students to submit nonbinding study cards one semester in advance of course enrollment for that term.[188]

The college uses *CUE Guide* ratings to identify poorly-performing TFs. "When a TF falls below 3.0 [on the *CUE Guide's* 5-point scale]," former Dean of Undergraduate Education William M. Todd III explains, "we write a letter in which we outline some measures the TF can take to improve his/her performance." Typically, about 50 TFs out of 1,000 receive letters recommending they seek assistance with their teaching.[189] Those TFs who receive poor evaluations for a second time—"fewer than a dozen," according to former Dean of Undergraduate Education Susan Pedersen ('81–'82), "are barred from further teaching."[190] Teaching fellows who receive low *CUE Guide* ratings are advised, but not required to get teaching help at the Derek Bok Center for Teaching and Learning, which provides extensive voluntary resources and services for all teachers in the FAS, from first-time TFs to tenured professors. The Bok Center holds voluntary teaching conferences before classes start each semester and conducts student evaluations for teachers' classes a couple weeks into each term. The Bok Center also offers walk-in clinics, seminars, and individual coaching sessions on topics like discussion leadership, lecture presentation, compilation of syllabi, English as a second language, and the use of technology in the classroom.[191]

Bok Center resources are used almost exclusively by graduate student teaching fellows, reports Lee Warren, Associate Director of the Bok Center. About 500–700 teaching fellows employed by the FAS attend one of the biannual Bok Center teaching orientations, and 200 more have their classroom teaching observed and evaluated by Bok Center professionals. All first-time TFs get some sort of training, but it usually amounts to no more than talking informally with a faculty member, Bok Center staff member, or another TF before teaching in the classroom. Though few junior faculty members and even fewer senior faculty members ever seek help at the Bok Center, Warren says there has been increasing interest in Bok Center resources among FAS professors from 1998–2002. In the end, notes former Dean Pedersen, professors are responsible for the kind of teaching that goes on in class sections. And few professors take the necessary time to prepare TFs, attend and evaluate discussion sections, and act on the advice of mid-term student surveys.[192]

Unlike most colleges, "Harvard is not a tenure-track institution," according to former Associate Dean of Affirmative Action Marjorie Garber. This means that untenured faculty at Harvard, like assistant and associate professors, are not automatically considered for tenure.[193] Under the current system, most Harvard junior faculty members spend an average of six or seven years at Harvard before getting fired and gaining prestige at other institutions. Departments seek only to tenure an individual who is already judged to be "the leading scholar/teacher available in the field," according to the 2000 FAS tenure statement. Just 35 percent of tenured positions in the FAS are filled by faculty members from within Harvard.[194]

But University President Summers, who has the final say on all tenure decisions, wants to modify the college's aim in deciding tenure cases. Summers wants to tenure professors less on the basis of reward for past achievement and more on the prospect of future work. He's urging departments to take greater risks on promising professors at early stages in their careers, so that Harvard's tenured faculty will do their best work while at Harvard, instead of at other institutions. This seems like a very good thing, especially because the FAS faculty lost several of its top young professors in 2002. The most notable departures were Assistant Professor of Government Keith J. Bybee, who left Harvard after being passed over for tenure to assume a tenured position at Syracuse University, and Assistant Professor of American History Brett Flehinger, who won the Levenson award for outstanding teaching in 2000, but who also left Harvard after being passed over for tenure. Flehinger assumed a tenured position at California State University—San Bernadino.[195]

Although in need of some tweaking, Harvard's tenure policy generally does a good job promoting effective teaching at the college. Harvard pays tenured professors more than other top colleges. In 1999–2000, the average salary for tenured professors at Harvard was $122,100, compared to $117,000 at Stanford, $114,900 at Princeton, $113,100 at Yale, and $107,000 at MIT.[196] Evidence of effective teaching is a required and substantial component in all promotion and tenure decisions, whether from assistant professor to associate professor or from associate or outside professor to tenured professor. The FAS tenure process begins when a department makes the decision to recommend one of its faculty members for tenure and sets about creating a "dossier" of recommendation letters on which the tenure candidate will be evaluated. The department then fields confidential letters of recommendation from professors within and outside of Harvard regarding the merit of the candidate's published work. The department chair also writes a letter of recommendation about the candidate's merits as a teacher, based on numerical evaluations and written comments from student evaluations—Harvard's *Committee on Undergraduate Education (CUE) Guide*, for example, or equivalent student evaluations done at other institutions.[197] When the letters of recommendations are complete, members of the department go before a review body to present the candidate's tenure dossier and testify on the candidate's behalf. The body that reviews each tenure case consists of the eight academic deans in the FAS, the university president, and an *ad hoc* committee of scholars appointed by the president. The university president makes the final decision on all tenure cases.[198] Although FAS deans are unable to quantify the amount of weight that teaching quality typically gets in tenure review, the fact that evidence of effective teaching plays a considerable role in every tenure decision provides professional incentive for FAS junior faculty to make effective undergraduate teaching a priority.[199]

The college also bestows special awards onto TFs, junior faculty, and senior faculty in recognition of exceptional teaching. Some awards have no financial component and some are one-time monetary prizes. None give long-term salary raises or involve special duties like the mentoring of less-experienced faculty. The Bok Center ceremonially honors the 15–20 percent teaching fellows who get *CUE Guide* evaluations of 4.5 or higher out of 5.0.[200] "Recognition as a good teacher is very important for…graduate students," notes former Dean Pedersen, "as they seek professional positions else-where."[201] The Undergraduate Council (UC) awards the Levenson Prize annually to one teaching fellow, one junior faculty member, and one senior faculty member. The Abramson Prize is a one-time money award for junior faculty. And Harvard College Professorships, awarded to senior faculty, are five-year appointments that bulk up a professor's official title and offer a choice of either one extra term of paid leave or the equivalent in research funds or summer salary.[202]

DIFFICULTY

Harvard academics require denser reading, longer exams, and a greater number of papers and problem sets than most colleges, making for a heavy and arduous academic workload. That said, more than one Harvard undergraduate notes, "You do not need to work nearly as hard once you're here as you did to get in."[203] Carefully selected from among a tremendous pool of academically qualified students, more than 99 percent of those admitted can handle the work at Harvard. And Harvard's delayed academic schedule affords students more time to get their work done.

In the 2000–2001 *CUE Guide*, students rated FAS courses on the basis of overall workload and difficulty on a scale of one (low) to five (high). Across the FAS, courses in the natural sciences on average require significantly more work and are significantly more difficult than any others. Courses in the core scored an average of 1.9 for workload and an average of 2.9 for difficulty; courses in the humanities scored a 2.2 for workload and 3.0 for difficulty; courses in the social sciences scored a 2.2 and 3.1; and courses in the natural sciences a 2.7 and 3.4.

How much time do Harvard undergrads spend on their academic work, and how much stress do academics cause them in college? Harvard students spend about 12 hours per week in formal classes, about three to ten hours in sections and laboratories, and about 30 hours outside of class reading, writing papers, doing problem sets, preparing homework, and studying.[204] While almost all Harvard students identify academic workload and grades as their foremost cause of anxiety at college, Harvard ranked 14 out of 17, and least stressful among all Ivy League schools except UPenn, in a 1996 study of the academic stress levels on the campuses of America's top universities.[205] Late exams allow professors to space out assignment deadlines and two weeks of Reading Period before final exams each semester allow students to fall behind in their reading during the term comforted by the knowledge that they'll have ample time to catch up before they are tested on the information.

Harvard students read a lot. Massive quantities of assigned reading range from 100 to 600 pages per course per week. "The amount of reading that most professors assign is," one undergraduate complains, "impossible to do … it is rare to find a humanities or social science course with a manageable reading load." Assigned reading is usually pretty dense—a diffuse collection of primary and secondary sources rather than successive, straightforward, annotated sections from one authoritative textbook. However, students figure out pretty quickly that you don't need to do all of the reading to get by. One student explains, "In high school, most Harvard students did all the work and did it excellently. Here, if you get in the mindset that you're going to read every last book on the list, you'll end up driving yourself crazy."[206]

Harvard undergrads write about as much in a given term as the collective musings of W. E. B. DuBois (Class of 1890), T. S. Eliot (Class of 1910), e. e.

cummings (Class of 1915), and other authors whose parents gave them names that were too long. Seventy-one percent of undergraduates write 10 or more papers each year and just 6 percent write fewer than four papers a year. Eighty-three percent are required to hand in at least 60 pages of final work each year and only 10 percent write fewer than 45 pages in a year. How much writing you're assigned to do depends on whether you're pursuing a degree in the arts or the sciences. Your average humanities or social science concentrator writes 14 papers a year, while your typical science concentrator writes just six. Students in the humanities and social sciences frequently turn in over 100 pages.[207]

Harvard undergrads are among the best and brightest in the world, but like all students, they cut corners where they can. Many skip or sleep through class on a regular basis. Professors take notice of such truancy only in smaller courses. Associate Professor of History James Hankins says that when students miss consecutive classes, "the usual reasons given are health or death in the family. . . . I once had a student who made the mistake of killing off her mother twice in the same semester." When students fall asleep in large classes with Professor of Chemistry James Davis, he asks the rest of the students to leave very quietly when the class is over and asks the next class to come in very quietly, so that the student wakes up in a different class. Resourceful loafers have developed several strategies to make their lives easier. Some students take only classes with low *CUE Guide* ratings for course difficulty and workload, others drop or withdraw from a course if they think it'll assign too much work or grade too demandingly, and the truly shiftless milk the liberal policy on Pass/Fail course enrollment. In order to minimize the amount the preparation they need to do to complete assignments, many students wait until the deadline for the first graded assignment before doing any work in a course. It's not uncommon for students to start writing papers at midnight that are due the next afternoon. Those who can't get a paper in on time or get a deadline extension aren't shy about sharing their tricks. When papers were due to be e-mailed to his teaching fellow, one computer science concentrator would send attachments with pre-made papers made of nothing but boxes, which made it appear as though the recipient's computer had failed to reformat the text. This method usually bought at least a few extra hours, he reports.[208] Few undergraduates do the "recommended" course reading or even the required "reserve" reading that must be obtained at the library. And after their first year, most students realize they need not necessarily do any of the assigned reading in a given week to be able "to make quasi-intelligent points during a core class section."[209]

Male students make up most of the slackers at Harvard. Although Harvard men number their fair share of anal-retentive workaholics, many work far less hard in college than they did in high school, primarily because they're confident in their ability to pull everything off and complacent with their Harvard acceptances and imminent Harvard degrees. While some of these slackers are women, most females are almost as painstakingly punctilious about their work as the four-color pen-wielding pre-meds of both sexes, who pack toothpaste and a change of clothes for consecutive all-night orgo sessions in Cabot Library. The typical female Harvard student is, according to one undergraduate woman, "an exceptional note-taker and a religious to-do list maker; she also arrives at her 10:00 A.M. lectures on time, attends office hours, and leaves herself enough time to outline her essays, in detail, before she begins writing them—and to have an extra day to revise them before the ultimate deadline."[210] Part of the reason why females undergraduates are so on top of their work may be that, compared to men, women, on average, deem themselves less academically able compared to their peers. A 1996 study of the top 20 American universities revealed that one-third of men, but only one-sixth of women, consider themselves smarter than the majority of their classmates.[211]

GRADES AND HONORS

The minimum academic requirements for any given term at Harvard are: (1) at least two satisfactory (C– and above) grades, one of which must be a letter grade in an FAS course taken for degree credit, and (2) at most one failing grade, which may not be accompanied by another unsatisfactory (below C–) grade. Students who don't meet these requirements in any one term are required to withdraw from Harvard for a year, even if their prior academic records are stellar. So how many can't hack it? Fifty-six students were required to withdraw for failing to meet academic requirements in the 2001–2002 academic year—fewer than one percent of the student body.[212]

Undergraduate course grades at Harvard are composed of weighted evaluations on a combination of papers, problem sets, labs, section participation, midterms, and final exams. In any class with more than 20 students, TFs grade all assignments and then meet with professors and other teaching fellows in an attempt to standardize grading procedures. But course grading is often inconsistent across teaching fellows, especially in larger classes, which have up to 30 TFs. One student complains, "[Y]ou can know the same amount of material as someone else and get a completely different grade."[213]

A couple weeks after final exams finish up, your grades are available online at www.registrar.fas.harvard.edu under the link for *Course and Grade Reports.* If you want to have a course grade changed, you need to provide two things: proof that the grade was substantially miscalculated in some way and a signed statement from the course instructor agreeing to the grade change. Most students with grade complaints approach their professors directly, and some appeal grades administratively through their freshman dean or senior tutor. But very few grades are ever changed.[214]

The highest general academic honor for Harvard undergraduates is the award of summa cum laude, given to five percent of graduating seniors each year. In order to have a shot at getting summa cum laude honors, students have to field the recommendation of their concentration department and exhibit a high grade point average, exceptional independent work on a thesis or oral exam, and outstanding performance in upper-level courses outside of their concentration. The decision about which students receive summa cum laude honors is made by a six-person subcommittee of the Faculty Council, with two representatives each from the humanities, social sciences, and natural sciences. After the honors are announced, a ceremony is held, wherein all the FAS deans give the award-winners rattails and wedgie bombs.[215]

Grades are inflated at Harvard. In the 2001–2002 academic year, Harvard awarded honors degrees to 90 percent of graduating seniors and an A or A minus for 50 percent of all grades, with only six percent of grades awarded below a B minus. Data compiled by Harvard's Educational Policy Committee (EPC) on Harvard undergraduate grades from 1985–1986 through 2000–2001 indicates that grades are higher in smaller classes than in larger classes and higher in the humanities than in the natural and social sciences.[216]

Some claim that higher overall grades accurately reflect a higher level of work produced by a more talented student body. They cite rising SAT scores among incoming freshmen, wider student availability to technological resources, deeper social emphasis on college preparation, and greater focus on classroom participation within the FAS. Indeed, Harvard students are very smart, work very hard, and have access to tremendous education resources. But none of these reasons fully account for the full one-point jump from 11.7 to 12.7 for grade point averages among Harvard undergraduates from 1985 to 2001 on the old 15-point grading scale (where A = 15, A– = 14, B+ = 12, B = 11, B– = 10, etc.). The increase in grades simply means that, at least to some extent, students have been receiving increasingly higher grades for roughly the same level of work.[217]

The important questions about grade inflation are: what caused it, why is it a problem, what is the college doing about it, and will the reform measures work? The answers are: the faculty's effort to keep undergraduates safe from the Vietnam draft, because it undermines academic progress, limiting honors, and probably not, respectively. As to the causes of grade inflation, former Dean of the College Harry R. Lewis ('68) aptly cites a "collapse of critical judgment" in evaluating undergraduate coursework, which originated in professors' desire to keep grades high so that students wouldn't be drafted into the Vietnam War. Grade inflation is a problem because of its impact on undergraduate education, not on career prospects; there is no evidence that grade and honors inflation has affected employer or graduate school perceptions of Harvard students. But grade inflation does undercut the usefulness of academic feedback for students, the incentive for undergrads to improve, and the accuracy with which students can measure their work against clearly defined standards of excellence.[218]

The faculty voted in favor of two reform measures in 2002 to combat grade and honors inflation at Harvard. First, the FAS replaced the old 15-point scale with a new 4.0 grading scale intended to clarify the meaning of Harvard's grades. Second, the faculty restricted the proportion of honors awarded each year from 90 to 60 percent of the graduating class. The grading reforms do not impose a mandatory curve or any formal constraints on faculty grading procedures, although Dean Gross ('71) will distribute information on "exemplary" grading practices to all departments, and will supervise the grades awarded by departments and individuals as a sort of "anti-inflationary presence." The faculty hopes that these changes will help to restore meaning to a Harvard A, defined by the *Handbook for Students* as "work of extraordinary distinction."[219]

But the college still has a long way to go to ameliorate grade inflation. Most Harvard courses lack the clearly defined grading standards and professorial oversight necessary to maintain consistent grading procedures among TFs, who often use disparate standards within a given section, course, concentration, or field. Some TFs give inflated marks due to the well-documented correlation between high grades and high student evaluations, which can influence TFs' salaries and teaching careers. Other TFs succumb to student pressure for higher grades, which has accompanied the growing competition for post-graduate employment and graduate school admissions. Harvard won't be able to totally fix grade inflation at the college until professors, departments, and the FAS exercise more rigorous supervision over the teaching fellows who actually issue the grades.[220]

MAJORS (CONCENTRATIONS)

While most colleges don't require students to declare a major until the end of their second year, Harvard students must declare their major, or "concentration," by the spring of their first year. The reason that Harvard students have to identify an undergraduate focus so early is because the college's sophomore tutorial program, which gives students intense experience within a particular concentration, requires early commitment to one of Harvard's 40 formal academic concentrations, listed online at www.fas.harvard.edu/academics/departments/.

According to the student handbook, "All degree candidates must fulfill the requirements of one of the recognized fields of concentration, an approved joint concentration, or an approved special concentration." There exists no degree in "general studies" for students who don't complete the requirements for any recognized or approved "concentration."[221] While a third of students change concentrations as upperclassmen, transferring between departments requires students to fulfill their new concentration requirements in less time, meaning they're able to take fewer elective classes. When choosing a concentration and planning a four-year plan of study, students rely on departmental literature, concentration meetings, the advice of upperclassmen, and the *Fields of Concentration* book, available online at www.registrar.fas.harvard.edu/hand-books/student/chapter3/, which outlines the specific requirements for each concentration.[222]

As an undergraduate at Harvard, you have to take between 10 and 15 courses within your chosen field of concentration, depending on the course requirements of your concentration department and on whether you go for concentration honors. Concentration departments recommend or require that students take an introductory concentration course in their freshman year, take concentration tutorials in their sophomore year, and take concentration seminars junior year. Most students pursuing an honors track within their concentrations are required to write a thesis in their senior year and to take two to five more courses within their concentration over their undergraduate career than nonhonors students. All concentrations offer the opportunity for honors, and some concentrations are honors-only: namely, joint concentrations, special concentrations, and interdisciplinary concentrations like literature, social studies, women's studies, applied mathematics, engineering sciences, history of science, chemistry and physics, history and literature, folklore and mythology, and visual and environmental studies. Most honors-only concentrations require students to apply for admission, rejecting between 20 and 45 percent of applicants. Students who get rejected from their honors-only concentration of choice have to pick a different concentration and can reapply the following year.[223]

In 2002 *Fifteen Minutes* polled undergraduates campus-wide in order to rank Harvard's 40 undergraduate concentration departments. The weekend student magazine based its ranking system on six broad categories: advising (25 percent), teaching (25 percent), classes (25 percent), honors (15 percent), social events (5 percent), and retention rate (5 percent).

The advising component of the ranking system focused on concentration's student-to-advisor ratio and seniors' rating (through surveys) of the quality of advising in their concentration department. The teaching component consisted of student-to-faculty ratio, percentage of tenured faculty, percentage of faculty teaching rather than on leave, and average student rating for classes taught by professors in a particular concentration department. The classes component was measured the size of sophomore and junior tutorials (small gets a higher rating) and the average student rating for concentration courses. The honors component was the percentage of concentrators who graduate with Latin honors—summa, magna, and cum laude. The social events component was simply the number of annual social events held by the concentration department, and the retention rate component was calculated as the percentage of first-years who declare themselves concentrators divided by the number of concentrators who actually graduate from that department three years later.

According to these criteria, undergrads ranked Harvard's 40 concentrations in the following order:[224]

Near Eastern Languages and Civilizations
Slavic Languages and Literatures
Classics
History and Literature
Women's Studies
Germanic Languages and Literatures
Sanskrit and Indian Studies
Literature
Comparative Study of Religion
Folklore and Mythology
Chemistry and Physics
Linguistics
Romance Languages and Literatures
Visual and Environmental Studies
Astronomy and Astrophysics
Physics
Chemistry
Biology
History and Science
Mathematics
Social Studies
Earth and Planetary Sciences
History

History of Art and Architecture

Environmental Science and Public Policy

Statistics

African American Studies

Psychology

Biochemical Sciences

Computer Science

English and American Literature and Language

Sociology

Philosophy

Engineering Sciences

Music

Government

Anthropology

Applied Mathematics

Economics

East Asian Studies

The five largest concentrations at Harvard are economics, government, psychology, social studies, and biology, ranked 39th, 36th, 28th, 21st, and 18th, respectively.

Of the 40 traditional concentrations available at Harvard, most students find one that accommodates their interests. But for those who want to study "nontraditional" fields, for which Harvard doesn't offer a concentration department, students can design their own interdisciplinary programs of study, called "special concentrations." A special concentration is ideal for students whose "academic interests don't fall squarely within one discipline," explains Assistant Dean of Undergraduate Education Deborah Foster, Head Tutor of the special concentration program. For students willing to forsake the structure of a traditional concentration department, special concentrations offer tremendous academic independence, allowing students to create their own classes, requirements, and syllabi, perhaps in one-on-one tutorials or cross-enrolled classes at one of Harvard's grad schools. Above all, Foster warns, special concentrators must be prepared to accept the responsibility of designing their own academic program.[225]

It's not easy to get special concentrations approved. The rigorous application process weeds out those who are less motivated. The ten-part, ten-page application for special concentrations, which is reviewed by the 14-person Special Concentration Standing Committee (SPSC), deters many prospective concentrators from applying. The application includes writing a statement of purpose, creating two proposed course plans, and finding a faculty advisor, which for most students proves the most difficult part of the application. Although there's no limit on the number of students who get approved for special concentrations, the SPSC accepts only those applications that meet the criteria set by the faculty committee and typically rejects all but five applicants each year.

Unsuccessful applicants are usually rejected because they fail to distinguish a unique program of liberal arts study or to convince the SPSC that they are not merely trying to evade tedious introductory coursework in a field that better suits their interests. Successful applicants say that they are pleased with the suppleness of special concentration curriculums. Approved special concentrations include education, computer graphics, children studies, health policy, urban design, and music therapy.[226]

Harvard's liberal arts and sciences academic tradition, based on intellectual study and theory, does not include the practice of crafts. "We aren't a professional school," says former Dean Pedersen. "We offer an 'arts and sciences' curriculum. I think students realize that when they apply here."[227] The FAS undergraduate curriculum has no professional or vocational concentrations, such as accounting, advertising, agriculture, architecture, business, commercial art, communications, criminal justice, education, journalism, law, nursing, theater, or musical performance. Concentrations like economics, music, and visual and environmental studies focus almost exclusively on abstract theory rather than on specialized training. Undergrads interested in pursuing professional career paths make up for Harvard's lack of vocational training by throwing themselves into pre-professional extracurricular activities.

"The extracurricular scene is so active and so alive," one undergraduate notes, "that in a sense the extracurricular is the education."[228] Aspiring journalists can write, edit, and publish for *The Harvard Crimson*, *The Harvard*

Independent, or *Harvard Magazine*; aspiring businesspeople can advertise, sell, and manage in the Financial Analyst Club, Women in Business, and Harvard Student Agencies; aspiring visual artists can draw, paint, and sculpt in Office for the Arts and House art studios; aspiring dramatists can act, direct, and produce with the Harvard-Radcliffe Dramatic Club, Hasty Pudding Theatricals, and Gilbert and Sullivan Players, and aspiring performers can sing, play, and dance either in a cappella groups, student bands, and pop dance groups or in the Dunster House Opera, Bach Society Orchestra, and Ballroom Dance Club.

But a pre-professional level of commitment to these or other extracurriculars often takes place at the expense of intellectual pursuits. "Performance opportunities on campus are great, but you don't have the same chance to practice and focus," says a student who took a year off from Harvard to study violin performance at Julliard. "Here [I] play two to three concerts a week, but at Julliard everyone practices for at least five hours a day."[229] Devoting that kind of time to pre-professional training at Harvard means considerable academic sacrifice from students taking four demanding courses each term.

Among prospective students, what the most serious performers often want to know is: can I make it big under Harvard's extracurricular education? Well, musicians like Leonard Bernstein ('39), Yo Yo Ma ('76), and Joshua Redman ('91) did. Actors like Jack Lemmon ('47), Stockard Channing ('65), and Tommy Lee Jones ('69) did. And comedians like John Lithgow ('67), Al Franken ('73), and Conan O'Brien ('85) did.

MINOR EQUIVALENTS

Harvard doesn't offer minors. Harvard students seeking to complement their concentration studies with a secondary field of academic interest can pursue joint-concentrations, citations, or certificates. About five percent, or 260, of upperclassmen in 2001 were registered as joint concentrators, which required that they divide their concentration studies between two academic departments and culminate their undergraduate education with a senior honors thesis uniting their two concentration pursuits. Citations, which are officially recognized on students' transcripts, are offered in any foreign language studies. To be awarded a citation, students must earn grades of B– or better in four semester-long courses in any single language department. The popularity of the language citation program has jumped markedly in recent years, from 56 students in 1998 to 183 in 2001 to 280 in 2002. Certificates, neither publicized in *The Handbook for Students* nor recognized on students' Harvard transcripts, are offered in four areas: African studies (4 students received certificates in 2001), Latin American studies (25), health policy (18), and mind, brain, behavior (70). The requirements to get each certificate vary, but all of them call for coursework and an honors thesis linking certificate studies to concentration studies.[230]

CORE CURRICULUM

Unlike some schools, Harvard does not require students to learn a specific body of knowledge or set of books. Instead, Harvard's core curriculum, developed in 1979, grounds a liberal arts education in eleven broad "approaches to knowledge" that are supposed to broaden the intellectual horizons of narrowly focused undergraduates who would not otherwise experiment among the different academic perspectives offered at Harvard. There are eleven areas in the core curriculum, of which students must take seven. Students are exempt from the four core areas that are most remote to their concentration studies, as determined by each concentration department. The full list of exemptions is available in the *Handbook for Students* and online on the Core curriculum website at www.courses.fas.harvard.edu/~core/.

The eleven core areas are

Foreign Cultures (language and culture)
Historical Study A (modern civilization)
Historical Study B (ancient civilization)
Literature and Arts A (literary analysis)
Literature and Arts B (art and music)
Literature and Arts C (cultural literature)
Moral Reasoning (ethical philosophy)
Quantitative Reasoning (statistics and logic)
Science A (physical science)
Science B (biological science)
Social Analysis (politics and society)

Core courses provide students with introductory approaches to knowledge in a format slightly unlike that of standard departmental introductory courses. Cores are watered-down so as to provide what the core program deems a "manageable quantity of knowledge."[231] Core courses also differ from departmental courses by virtue of the core program's oversight for consistency in workload and difficulty among core offerings.

Senior faculty members teach 93 percent of cores, and students gave core instructors an average rating of 4.2 out of 5.0 in the 2000–2001 *CUE Guide*. Noting several problems with the core curriculum, students gave core courses a good but not great average overall rating of 4.0 out of 5.0.

Students clamor for a greater number and wider diversity of core offerings. The FAS has not yet met its 1997 goal of offering 12 courses per year in each core area. Insufficient availability of alternatives within several core areas severely curtails students' curricular choices. *The Harvard Crimson* explains, "when only three or four courses that fulfill a particular core requirement are offered in a term, students are often forced to pick a class that fits more conveniently into their schedules rather than one that truly interests them."[232] Students also lament the shortage of departmental courses cross-listed for core credit, especially those students with a strong background in a core area who want to explore upper-level department coursework remote from their concentration.[233] While some courses in each department don't fulfill the core's goal of teaching "approaches to knowledge," students argue many more departmental courses in fact do teach broad approaches to knowledge than are currently cross-listed for core credit. As of the 2002–2003 academic year, there are no departmental courses offered that satisfy any of the social analysis, historical studies A, or literature and arts A, B, or C requirements. While students may petition the Standing Committee on the Core Program to request credit for a non-core class, petitions are usually approved only for students who have extenuating academic circumstances (like changed or joint concentrations) that prevent them from otherwise fulfilling a given core area requirement, rather than for students who want to get core credit for a smaller, more challenging, or more focused departmental course that teaches an "approach to knowledge" closely resembling those in a given area of the core.[234]

WRITING REQUIREMENT

To fulfill Harvard's writing requirement, all freshmen have to get a passing grade in one semester-long 15-student course in Expository Writing 20 (Expos), which offers more than 60 different courses, such as Expos 2, "Objects of Desire;" Expos 48, "The Culture of Consumption;" and Expos 51, "Cyborgs, Monsters, and the Limits." All Expos 20 course offerings require students to write four essays, each between five and ten pages long, which call for interpretation of textual evidence and proper integration and citation of sources. Expos instructors, called preceptors, smother students with personal attention. By carefully dissecting and scrutinizing the writing process with pre-essay exercises, post-essay revisions, and frequent meetings with preceptors, students report they significantly strengthen their writing ability. They also devote more time and effort to Expos 20 than almost any other course at Harvard. The expository writing faculty recommends that 150–180 freshmen each year take Expository Writing 10 in the fall semester as an introduction to Expos 20, based on their performance on the Freshman Writing Test (taken by all first-years). But students can decline the Faculty's recommendation to take Expos 10 if they want; about 100 freshmen actually take Expos 10 each year. Only two to four students each year don't pass Expos 20; these students have to take Expos 20 again and almost always pass it on the second try.

LANGUAGE REQUIREMENT

The 35 percent of incoming freshmen each year who haven't already met Harvard's foreign language requirement have to take two semester-long language courses during their first year. Minimum test scores that satisfy the foreign language requirement include: a 600 on any SAT II language subject test that has a reading component, a four on any Advanced Placement (AP) language exam, a six on any International Baccalaureate (IB) language exam, or a passing score on a language placement examination administered by Harvard language departments during the first week of school in the fall. Students whose native language is not English and who are proficient in both languages are exempt from the language requirement.

Students who have to take a year of language courses at Harvard in order to fulfill the requirement report having an overwhelmingly positive experience.

Language studies concentrations rate among the best at Harvard, although relatively few students devote substantial portions of their studies to work in a foreign language or literature. For most Harvard students, studying a foreign language is simply a requirement to be gotten out of the way as painlessly as possible. Yet 60 percent of students who take classes in a foreign language or literature describe them as "hard work but pure pleasure." These classes get such high marks because they most effectively engage students inside and outside of the classroom. Class sizes are small, almost always under 15 students, and language instructors insist that all students contribute regularly. Students are encouraged to work in small groups outside of class and are required to complete frequent written assignments and quizzes, providing students with opportunities for constant feedback and midcourse improvements. So having to take courses to fulfill the language requirement isn't all that bad.[235]

FRESHMAN SEMINARS

Freshman seminars give first-years close academic contact with full-time members of the Harvard faculty within discussion-oriented classes of 8–12 students that examine specialized subjects of mutual interest to professors and students. Faculty members teach two-thirds of freshman seminars, all of which are graded on the basis of satisfactory/unsatisfactory, so students can engage in meaningful academic conversation without pressure or competition for grades. Just as in sophomore tutorials and in junior and senior seminars, faculty in freshman seminars don't lecture; they guide discussion and encourage student participation by asking questions and drawing attention to key points. Students often have opportunities to teach, lead, and direct classes in these small discussion-oriented settings, which usually take place at round tables that facilitate dialogue. Freshman seminar offerings include: Freshman Seminar 5, "Calculating Pi;" Freshman Seminar 35, "Are We Alone? The Idea of Extraterrestrial Intelligence from the Scientific Revolution to Modern Science Fiction;" and Freshman Seminar 96, "The Baroque, Classical, and Romantic Concertos: The Evolution of a Quintessential Instrumental Genre from Bach and Handel to Liszt and Brahms." Students have to apply to take freshman seminars, and only one-third are accepted and allowed to enroll. Even though the FAS doubled the number of freshman seminar offerings to over 60 courses in 2002, there are still too few freshman seminars available for first-years yearning for direct contact with professors. Because of a lack of space in the Freshman Seminar Program in fall 2002, 470 of the 700 first-years who applied to enroll were denied access. That's 230 first-years who were deprived the opportunity to quintessentially resolve extraterrestrial Pi.

INDEPENDENT STUDY

Harvard upperclassman can petition to do up to four semester-long independent studies, ranging in content from field research to artistic performance to academic study not offered by the FAS. 54 students did independent studies in 2001–2002, most of them through internship programs. Independent study proposals are approved and projects evaluated by an individual faculty member who provides guidance but not instruction for each independent study. One of the toughest parts of an independent study is finding a faculty member to approve, sponsor, and oversee the project. Once a student finds a faculty advisor, the independent study project is graded on a pass/fail basis.

CROSS-ENROLLMENT

At no extra charge, students can get credit for courses offered outside of the FAS either at Harvard professional schools or at MIT, but not at Harvard graduate schools or at other Boston-area universities. About 500 undergraduates cross-registered for accredited non-FAS courses in the 2001–2002 academic year.[236] There are a few deficiencies in the FAS' liberal arts curriculum that students every year look to make up for elsewhere. For example, about 50 students each year cross-enroll for accounting courses offered at MIT. Approval for credit depends on whether the proposed cross-enrolled courses have sufficient ties to students' concentration studies. When students cross-enroll, their Harvard tuition is reduced on a per-course basis. Financial aid recipients can apply scholarships to the cost of studying at other institutions.[237]

STUDY ABROAD

Harvard allows undergraduates to study abroad in the fall, spring, or summer. The majority of Harvard students who study abroad do so in the fall or spring of their junior year. Others study abroad during spring term of sophomore year, fall term of senior year, or during the summer. Because Harvard's schedule runs later than most schools, those who study abroad second semester usually have to take fall term final exams away from Harvard after they arrive at their international host university. Most of those who study abroad do so for one semester, but some spend an entire academic year studying overseas. Three-quarters of Harvard students who study abroad do so through Harvard-approved study abroad programs sponsored by universities and educational organizations in the United States. One-quarter of those studying overseas apply directly to foreign institutions as visiting students, usually in English-speaking countries. A study-out-of-residence advisor helps students select a study abroad program or overseas university, explore course options, and complete the petition process for study abroad. Harvard allows students to apply their financial aid packages to study overseas. But whether the cost of study abroad is greater or less than living on campus depends on the particular country and academic program selected.[238]

Harvard is not as study-abroad friendly as most other top schools and sends far fewer students overseas. Roughly 160, or about four percent, of Harvard undergraduates study out-of-residence each year. The overwhelming majority of Harvard students who have studied abroad say that the experience was enormously valuable to their undergraduate experience. So why do so few students choose to study in another country during their undergraduate years at Harvard? Some are reluctant to leave Cambridge for fear of compromising campus ties—from blocking group friendships to extracurricular leadership positions. And some students are less than enthusiastic about abandoning their undergraduate quest to become an impact-making, important-sounding, re-sume-padding, power-tripping person-in-charge-of-something at Harvard.

Extensive concentration and core requirements mean that you have to plan several semesters in advance of study abroad in order to have fulfilled requirements by the time you graduate. While Harvard provides a pre-approved list of programs abroad, the college doesn't sponsor its own overseas study programs like other top colleges do. Eighty percent of study abroad students receive either concentration or elective credit for coursework abroad, but foreign cultures is typically the only core area for which students are able to get credit for work overseas.[239]

For a long time, administrative red tape was also responsible for dissuading many students from studying abroad during their time at Harvard. But under the supervision of University President Summers—who in March 2002 declared, "I look forward to the day when essentially every undergraduate student has a meaningful foreign experience during their time in college"—the FAS is taking measures to make study abroad a more feasible and attractive option for students at Harvard.[240] Until 2002, a student seeking approval for study abroad had to turn in paperwork at the Standing Committee on Study Out of Residence, the core curriculum office, his or her housing office, and concentration tutorial office.[241] Now Harvard is in the process of reducing administrative obstacles to study abroad not only for the personal enrichment of undergraduates, but also in order to relieve the pressure on housing availability on campus.[242] Students are no longer required, for example, to study their host country's language for two years before leaving campus or to provide documented evidence that their study abroad constituted a "special opportunity not available at Harvard."[243]

TIME OFF

Twenty percent of undergrads at Harvard take time off during college, a much higher percentage than at other schools. Part of the reason that so many Harvard students take a semester or more away from Cambridge is because it is so difficult to receive academic credit for study abroad at Harvard. When students take time off, they can go wherever they want and study or not study whatever they want without worrying about administrative hassles, academic requirements, or college bills. Although students are allowed to take a leave of absence from Harvard after a term has already begun, those who decide mid-semester to take time off are charged for tuition, room, board, and fees up until the end of the semester in which they leave. During their time off, Harvard students do things like spend time with family, serve in the military, relax, work, travel, and study in a wide range of interests all across the world. Although some students who take time off find it difficult to readjust to college life after returning to Harvard, most are happy for having taken time off, and many report that the time away helped them better enjoy life at Harvard once they returned.[244]

Advanced Standing

Harvard does not give credit for any coursework completed before coming to Harvard. But typically about one-half of the students in each freshman class are eligible for advanced standing by virtue of having at least four test scores of five on certain AP exams or scores of seven on certain IB exams. Students must decide after their first semester at Harvard whether or not to accept advanced standing. The advantages of advanced standing are: fewer course requirements, advantages in housing and core lotteries, and the option of graduating in three years or receiving a master's degree in four. The disadvantages are: having to submit a nonbinding plan of study, having to declare a concentration a semester earlier than nonadvanced standing students, having to take sophomore tutorials or research labs freshman year, and being ineligible for some Harvard scholarships. Typically about 25 percent of each freshman class, half of those eligible, claim advanced standing status in their freshman year, but only about 30 students each year graduate in three years, while 15 to 20 students earn a master's degree in four years, and 30 use their advanced standing status to study abroad for elective credit and return to Harvard with enough concentration and core credits to graduate with their entering class.[245]

Senior Theses

While writing a thesis is required of all concentration honors candidates, many students at Harvard decide not to write one. One advantage of writing a thesis is the achievement of tangible closure for the completion of your undergraduate career in a particular concentration. Another advantage is the door that writing a thesis may open for you after college: "An important reason to do a thesis" says Associate Professor of Linguistics Bert Vaux "is that you have something to show for yourself when you apply to grad schools or other sorts of jobs."[246] A third advantage is the opportunity for self-knowledge. As one student puts it, writing a thesis is a good idea "not just in terms of what I learn about my topic, or even what I learn about the field and research methods I'm becoming involved in, but because of what I learn about myself, my habits, talents, and weaknesses along the way. . . . How good am I at committing to self-imposed deadlines? Am I the sort that gets lonely working alone so much, or will I thrive on the opportunity for uninterrupted independent thought?"[247]

The major disadvantages of writing a thesis are sacrificing elective courses and leisure time during senior year. For slackers, reasons not to do something just don't get much more compelling than that.

In addition to writing a thesis for concentration credit, many noncredit opportunities are available to Harvard undergraduates for one-on-one, faculty-mentored research projects. Students can work with one of over a hundred faculty involved in mentoring programs, including visiting research scholars and research specialists hosted by concentration departments, campus organizations, or interdisciplinary academic centers on campus, such as the Latin American Studies Center, the Russian Research Center, the Center for European Studies, the DuBois Institute for African American Studies, and the Center for East Asian Studies.

ACADEMIC ADVISING

The story of all support services at Harvard comes down to this: unending assistance is available, but students have to ask for it, and many don't.

If you recognize that you need help, if you know what kind of help you're looking for, and if you're willing to go out and get it, then far-reaching resources are available to you. But Harvard's remarkable breadth of human resources often serves only as a missed opportunity for undergraduates in need of guidance. Many undergrads find that Harvard's get-it-yourself attitude to academic (and career, financial, and medical) advising is intensely impersonal. Students joke that, at Williams, they walk you into the water holding your hand; at Yale, they teach you to swim by watching from the sidelines; and at Harvard, they throw you into the water and check in four years later to see how it went. "Mother Harvard doesn't coddle her young," one undergraduate affirms. "If you want something, you've got to go get it. It's not necessarily a bad thing. It trains Harvard students to be the best."[248] Although each student is provided with numerous advisors, many undergraduates go through four years at Harvard with no more than half-an-hour of formal academic advising. For most students, the lack of advising isn't a big deal: lots of undergrads are fiercely independent and simply don't need or want any help.

But a big part of why students receive formal advising so infrequently at Harvard is that they're dissatisfied with the quality of advising they get. On a scale of 1 (worst) to 5 (best), seniors in the Class of 2001 ranked advising across all concentrations an average of 2.83. The advising survey asked students, among other questions, about the general availability of advice and whether students received guidance on courses appropriate for their interests and backgrounds, explanations for concentration requirements, and counseling on possible summer and postgraduate plans. On the whole, most Harvard students have minimal faculty interaction within the advising system. Just one-half of students have faculty members as concentration advisors.[249] "Academic guidance, particularly in several large departments," former Dean Lewis ('68) wrote in his *Report on Harvard College, 1995–2000*, "is at a level below the reasonable expectations of both students and faculty."[250]

Huge variation exists in the quantity and quality of advising across concentration departments. In smaller concentrations, students have more contact with faculty advisors and are able to get academic advice more quickly from their concentration department; in larger concentrations, most students never meet with a concentration advisor and few are able to get academic advice without waiting a long time or making an appointment days in advance. Advisors in large concentrations don't know much about their students. Fewer than half of undergraduates in concentrations with over 200 students report that their advisors know anything about their academic records or intellectual interests.[251]

Luckily, there is a vast network of human resources beyond concentration department advisors that students can turn to for academic advice. Freshman can find help choosing courses or planning their overall academic programs in proctors, prefects, upperclassmen, or the Freshman Dean's Office. Upperclassmen can go to sophomore advisors, nonconcentration academic advisors, entryway tutors, senior tutors, and the House Master. And all students can find help in section leaders, professors, and the staff at the Bureau of Study Counsel (BSC) and Office of Career Services (OCS). That academic advising involves so many different people and places at Harvard ensures that if a student feels uncomfortable with any one advisor, there are always plenty of other sources to which to turn. But more than one student feels "overwhelmed by the plethora of advisors" that makes it "difficult to discern who [one] should see for what."[252] In fact, when Harvard students seek out academic advice, they get it less often from formal resources like concentration advisors and academic tutors than from fellow students, parents, departmental websites, and printed materials, such as the *CUE Guide*, *Courses of Instruction*, and the *Handbook for Students*.

The first tier of academic advising at Harvard is more relaxed than at most schools. Residential proctor advisors in freshman dorms and residential tutor advisors in upperclass Houses are supposed to prevent dorm life from being an escape from academic life. Freshman advisors (resident proctors or nonresident advisors) are assigned on the basis of students' residence rather than on the basis of students' intended majors. Freshmen report that some proctors, particularly those who attended undergraduate institutions other than Harvard, don't know enough about Harvard to provide the help that students need, even after attending a mandatory seven-day training program before students arrive at school. Upperclass residential advisors, called tutors, are assigned on the basis of students' chosen field of concentration. Students typically get little academic help from either dorm proctors or House tutors, who remain busy with graduate commitments and who possess varying degrees of specialized knowledge about how students can pursue their academic interests at Harvard.

The most useful and underutilized academic resource for students is the BSC, which offers a wide range of academic and psychological services. Twenty full-time staff members work at the BSC office in Harvard Square. Academic services range from free weekly study workshops to bound volumes of past final examinations to personalized assistance with study skills like concentration, time management, note-taking, exam-preparation, and logical problem-solving. BSC also offers the not-for-credit Harvard Course in Reading and Learning Strategies, which costs $100 and meets an hour every day for three weeks. The 300 undergraduates (mostly freshmen) who enroll each year say that the course helps greatly with speed-reading, reading comprehension, and critical thinking skills necessary to manage the massive quantities of reading assigned in the FAS courses at Harvard. BSC also offers one-on-one peer tutoring for $4 an hour with undergraduates who have received A's in those courses.

Other helpful academic resources for undergraduates include the Writing Center, the Language Resource Center, the Radcliffe Institute for Advanced

Study, and the Office of Career Services (OCS). The Writing Center offers free one-on-one writing conferences with specially trained upperclass undergraduates. Students can make appointments online or just attend drop-in hours for help with any stage of the writing process. Writing Center consultations take place either in the Barker Center just outside Harvard Yard or in Hilles Library in the Radcliffe Quadrangle (the Quad). The Language Resource Center on the sixth floor of Lamont Library has 46 computers for student use, high-tech listening facilities, and a large collection of digitized videos and foreign-language periodicals.

The merger of Radcliffe College with Harvard College in 1999 stripped Radcliffe of its co-authority over female undergraduates at Harvard and transformed Radcliffe into an "Institute for Advanced Study." Now, Radcliffe offers externships, mentoring opportunities, speaker series, Ann Radcliffe Trust Grants, and the Schlesinger Library for Gender Studies, which is rumored to be in contention for the purchase of Boston's pro baseball team, which would become the Schlesinger Library for Gender Studies Red Sox.

CAREER ADVISING

The Office of Career Services (OCS), located in Harvard Square, provides vast resources and services to help students with resumes, cover letters, interviews, and networking skills for term-time, summertime, study abroad, time off, and post-graduate internships, jobs, and career planning. You can go to OCS to dissect a resume, videotape a mock interview, or discuss opportunities and strategies for finding work. OCS has 17 counselors, each of whom is "a generalist in career planning and a specialist in areas such as fellowships, health careers, government, business, work and study abroad, law, communications, public service, career explorations, science and technology, academic careers, minority concerns, and nonacademic careers for PhDs." You can check out Harvard's career resources by field online at www.ocs.fas.harvard.edu/resources/resource.htm. OCSs library maintains an "extensive collection of career descriptive literature, national and international directories, employment and internship reference books, domestic and foreign catalogues, and reports of Harvard graduates on their graduate schools, leave of absence experiences, and work and travel abroad.[253] OCS also publishes a weekly newsletter, distributed to all upperclass Houses and available online at www.ocs.fas.harvard.edu/, which outlines the latest opportunities for jobs, fellowships, and internships. Harvard almost never grants academic credit for internships. The OCS Career Advisory Service provides an alumni/ae database that undergraduates can use to get advice on career planning or to make connections in their field. The Fellowships Office at OCS provides first-rate advising on the 150 Harvard-based undergraduate prizes and the various national grants and fellowship competitions.

Career forums each fall and spring bring hundreds of companies to campus to recruit Harvard seniors whose primary goal, according to one senior, is "to get to the cookie platter by maneuvering around the grinning, Brooks Brothers-clad yuppies eagerly awaiting a handshake and a Q-and-A session."[254] The opportunity to drop off resumes, have interviews, and talk first-hand with company representatives attracts most of the senior class to participate in the on-campus recruiting process each year.[255] But many are dissatisfied with the narrowness of career options that Harvard attracts to its campus. Fully two-thirds of the companies at the annual career fair are involved in consulting, investment banking, or financial services.[256] "If you want to make money, there's a well-paved avenue available to you," says one student. "It's called 'Harvard recruiting.'" Tons of Harvard seniors land high-paying jobs right out of college, but those interested in less lucrative lifestyles are often left wanting more from Harvard's post-graduate services.[257] As one student puts it, "Harvard is ... a belief that success by conventional standards should precede all else."[258]

LIBRARIES AND PLACES TO STUDY

Harvard's library system, the oldest and largest in America, contains 14.4 million books, manuscripts, microforms, maps, slides, photographs, and other materials in more than 90 individual collections and accessible through the University's online library catalog, called Harvard Online Library Information System (HOLLIS) at http://lib.harvard.edu/. HOLLIS also offers undergraduates an extensive collection of free electronic resources and online journals they can access from their dorm rooms like LexisNexis, OVID, ProQuest, and World Cat. Harvard libraries are open to anyone with a Harvard ID or to non-

ID-holders who obtain a visitor's pass for research purposes. In order to ensure a distraction-free environment for undergraduate studying, no public visitation is allowed for nonresearch purposes. The on-campus libraries most frequented by undergraduates are Lamont, Widener, and Cabot in the Yard, the individual River House libraries, and Hilles Library in the Quad. All students go to Widener to do research, most go to cozy Lamont to study, pre-meds hit the books in sterile Cabot, and students living in the Quad go to nearby Hilles for both research and study purposes. Although House libraries are comfortable and convenient for upperclassmen living in River Houses, most run out of study space during exam periods and maintain book collections that are too narrowly focused to be useful for undergraduate research. The Eliot House library, for instance, boasts one of the largest collections, which ranges in scope "from British history to British literature."[259]

The showpiece of the Harvard library system is Widener. Affectionately referred to by the *Unofficial Guide to Life at Harvard*, as "The Big F***** with the Steps," Widener Library maintains the world's largest and most comprehensive collection of research materials in the humanities and social sciences and is the second largest library in the world behind the Library of Congress. Widener houses five million volumes in more than 100 languages among 10 floors and more than five miles of open book stacks. Elevators at Widener descend to the bowels of the earth, where students rummage for information through dimly-lit stacks of materials, at once a creepy and awe-inspiring experience. But Widener isn't just impressive; it meets needs of undergraduates. The collection reflects the scope of each FAS department and provides everything necessary for undergraduate research. Professional reference librarians are available during all open hours to help students find the information they need.[260]

The vast collections of Widener books, journals, microforms, films, pamphlets, posters, audio recordings, and electronic resources selected to be placed in Harvard libraries are supposed to be "selected only if they are relevant to a course or program," according to Bill Thauer, an administrator in Widener's Collection Development Office. But Widener also maintains a wide range of commercial fiction and most of the books that made *The New York Times'* most recent bestseller's lists. Although leisure books are available by authors like

John Grisham, Dave Barry, Oprah Winfrey, and Pat Riley, "research-based" materials account for "99 percent" of what students take out of Harvard libraries, according to one undergraduate book-checker at Widener.[261]

Students don't read much for pleasure because they keep themselves exceedingly busy with jobs, extracurriculars, and, most of all, studying. Most students regularly go to congested Lamont and Cabot libraries to study. Very few ever visit (or even know about) the idyllic study alcoves to be found on campus at the Business School Chapel, Law School Library, or Loeb Music Library. Early-closing library hours don't accommodate the large number of students who study late into the night. Lamont Library, where students flock every night to rent out laptops and study in lighted cubicles, four-person tables, and cushy window-side chairs, sounds an alarm every night at 12:45 A.M. to let students know that its time to find somewhere else to go if they want to keep studying. Many students work until two or three in the morning, but all libraries close before one. Libraries don't stay open past one because, administrators say, it costs too much to staff libraries into the early morning. The one exception is during Reading Period, when Cabot Library in the Science Center stays open (and well-populated) 24 hours a day. When libraries close, students can retreat to either dorm rooms or to upperclass dining halls.

Other places that students go to study are Loker Commons, Harvard Yard, and Harvard Square coffee shops. Rolling knolls of lush green grass in Harvard Yard and House courtyards are littered with book-wielding students during daylight hours in the fall and spring, but few manage to be productive outside. "The Yard and other outdoor locales may be picturesque," warns one student, "but the temptation to sunbathe and/or fall asleep can be overwhelming." For freshman in the Yard, Annenberg dining hall is closed off for students to study in between meals, and Loker Commons, located beneath Annenberg, is always packed, but is often too loud for some students to study there comfortably. Upperclass dining halls stay open 24 hours a day, but students who want to study there must put up with student foot-traffic and snacking diversions available there after 9:00 P.M. Gently bustling coffee shops in Harvard Square are highly underutilized study spots, but most close by nine or ten at night. Students can always retreat to their dorm rooms to study. But, complains one student, dorm rooms "hold a million distractions: the phone, the Internet, the roommate who has given up on schoolwork altogether and who wants a sympathetic ear for her adventures from last weekend."[262]

COMPUTER FACILITIES

Harvard students are wired. Undergraduates can use computers from their dorm rooms to send email, go online, or search the library system's card catalogue through Harvard's FAS computer network. Almost all students on campus have their own laptop or personal computer, but there are enough public terminals on campus that students could get by without their own computer at a moderate inconvenience. The upperclass House computer rooms, university libraries, and Science Center basement all have computers and laser printers available for student use. The Science Center has 60 Macs, 60 IBMs, and 25 Alpha Stations available 24 hours a day for students to check e-mail, surf the Internet, or write papers. Handfuls of public stand-up terminals are also scattered around campus at places where classes and study-groups typically meet like Loker Commons, the Barker Center, Boylston Hall, and Sever Hall. If you wanted to, you could check your email at public terminals at a dozen different buildings in a single stroll around Harvard Yard.

When computers go bad, there are lots of places for students to get help. The Harvard Computer Society (HCS) puts out a 100-page handbook each year called *Computers at Harvard*, which offers user-friendly assistance on any type of computer question. University Information Systems (UIS) also offers excellent IBM and Macintosh computer classes for beginners at the UIS office just outside of Harvard Yard. When students have computer problems, most seek help from roommates or the computer science concentrator on the second floor of their building. But all freshman dorms and upperclass Houses have resident undergraduates User Assistants (UAs) that make free dorm room calls when students make appointments online or by phone. Help is also available by contacting HCS online at help@fas.harvard.edu or by visiting the Computer Help Desk in the basement of the Science Center.

Harvard Arts and Sciences Computer Services (HASCS) runs the FAS computer network. Incoming freshmen and transfer students are given FAS e-mail addresses that read: lastname@fas.harvard.edu. Harvard's e-mail network is fast, secure, and equally accessible on and off campus. Most students use Telnet, Eudora, or Outlook browsers to check their e-mail on campus, (where almost all computers provide secure telnet access), and, when off campus, use Webmail, available online at webmail.fas.harvard.edu, which allows students to check e-mail through any normal web browser and from nearly any computer with Internet access.[263]

MUSEUMS

You'd be hard-pressed to find another college in America where you've got free access within just a couple of blocks to original van Goghs, 4,000-year-old Chinese jade statues, an exhibit of 3,000 hand-crafted glass flowers, and a reconstructed Byzantine chapel filled with the sounds of recorded Gregorian chants. The Harvard University Art Museums, all located in Harvard Yard, maintain a permanent collection of over 150,000 works and regularly sponsor special exhibitions. Harvard's museum collection includes: ancient, Asian, Islamic, and Indian arts at the Sackler Museum; European and North American painting, prints, and photography at the Fogg Museum; German Expressionist painting at the Busch-Reisinger Museum; and archaeology, geology, ethnology, zoology, and botany at the four-story Harvard Museum of Natural History.

SPECIAL LECTURES, SEMINARS, AND PERFORMANCES

Another unique perk of going to Harvard is the opportunity to listen to and interact with fascinating people ranging from authors, artists, and athletes to physicists, politicians, and pop idols. Harvard hosts a number of visiting faculty and special guests at public events open to all undergraduates. The Institute of Politics (IOP), Harvard Foundation for Intercultural and Race Relations, and student organizations on campus regularly bring among the biggest names in the news to the Harvard campus, including Will Smith, Halle Berry, Jackie Chan, Denzel Washington, Queen Latifah, Tom Brokaw, Peter Gammons, Henry Cisneros, Gerald Ford, and Dan Rather. Just since 2000, undergrads have had the chance to stop by after class in shorts and a T-shirt to talk with and get books signed by Nobel Peace Prize winning author Elie Wiesel, listen to the latest developments made by leading AIDS researcher David Ho, ask advice of and make connections with CNN Primetime Anchor and Senior Correspondent Bertie Ahern, or eat free pizza and discuss human rights with United Nations Secretary General Kofi Annan.[264]

CHAPTER FOUR
RESIDENTIAL LIFE

FRESHMAN DORMS

Harvard requires all 1,650 freshmen to live on campus. Of the 17 freshman dormitories, 13 are located in 22-acre Harvard Yard, one is in nearby Harvard Square, and three—called the Union dorms—are converted apartment buildings on Harvard and Prescott Streets, adjacent to the Yard. Originally used as a grazing pasture for the university's cows, Harvard Yard has the nicest housing, biggest green, closest proximity to classes, and most logistically convenient social life of any residence on campus. The 13 dorms that are located in Harvard Yard are Canaday, Grays, Hollis, Holworthy, Lionel, Massachusetts Hall, Mathews, Mower, Stoughton, Straus, Thayer, Weld, and Wigglesworth. All but the newest Harvard Yard dorm—Thayer—feature elegant red brick façades. The Apley Court dorm in Harvard Square, home to 34 lucky freshmen each year, is replete with bathtubs, oak floors, and marble staircases. The Union dorms—home to 250 freshmen each year—are Greenough, Pennypacker, and Hurlbut.

Silhouetted by the architectural wonders that are Widener Library, Memorial Church, and Memorial Hall, Harvard Yard is among the top five tourist sites in Boston.[265] Paved walkways, expansive greens, and massive oak trees are the playground of the Harvard freshmen who live in dormitories all around the Yard. The constant stream of locals, shoppers, joggers, and tourists give Harvard Yard a Disney World-like feeling.

Throughout the day, undergraduates give free guided tours of the Yard, stopping in front of University Hall to explain three lies inscribed on the John Harvard statue: (1) the statue's image isn't John Harvard, of whom no documented pictures exist; (2) the college was founded in 1636, not 1638; and (3) Harvard was founded not by John Harvard, but by the Great and General Court of Massachusetts Bay Colony. Captivating. Although maneuvering tourist bottlenecks sometimes inconveniences students on their way to class, having people come from all over the world to check out your school is enormously flattering. Besides, watching hundreds of people every day rub John Harvard's bronze foot for good luck foot is always worth a chuckle, considering that more than six percent of the 6,600-person student body has urinated on the statue, according to a 2000 survey by *Flare* magazine.

All freshman dorms are within a two-minute walk of each other. Each dormitory building has between one and twelve vertical entryways, which consist of a single door and stairway leading up to four or five floors of single-sex student suites. Each entryway houses between 15 and 40 students. First-year suites are enormous compared to those at most schools. About one-quarter of freshman bedrooms are singles, and no more than two people live in a bedroom. Most freshman rooms have their own common room and bathroom. Only one freshman dormitory—Thayer—has horizontal hallways and communal bathrooms like at most schools. Where a fire-door connects adjoining suites (in about half of freshman dormitories), students often choose to keep the fire-door open, forming a larger informal living group. Neither pets nor smoking are allowed in any residential building on campus.

First-years have no choice of where or with whom they live. The Freshman Dean's Office (FDO) assigns all first-years to suites within each dormitory entryway. In making these assignments, the FDO take special care to match students according to extensive student rooming questionnaires that include questions about preferences for number of roommates and roommates' personalities, interests, sleeping patterns, musical tastes, and living styles. Assistant deans say that the most important criteria used in making roommate assignments are usually how many roommates students want and how social they want their room to be. Because the FDO intends for roommates to learn from each other, rooming and entryway assignments are also made with the goal of creating a "diverse undergraduate community."[266] Most freshman rooming groups include students from different backgrounds. Each entryway exhibits substantial racial, ethnic, religious, economic, political, and geographical diversity, such that first-year students must live, eat, and interact with students unlike themselves. When students are unhappy within a particular suite or room, the college recommends a number of mediation and counseling resources to help them resolve their problems, but encourages them to remain in their current living situation. If repeated attempts at resolution fail, then students are reassigned to "psycho single" suites that provide a private room and a good deal of social stigma. The Freshman Dean's Office doesn't release information on how many freshmen are assigned to psycho singles each year.[267] Although naturally some students have difficulties with their first-year rooming situations, the overwhelming majority of Harvard upperclassmen report that their first-year living experiences set a positive tone for future interactions with students of different backgrounds.[268]

While most colleges designate upperclass Residential Assistants (RAs) to live in freshman dorms, Harvard assigns a Harvard graduate student or university employee—called a "proctor"— to live in each entryway along with 20–30 first-years. Proctors are responsible for advising academics, enforcing university regulations, and making students aware of campus resources they might find useful. The residential proctor system is supposed to provide first-years with easy-access advising, counseling, and friendship, but some proctors are so busy with other commitments that they are rarely available to spend time with undergraduates. The large age difference between proctors and students sometimes makes it difficult for students to relate to proctors on a social level. Whereas RAs at other institutions are only a year or two older than most first-years, proctors typically range in age from 23–33 years old. First-years are also hesitant to approach proctors with some of their personal problems because of the proctor's role as a university official with disciplinary powers. "We could get in trouble if we brought up things, like drinking," one student says, "that make a big difference in our Harvard experience."[269] Former proctor Sarah Burmingham Drummond explains, "I could never turn my head if I knew students were drinking in the dorm; I could never walk by John Harvard['s statue] if students were peeing on it." "I love my students," Ms. Drummond says, "but they could never be my 'friends.'"[270]

Besides settling for distant relationships with their proctors, many first-years feel divorced from the rest of the undergraduate community. Freshmen interact with upperclassmen in extracurriculars and in most classes, have keycard access to all upperclass Houses, and are free to take meals in upperclass dining halls; but they live in their own dormitories located on their own section of campus and eat in their own dining hall. "Prefects"—two or three upper-classmen assigned to each freshman entryway—are supposed to bridge the gap between freshman and upperclass life. Prefects plan weekly study breaks and monthly social events and are available upon request for one-on-one advice about academic and personal concerns. But their effectiveness in relating to freshman is limited by university policies barring them from drinking—or even discussing alcohol—with the freshman to which they're assigned. The upperclass presence that prefects provide in the lives of freshmen is constrained by the difficulties of sustaining entryway enthusiasm for social events and of balancing prefecting duties with their other undergraduate commitments. Prefects don't do much to make freshmen feel a part of the community of upperclassmen on campus.

Dean of Freshmen Elizabeth Studley Nathans explains that separation between freshmen and upperclassmen is intended to encourage unity as an entering class.[271] But whatever community is formed among each class is often lost after freshman year when first-year friends are randomly scattered across the campus into upperclass residential Houses. As busy upperclassmen, when undergraduates no longer run into first-year friends in the dining hall or around Harvard Yard, many find it too difficult to keep first-year friendships active. And the lack of casual contact that freshmen have with upperclassmen makes the second-year transition from Harvard Yard to the upperclass House system a difficult one for some students.[272]

The changes that students experience between freshman and sophomore year are substantial. Whereas Harvard Yard has a very public feeling to it, the Houses have a much more secluded air, with locked gates, few outside visitors, and residential structures that are less conducive to social interaction with each entryway. Besides living in a new place with new people, students are also given much more trust after their first year.

Although all undergraduates can come and go as they please with no curfews or formal supervision, only upperclassmen are allowed to take food out of the dining hall, manage fireplaces in their dorm rooms, and drink alcohol openly without regulation or punishment. After freshman year, one student says, "it's like you have transferred to a different school."[273]

UPPERCLASS HOUSING ASSIGNMENTS

Unlike most colleges and universities, Harvard has no themed upperclass residences designated as minority, religious, athletic, single-sex, or substance-free dorms where students can choose to live. Instead, in the spring of their first-year, students pick up to seven friends with which to form a "blocking group."

Each blocking group is then randomly assigned to an integrated upperclass House, where students live for the next three years.

Because the blocking process forces freshmen to prioritize their friends, it can lead to tense spring months spent living with those who were voted out of a blocking group. One undergraduate complains, "[Y]ou get into a situation where you either block with a person or you're no longer friends."[274] Many form blocking groups that are racially, ethnically, religiously, athletically, or extracurricularly homogenous. The 40 or so rising sophomores each year who don't block with anyone are called "floaters."[275] Those who float in the housing lottery are randomly assigned to a blocking group with fewer than eight people. Some students float voluntarily—either because they don't want to deal with the stress of blocking or because they want to live with people they don't know. Most floaters are either less social students who don't know anyone who wants to live with them or "students whose friendships split along awkward fault lines."[276]

Computer-generated housing lotteries began in 1995 when former Dean of the College L. Fred Jewett ('57) randomized the House selection process from the prior system in which blocking groups were assigned in accordance with their top four House choices. Students today have no memory of the days before randomization when "[m]usicians gravitated toward the Steinway pianos at Winthrop and Cabot, while athletes appreciated the close commute to practice from Kirkland. Dancers sought out the studio at Currier, while visual and theater artists made use of the exhibition and performance space at Adams … [and] large number of students of color chose to spend their remaining three years at Harvard in the Quad or Quincy."[277] Or, as Al Franken ('73) recounted in his 2002 Commencement Speech, "Dunster House was known as the music-drug-theatre house. Mather House was known as the drug-jock house. Adams was the artsy-drug house … Quincy was just the drug house. As were Leverett, Kirkland, Winthrop, and Lowell. Eliot was considered the preppy-drug house, but was also sometimes just thought of as the drug house. There was no Quad then, but people used to sneak up there to do drugs." Now E has replaced LSD as the acronym drug of choice on campus and motley crews have replaced high concentrations of homogeneous student groups within Harvard's housing system.

The college administration randomized the housing assignment process in order to combat rampant self-segregation across the residential buildings on campus. Randomization helped make each House a diverse "microcosm of the college," but also undercut the communities of shared backgrounds and interests within each House. Many African American and queer students opposed randomized housing when it was first instituted on the grounds that it denied them the opportunity "to live in a community that shares their cultural, political and social values."[278] But ever since the first class of randomized students graduated from Harvard in 1998, senior surveys among majorities and minorities alike show greater satisfaction with the housing assignment process and the overall House system than before randomization. Also, inter-house transfer applications have been steadily on the decline since 1995–1996.[279]

While the blocking process is often the most stressful aspect of first-year life at Harvard, blocking isn't as big a commitment as freshmen typically assume, primarily because most students' social circles shift a great deal throughout college. Although many students socialize with their blocking groups more than any other crowd and most end up sharing a suite with their blockmates, you can obviously hang out with whomever you want and are allowed to choose your suitemates from among anyone in the House from your graduating class. Upperclassmen may or may not remain friends with those with whom they originally blocked and may or may not choose to keep in touch with first-year friends with whom they chose not to block. The only social phenomenon you can count on is meeting new people and making new friends throughout your time at Harvard, both within and outside of the House system and freshman blocking groups.

UPPERCLASS HOUSE LIFE

Harvard guarantees four years of on-campus housing to all undergraduates. About 4,800, or about 95 percent, of all upperclassmen choose to live on campus in 12 Houses of 330–450 students. Sophomore, junior, and senior students living on campus are assigned to either Adams, Cabot, Currier, Dunster, Eliot, Kirkland, Leverett, Lowell, Mather, Pforzheimer, Quincy, or Winthrop House. While most of the Houses were built of red ziggurat brick in elegant nineteenth-century architectural designs, hideous Mather House "was designed by the same firm that built Hitler's bunker," quipped Conan O'Brien ('85) in his 2001 commencement speech. "In fact, if Hitler had conducted the war from Mather House, he'd have shot himself a year earlier."

The Houses are located in two main locations. Nine are scattered along a quarter mile stretch of the Charles River, just a few blocks south of Harvard Yard. These "River Houses" are Adams, Dunster, Eliot, Kirkland, Leverett, Lowell, Mather, Quincy, and Winthrop. About one mile northwest of Harvard Yard is the Radcliffe Quadrangle, called the "Quad," which consists of Cabot, Currier, and Pforzheimer Houses. DeWolfe and Claverly Halls, located in Harvard Square, provide overflow housing for River Houses and the Jordan Co-op near Currier House provides overflow housing for Quad Houses.

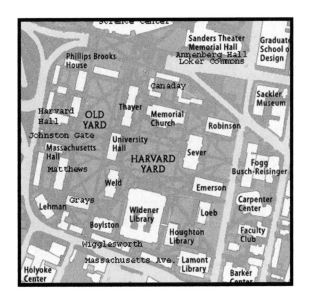

Graphic by Garrett Grolemund ('03), reprinted with permission from *The Harvard Independent*.

Few first-years want to get assigned to Cabot, Currier, or Pforzheimer Houses because of the Quad's physical isolation from Harvard Yard, Harvard Square, and the River Houses. In order to avoid getting Quadded, some first-years make sacrifices to the "River House Gods" by burning their fall-semester textbooks along the shore of the Charles River.[280] Despite substantial anti-Quad sentiment among freshmen blocking groups, those who end up there are usually happy with their living situation. The Quad Houses have the best library, the best party rooms, and the best courtyard—what one student calls "a mirage in the dense residential area [of Old Cambridge] that surrounds it."[281] Plus, the Quad's geographic separation from everything else on campus furnishes Cabot, Currier, and Pforzheimer Houses with a degree of solidarity not found in other dorms on campus. But if the seclusion is too much, it's a pretty painless process to transfer Houses—just one form and a couple of phone calls.

All Houses have their own laundry room, dining hall, and grassy courtyard, where students can be found in warmer weather playing Frisbee®, football, and wiffle ball. Each River House has its own small library, while Quad Houses share the larger Hilles Library. House libraries offer a quiet place to study and free video rentals, but few books. Almost every House also has its own kitchen, grille, weight room, computer lab, darkroom, art studio, music practice room, wood shop, widescreen television room, vending machines, video games, and pool, foosball, and table tennis. A few Houses also have a theater, woodworking shop, pottery studio, sound studio, and dance studio.

Harvard's upperclass housing system was developed by former University President Abbot Lawrence Lowell in the 1930s in the model of the Oxford and Cambridge University systems, where undergraduate students and graduate tutors lived together in residential communities. The overall well-being of each House is overseen by a House Master, who lives in the House with his or her family. House Masters, nominated by the dean of the college and appointed by the president of the university, are senior faculty members or senior administrators whose spouse or partner serves as Associate Master of the House. House Masters appoint tutors, sponsor House-wide activities, and appear sporadically at open houses, special functions, and regular dining hall meals to gather with students. Several even memorize the names of every incoming student in the

House before they arrive in the fall. While there are a few House Masters who are dynamic residential leaders and community builders, most House Masters have little tangible impact of the lives of upperclass students. Other adult employees in the House include guards, custodians, dining hall workers, the Allston Burr Senior Tutor—who helps students with special disciplinary or academic issues—and the superintendent—whom students seek out to borrow vacuums, unlock doors, and repair rooms. The adults in the House who are most important for undergraduates are the 15–30 resident tutors.

The House tutor system includes resident tutors, nonresident tutors, and faculty affiliates. But because students rarely see nonresident tutors or faculty affiliates, the tutor system is in fact comprised only of those graduate students or junior faculty members who live in suites alongside undergraduates within the House entryways. Each resident tutor serves as academic advisor, entryway-wide social event coordinator, and House-wide community builder. This three-pronged role amounts in practice to (1) scheduling one mandatory advising meeting per year with each of 15 or so assigned students, usually just to reaffirm course choices, (2) hosting one-hour study breaks in their dorm rooms once a month, and (3) turning students into the Allston Burr Senior Tutor when the marijuana aromas waft through the entryway. Students have similar complaints about House tutors as they do about dorm proctors: "[t]utors are busy law or medical or doctoral students whose primary commitment is to their own work," says one student. "And undergraduates often feel a conflict about confiding in the people who control their files and are supposed to be writing their recommendations."[282]

When students have problems of any kind, resident tutors are nearby adults willing to listen and capable of referring students to more expert resources. They provide friendly older faces, interesting meal-time conversations, occasional nuggets of wisdom, and diverse artistic, musical, public service, and professional experiences. But for the most part, tutors play a negligible role in the lives of all except the few who seek them out for special academic or personal help. Accordingly, University President Summers has undertaken plans to reevaluate, restructure, and possibly eliminate the tutor system, initiating in 2003 a series of undergraduate surveys intended to gauge student satisfaction with the residential tutors in the upperclass Houses.[283]

Social community within the Houses has diminished greatly since the college randomized the housing assignment process. Since randomization, the students inhabiting each residential House no longer have any common culture/interest, long-term House-wide project, or inter-House spirit/rivalry to unify them as a House community.[284] Self-created ethnic, religious, athletic, extracurricular, and blocking social circles, rather than randomized House communities, are now the most common sources of close friendships at Harvard. Neither House dining halls and laundry rooms, nor annual House formals, brunches, teas, open houses, and sophomore outings are enough to sustain House community. Students have a good time at special events like the Eliot House Fete, with its chocolate-covered strawberries, champagne fountain, and live swing band and are sure to run into each other leaning over the sneeze shield at the salad bar and folding underpants in the laundry room basement. But one-time social events are soon forgotten and friction does not always bring about friendship. Only House email lists, intramural (IM) sports programs, and House Committees, known as HoCos, help bring Housemates together with any consistency. The community-building character of these endeavors varies greatly from House to House. Although certain IM sports in certain Houses garner a lot of support, for example, the intramural program is most Houses is often a "hodgepodge of last-minute sign-ups and forfeits."[285]

SUITES AND SPECIAL SERVICES

Most of the rooming accommodations at Harvard are luxurious compared to those at other colleges. The majority of student suites are comprised of private bathrooms, massive common rooms, and spacious one- or two-person bedrooms. Each student gets a desk, chair, dresser, bookcase, closet, and extra-long twin bed. And almost every upperclass suite has its own working fireplace for student use. Posh freshman suites, assigned by the FDO, are usually the nicest of all rooms on campus, sophomore suites are a significant downgrade, and junior and senior rooms get bigger as students get older. Most Harvard seniors are guaranteed their own generous-sized bedrooms. Each House determines its own procedure for upperclass rooming assignments, but typically the way it works is that incoming juniors and seniors get to choose which suites they want for the following year according to the order they draw in the spring housing lottery. After juniors and seniors take their picks, the House then assigns the leftovers to rising sophomores.

The two downsides of Harvard suites are the lack of privacy and overcrowding in some Houses. Several college dormitories are congested. Former Dean Lewis ('68) admits, "We would be well served to recognize that with the present housing stock we should be housing about 100 fewer students in the Houses than we now are."[286] In the short term, administrators hope that study abroad reforms will ease some of the current housing crunch; in the long term, campus developments in Allston may free up some space for additional undergraduate housing. Students are less than fond of the sound-carrying firedoors that connect adjacent walk-through suites. "I've gone through every variety of ear plugs," complains one student. "But this girl who lives through the firedoor … talks on the phone all day, so I know everything about her—her love life, her menstrual cycle, you name it."[287] Students whose firedoors connect suites through one or more bathrooms know when their neighbors have drank too much alcohol or eaten too much fiber. And thin walls, small bunk beds, and double bedrooms diminish romance and increase tension among partners and roommates. Students are frequently "sexiled" out of their doubles when suitemates are getting freaky.

Students are dissatisfied with television, telephone, laundry, and mail service on campus. There's no cable television at Harvard because the dorms are much older than those at colleges where cable wiring is completed during construction. Cable installation would be prohibitively expensive and time-consuming, according to Associate Dean of the College David P. Illingworth ('71). The Harvard Student Telephone Office (HSTO) provides cheap phone service from all campus dorm rooms, but if you've got a problem, there's a better chance that Larry Summers and Cornel West will get together for golf than that you'll get hold of HSTO for help.[288] Freshmen pick up their mail in the Harvard Yard Mail Center deep in the basement of the Science Center, and upperclassmen get theirs in their House mailrooms. University mail is notoriously slow; it takes up to two weeks for mail to get delivered across campus. There are laundry rooms in the basement of a few freshman dorms and one in each upperclass House. Crowded laundry rooms, clothing thefts, busted machines, and costly service can make doing laundry at Harvard a pain. Washers cost a buck a load and dryers are 75 cents. Rather than using quarters, most students pay for laundry service with their electronic Crimson Cash accounts. You can dish out a couple hundred bucks a semester to have a Harvard Square laundromat or Harvard Student Agencies (HSA) do your laundry for you each week, but lots of students have their clothes lost or damaged in the care of local services.[289]

At any time during the year, students can add money to their Crimson Cash account, which is stored on central university computers and accessed with students' university identification (ID) cards. The student ID gives students formidable swiping access to dorms, libraries, and dining halls on campus in addition to laundromats, vending machines, and photocopy machines. The photograph that freshmen have taken during registration remains on their ID cards throughout college, unless they request a new one. Replacement IDs are $20 for lost cards, free for stolen cards accompanied by a police report, and free for broken ID cards with chunks, hunks, shards, ashes, evaporate, or liquefied equivalents of the old card.

When they first get to Harvard, most students open a bank account in their own name at one of the local banks in Harvard Square. Doing so allows students to avoid ATM transaction fees and to write checks for various services on campus. There are dozens of banks from which to choose, each offering different perks. Cambridgeport Bank, located on Massachusetts Avenue in Harvard Square across from Wigglesworth dorm, offers a free checking account. USTrust Boston and BankBoston don't charge for check writing or ATM use. And Cambridge Trust Company offers students a free dictionary for opening an account there. Most undergraduates choose a bank that doesn't charge them for dipping under a minimum balance.[290]

FOOD SERVICES

The $3,500 "board" portion of Harvard college fees includes meals in any Harvard dining hall, bag lunches, Fly-by lunches, kosher dinners at Hillel, and Brain Break snacks after 9:00 P.M. on Sunday through Thursday nights. Harvard students living on campus have no choice but to purchase the 21-meal-per-week dining plan, even though the average student eats just 13 to 14 of those meals.[291] The mandatory meal plan is pricey at $7 for breakfast, $10 for lunch, and $11 for dinner, and Harvard offers no reduced-meal option, so students lose money for any meal they miss. But at least students can eat as much as they want during mealtimes and reenter the dining hall as often as they want during open dining hall hours.

Dining halls on campus are open for meals Monday through Saturday 7:30–10:00 A.M., 12:00–2:15 P.M., and 5:00–7:15 P.M., and on Sundays from 11:30 A.M.–2:00 P.M. and 5:00–7:15 A.M. Quad Houses open and close lunch and dinner 15 minutes later (to accommodate shuttle rides back from classes in the Yard), and most River Houses keep their dining hall doors open between meals, when you can get drinks, fruit, bagels, cereal, and leftover pastries. Some students find that restrictive meal hours leave them either hungry or broke. One student complains, "neither my internal clock nor my class schedule mesh with the dining hall services meal hours."[292] Students who can't make mealtimes can get bag lunches, which must be reserved a day in advance and must be picked up at the dining hall between 7:30 and 10:00 A.M., both significant inconveniences to students with busy and unpredictable schedules.

Most students at Harvard rate their overall dining experience somewhere between "average" and "very good," according to the 2002 residential dining satisfaction survey. Serving area and dining room appearance and cleanliness are "excellent," as are speed of service and friendliness of dining staff. But complaints about the food itself persist. Students say that food quality, taste, and appearance are merely "average," as are menu variety and selection. Harvard students who have visited friends at other Ivy League schools say that Harvard's food pales in comparison. Some complain that the ethnic food on the menu, especially Asian American cuisine, lacks in authenticity. And one alert student points out, "whatever was served the night before is transformed into the next day's entree. Beef tips one day, beef stew the next day."[293]

The Harvard University Dining Services (HUDS) menu rotates every couple weeks and can be found online at www.dining.harvard.edu. Every day, the menu features fresh fruit, hot vegetables, a salad bar, two soups, cereal, pasta, cold cuts, a frozen yogurt machine, and a grill with hotdogs, chickwiches, hamburgers, and vegetarian burgers. Ice cream is served only on Sunday nights and, even then, in only one flavor. The salad bar offers a fresh assortment of organic ruffage and the chickwiches are always a dependable fallback for any weak lunch or dinner menu. Your typical breakfast consists of (1) scrambled eggs, (2) muffins, (3) grits/maypo/oatmeal/cream of wheat, and (4) hash browns/donuts/pancakes/French toast/Belgian waffles. Lunch entrées include: pizza, lo mein, chicken Caesar wraps, smoked turkey Reubens, and tomato basil cod filets. And dinner entrées are: roast sirloin, sweet and sour pork, buffalo chicken wings, barbequed spare ribs, and blackened mahi mahi. Perennial menu favorites and least favorites revolve around the chicken selections: an article in the April 2002 edition of Flare magazine carried out a heated dialogue between the fêted chicken parmesan and detested General Wong's chicken.

Hot vegetarian and vegan options are available at every meal, but the selection isn't very good. Entrées include falafel sandwiches, tofu pad Thai, Asian vegetable stir-fry, portobello mushrooms with baked tofu, and polenta with mushrooms and spinach. The "tofu-tomato sizzle" tastes much like the 1987–1988 Courses of Instructions book smothered with tomato paste. Protein options for vegan students at Harvard include soy-based burgers, hotdogs, milk, and yogurt. Jewish undergrads who keep kosher can eat either at the Hillel Kosher Kitchen in Harvard Square, which serves dinner six nights a week, or at any of the dining halls' kosher sections, which include kosher toasters, microwaves, and refrigerators, as well as a meager selection of hot and cold items for personal preparation. Muslim students who eat only halal meat, however, are poorly accommodated and are often forced to become vegetarian when eating in Harvard dining halls. HUDS also makes six festive meals throughout the year, which range from the sickening to the spectacular: "Cinco de Mayo" features an unsavory array of imitation enchiladas and quesadillas, while the "New England Clambake" boasts mouth-watering fresh steamers and lobsters.[294]

HUDS has an excellent record of responding to what students have to say about campus food. "Anything we do in dining services, we encourage student input," says HUDS Executive Chief Chef Michael D. Miller. Recent student comments have resulted in the reduction of salt content in soups, extended hours for hot breakfast service, and the elimination of unpopular knockwurst and pupu platter entrees. Preference surveys, distributed and collected once a month at each dining hall, ask students which cereals, beverages, and salad dressings they'd most and least like to see in the dining halls. Feedback cards are available in every dining hall for students to write suggestions directly to head HUDS staff. If you take the time to share your culinary thoughts, you can expect an e-mail response within 24 hours. One unique and much-appreciated aspect of dining services at Harvard is the presence of full nutritional cards for almost all food served in the Harvard dining halls, even if the information on the cards isn't always accurate.[295]

HUDS' special services help meet students' individual dining needs. Fly-by lunches are available in Loker Commons for upperclassmen who aren't allowed to eat in Annenberg Hall and who don't have time to go back to their Houses to eat in between classes that are held in or around Harvard Yard. Fly-by lunches consist of bottled water, fruit, soup, cookies, and a pre-prepared cold cut sandwich. Brain Break is held in Loker Commons and House Dining Halls a couple of hours after dinner ends on every night except for Friday and Saturday. Brain Break features a decent late-night selection of fruit, bagels, pastries, and drinks, but all the food usually gets eaten up within 45 minutes after it is set out at 9:00 P.M. A mandatory $50 "Board Plus" charge is added to students' board fees each semester for discretionary food spending. Board Plus can be used either to treat guests at any dining hall or to get food at any of the nine campus restaurants, including the Barker Center, Loker Commons, and the Science Center Greenhouse Café, all located just outside the gates of Harvard Yard. Barker, Loker, and the Greenhouse feature exceptional fare, much better than at dining halls, from Loker's stir-fries and smoothies, to the Greenhouse's calzones and sicillian pizza, and Barker's sushi and panini sandwiches. Unspent Board Plus balances carry over from fall to spring semester, but are lost at the end of the year.

You'll be blown away by Annenberg, the 9,000 square-foot freshman dining hall that bears an uncanny semblance to Harry Potter's banqueting hall at the Hogwarts School of Witchcraft and Wizardry.[296] Marble busts surround row after row of long oak tables. The hall is lit by 50-foot high chandeliers and reflected sunlight gleaming in through intricate stained-glass windows set within hammerbeam trusses, stenciled ceilings, and walnut paneling. Most upperclass House dining halls are also attractive, but none come anything close to Annenberg. Most of the Houses have recently renovated food service areas that blast Boston's Top-40 radio station, Jammin' 94.5 FM. Annenberg and House dining halls serve the same menu, but food generally tastes better in the

Houses, where chefs prepare for one-quarter the number of students who eat in Annenberg.

The Harvard campus recently became uneasy about food sanitation when incidents of food poisoning broke out in the Cabot House dining hall in 2001 and in the Dunster and Mather House dining halls in 2002. But students need not worry about the freshness and cleanliness of the food they're served; the 2001 and 2002 cases of food contamination are exceptional aberrations in HUDS' otherwise spotless long-term track record of effective dining inspection. Every food dish uses a thermometer to ensure that its temperature remains within a healthy range. Silverware and flatware are washed three times, once loose, once with eating end up, and once with eating end down. Every three days, the kitchens are soaked in water, sprayed with chemicals, and rinsed to remove dirt and germs. Storage refrigerators print out temperature readings throughout the day to ensure that food always remains between 25 and 40 degrees Fahrenheit. Dining hall workers undergo intensive training in food safety. They wash their hands twice an hour, change their rubber gloves frequently, and are watchful for cross-contamination. Food is monitored throughout the preparation and service process. The City of Cambridge sends an inspector to do a preliminary check of all of Harvard's dining halls and Environmental Health and Safety Department food safety officers inspect each dining hall twice a year.[297]

CRIME AND SAFETY ON CAMPUS

Crime is fairly common on Harvard's urban campus. A half dozen assaults on female students in 2003–2004 made university-wide e-mail crime warnings common. In a fuller 2001 report, the Harvard University Police Department (HUPD) reported zero instances of arson, manslaughter, or homicide on campus, 22 forcible sex offenses, five aggravated assaults, two instances of robbery, 342 of burglary, 232 of larceny, 15 of motor vehicle theft, seven drug law violations, and zero bias crimes with or without prejudice.[298] The 1999 College Community Crime Risk Assessment ranked Harvard the 541st most dangerous out of 1,497 campuses studied.[299] The college got a seven on a "risk scale" of one to ten, meaning that Harvard students face about double the average national risk of being victims of violent crime, according to the Risk

Assessment. Among Ivy League colleges, Harvard was ranked less safe than Princeton and Dartmouth, and safer than the University of Pennsylvania, Columbia, and Yale, each of which all scored a nine on the risk scale.[300]

Cambridge has one of the highest rates of bike and laptop theft in the country, but neither item is as popular a target as yellow-stained university-issued pillows. In order to ensure the safety of their property, students can secure their bikes with U-locks, keep their dorm rooms locked, and register their laptops and bicycles through Harvard University Police Department's Security Tracking of Office Property (STOP) program. That way, if police recover stolen items, they can be returned them to their owners. Many students every year just have to suck it up and buy new stuff.

Almost 95 percent of students report feeling safe on the Harvard campus.[301] HUPD officers—who are sworn State Police special officers with deputy sheriff powers—roam the campus premises on bike and foot. The large metal gates surrounding Harvard Yard stay open during the day, and all but the major gates close after 7:00 at night. Harvard dorms are designed so that there are two doors between a student in his or her room and the street, which the college advises be kept closed and locked at all times. Harvard University IDs are required to get into all dormitories on campus, although it's not difficult for non-ID holders to follow students into dorms or get unsuspecting students to let them in. HUPD officers respond to several reports each month when unauthorized persons manage to get into Harvard dormitories.[302]

"Blue Light" police assistance telephones, located at every turn all over campus, provide immediate communication to police dispatchers and speedy responses by university police officers. Though traveling across the farthest reaches of the campus takes only a maximum of 15–20 minutes by foot, the college advises students not to walk across campus alone at night. The safest way to travel around the Harvard campus is by taxi, a dozen of which congregate regularly in Harvard Square outside Fleet Bank. But a cab ride even from the Science Center to the Quad runs up a sizable $4 tab. Free Harvard shuttle buses, serving throngs of Quadlings, take students all over campus every 20 minutes on weekdays from 7:30 A.M. to 1:00 A.M. and on weekends from 9:45 A.M. to 5:00 A.M. Pocket-sized schedules are available at libraries, dining halls, House offices, shuttle buses, and the Holyoke Center Information

Office. Students willing to wait 10–45 minutes can call Evening Van Shuttle Service for free on-campus transportation until 2:40 A.M. every night. After 2:40 A.M. on a weekday, students can call HUPD for a free police escort.

OFF-CAMPUS HOUSING

Fewer than four percent of all Harvard upperclassmen live off campus each year, partly due to student satisfaction with living conditions in the House system and partly due to the shortage of available off-campus housing. While off-campus apartments tend to remove students from much of the Harvard community, they offer more space, peace, and quiet than undergraduate Houses. "Of the 200 off-campus students," Former Dean Lewis ('68) notes, "a significant number are either married, and hence ineligible for residence in the Houses, or are older, having returned to complete their degrees after long absences, and may therefore find the residential experience less appealing."[303]

Most of those who live off campus rent apartments from the Harvard Affiliated Housing department, which leases from among its Cambridge complexes a couple hundred one- to three-bedroom apartments to undergraduates each year. Somerville, Central Square, and Porter Square complexes, all within a fifteen-minute walk to Harvard Square, also make apartments available to students. Apartments vary in price and may or may not cost more than on-campus housing, depending on location, size, and accommodations.[304]

Here's how college payment works if you opt to live off campus: Harvard charges you only tuition and Student Services fees and calculates your financial aid award as if you have the same room, board, and personal expenses as students living on campus. Harvard provides no extra financial help (or special housing arrangements) for married students. Harvard's Financial Aid Office treats married students living together off-campus as if they were single students, expecting the students' parents or spouse to provide any necessary extra support. Harvard does, however, provide special assistance to undergraduate parents to help meet the financial burdens of raising a child, such as off-campus housing, day care, and health care.[305]

For those dissatisfied with Harvard's House system, but unable to pay for an off-campus apartment, the Dudley Cooperative (Co-op) offers reduced room and board in exchange for food preparation and household chores. The

Dudley Co-op is a self-sufficient community of 35 undergraduate students living in two wooden Victorian houses in Harvard Square, on the corner of Sacramento Street and Massachusetts Avenue, about a half-mile north of Harvard Yard. The Co-op has 29 student rooms, two tutor rooms, a living room, and a well-equipped kitchen. The movie *With Honors* was based on the true story of Dudley Co-op residents who allowed a homeless man named Damon Paine to live with them for several years. Founded in 1958 to provide alternative housing for low-income Harvard men, the Co-op now provides residential housing that's about $2,000 cheaper per semester than university housing. Students living at the Co-op have to clean their own bathrooms, churn their own compost, and make their own food, chores that require about six hours a week of Co-op members' time. Twice a day, the Co-op's overwhelming vegetarian community comes together to make organic dishes, fresh-baked bread, and homemade granola for Dudley residents and 7–15 guests per meal. While Co-op residents are well-represented among Harvard's progressive political activists, they insist that they are not, as *The Unofficial Guide to Life at Harvard* reports, eager to "stick it to The Man." *Fifteen Minutes*, the weekend magazine of *The Harvard Crimson* daily, reports that at the Dudley Co-op, "hair more frequently flows long, shoes tend to be clogs, jeans are fringed at the bottom, bras are less common [and] … [s]ome even knit their own clothes from knitting company's samples."[306] A significant percentage of students at the Co-op are gay or lesbian. Unlike on-campus houses, the Co-op allows pets.

SUMMER HOUSING ON CAMPUS

Several hundred Harvard College students stay over the summer in Harvard housing free while working for college-recognized student groups. The Harvard Summer School Office offers free summer on-campus housing (including room, board, and a Harvard course) to 100 undergraduates (out of 400 that apply and engage in a hellish interview process) who fulfill minimal duties as proctors to high school or college students at Harvard Summer School. About 350 Harvard undergraduates also enroll in Harvard Summer School as students, along with 1,200 high school students, 1,100 students international students, 600 students from other American colleges, and 350 students from Harvard's graduate and professional schools, all of whom live on the Harvard campus from June through August, choosing from among 200 Harvard courses offered by resident and visiting faculty. Another 100 Harvard undergraduates live on campus in the summer while leading recreational and educational camps for children through PBHA's Summer Urban Program. Harvard students unaffiliated with the Summer School or summertime extracurriculars, but who want to stay in Cambridge for the summer, can check out either bulletin board postings all around Harvard, local newspaper classified sections, or the Harvard Housing Office, which rents Harvard-owned apartment complex near Harvard Square and posts independent listings for Cambridge-area apartments or sublets.

CHAPTER FIVE
EXTRACURRICULAR LIFE

Harvard graduates report having far more vivid college memories in out-of-class activities than in classroom pursuits. Nearly every student at Harvard makes a substantial term-time commitment to one or two activities outside of coursework, whether paid work, ROTC, athletics, public service, performing arts, politics, activism, student publications, and special-interest groups. A list of online links to all undergraduate student groups at the college can be accessed at www.college.harvard.edu/student/organizations/.

The most popular out-of-class commitments are paid work, volunteer work, performing arts, athletics, and politics, in that order. Harvard students usually don't have too much trouble balancing extracurricular activities with their coursework. Harvard Statistics Professor Richard Light determined in interviews with more than 1,500 Harvard undergraduates that up to 20 hours per week of out-of-class activities had little or no relationship to students' grades.[307]

Even students with the most unusual interests, like mime/daredevil Montana Miller ('96) have ample opportunities at Harvard to test their talents and pursue their passions. The 250 extracurricular student organizations at Harvard range from the Harvard Juggling Club to the Onion Weavers Puppet Theater. The enormity of the biannual Harvard Activities Fair reflects not only the cosmic hodgepodge of student interests on campus, but also the unconstrained ambition of those competing for the top spot. While most students take on extracurriculars as natural extensions or personal expressions of their individual interests, others on campus pursue activities mainly in order to claim the title of director, chairperson, or president. In the words of one undergraduate: "Leadership at Harvard is an interesting phenomenon. In a community with unheard of number of per capita high school class presidents, no one is used to or satisfied with being 'just a member.' We all aspire to lead, to plan, and to be in charge. And, if you cannot rise the ranks of your organization, the natural response is to start your own."[308]

Harvard students create as much exclusivity in their extracurriculars and social organizations as the college created in admitting them. Those activities with a performance or production element are, in general, far more competitive than those same activities are at other colleges where students can gain membership just by signing up. At Harvard, students have to successfully complete a highly selective "comping" process, during which students compete for membership in campus organizations. Comping entails several rounds of athletic, musical, artistic, or writing auditions at the start of each semester. Many a church choir soloist, debate team captain, school paper editor-in-chief, Model UN president, and regional Tae-Kwan-Do champion get more rejections in their first two weeks at Harvard than they have in 18 years prior. The competitive nature of Harvard extracurriculars works better for some students than others. According to one student: "The [extracurricular] system works well for those who have talent and want to compete and achieve individually in large, hierarchically-arranged organizations. There are fewer opportunities for those who want to split time among a variety of groups, fewer still for those who really enjoy doing something at which they have little talent."[309]

PAID WORK

More than half of all Harvard undergraduates work part-time for money, whether to fulfill the requisite self-help portion of their financial aid award or to make some spending cash for themselves. Students typically work between seven and twelve hours per week. More women work than men, and more upperclassmen than freshmen. Students work at a wide variety of jobs, the most popular of which are administrative/clerical, custodial, and computing/technology, respectively. Three-fourths of Harvard students who have term-time jobs say that working has a positive effect on their overall satisfaction with college, including coursework, friendships, and romances. Only six percent say that working has a negative impact on their college experience.[310]

The Student Employment Office (SEO), located in the basement of Byerly Hall and online at www.seo.harvard.edu/, posts on their website a wide range of part- and full-time work on- and off-campus. The SEO oversees the Federal Work-Study Program, the Faculty Aide Program, and all undergraduate research grants, which provide funds for faculty members to pay undergraduate research assistants. The SEO also maintains a "special skills" file of student abilities and availabilities for those interested in work as typists, translators, musicians, or babysitters.

Undergraduate entrepreneurs are allowed to operate businesses out of their Harvard dorm rooms as long as they register their intent with college. According to Dean Illingworth ('71), two or three dorm-run business proposals are approved each year, most of which are computer and technology related. Examples include Nicholas Palazzo's ('03) sports publication, *StacK Magazine*; Alastire Rampell's ('03) software design company, Rampell Software; and Aaron Greenspan's ('05) computer education service, Think Computer Corporation.[311] The administration's primary concerns with undergraduates conducting enterprises out of Harvard dorms are that student-business-people not disturb other students, not overuse Harvard's computer network, and not compromise the nonprofit status of the University. The only undergraduates whose business ideas are ever rejected, says Dean Illingworth, are those who misrepresent their affiliation with the trademarked Harvard name.

Harvard Student Agencies (HSA), located in Harvard Square, provides cashflow and managerial experience to 900 part-time or full-time undergraduates annually. Among services like food-catering, dry-cleaning, and book publishing, the most successful of HSA's programs is the *Let's Go* travel guide series, a $6.2 million corporation that employs 200 students, runs 10 student-run businesses, and sponsors several career-oriented Harvard programs such as Career Week, the Business Leadership Program, and HSA Entrepreneurial Contest. *Let's Go* receives hundreds of applications each spring from students looking for a free summertime trip to Namibia, Malaysia, or the Ukraine in exchange for updating *Let's Go* tourist reports. But many former *Let's Go* writers say that the work was tougher than expected. One student explains, "It's fun to be on the road, but when you go back to your hotel room, and you're faced with four hours of writing, and you can't call your family because it's too expensive and your editor hasn't called in a while, it can get pretty hard."[312]

Students who get As in math and science courses can teach or tutor other students for money. Undergraduate teaching assistants make about $1,000 a semester for 20–40 hours of work each week spent teaching an hour-long section, holding at least two hours of office hours, attending three hours of lecture, responding to student emails, and grading problem sets. Peer tutors make $12 per hour and get to arrange their own hours with undergraduate tutees. Computer savvy user assistants (UAs) get $10/hour to answer student questions for a few hours a week in the Science Center computer lab, maintain the computer lab within their House, and make on-call visits to fix Housemates' computers. UAs also get optional free on-campus summer housing in exchange for answering questions and fixing computers for students enrolled in Harvard Summer School.

Students who work with the Language Resources Center (LCR) and Audio Visual Services (AVS) are paid $9.50 an hour to provide technical support for students and faculty. The Crimson Callers group offers students $10 per hour to milk alums for donations. Students ushers get $8 an hour and a free performance to take tickets, hand out programs, and help audience members find their seats. The Malkin Athletic Center (MAC) employs students to swipe ID cards, wash towels, and lifeguard at the pool. And student guinea pigs can earn $10–$100 in ten minutes to three hours as test subjects for one-time psychological experimentation. Listings are posted in the lobby of William James Hall, the 15-story building located a couple blocks beyond Harvard Yard.

The Harvard libraries, particular Widener, Lamont, and Cabot in the Yard and Hilles Library in the Quad, hire hundreds of students each year at $8.00–$9.50 per hour for work ranging from checking ID cards to signing books out to tracing misplaced books deep in the stacks of Widener, a job that sounds like a lot of fun. According to the SEO website, the job of "tracer" requires "some heavy lifting," "at least two languages," "ability to work independently," and "attention to detail" for $8.60 an hour. In other words, the tracer position requires "someone qualified enough to run a small country with dual national languages" for the same compensation as the kid who washes towels at the MAC. House libraries offer the most low-key of all campus employment, giving work-study students plenty of time to do coursework on the job.

Hands-on work is also available. A number of labs, offices, and mailrooms on campus employ students to mix, shuffle, and sort stuff for $8–$10 an hour. Harvard University Dining Services (HUDS) hires dozens of students each semester for flexible three-hour shifts to serve food, bus trays, and wash dishes at $9.40 an hour after the first semester at $8.85. Undergraduate waiters and waitresses at the Faculty Club are among the highest paid student workers on campus at $13 per hour. Students working at the campus' child care centers help prepare snacks, make arts and crafts, and supervise kids on the playground for $9.50 an hour. And if you're willing to clean your classmates' dirty toilet seats, dorm crew employs over 100 term-time undergraduates to do "wet" and "dry" cleaning work in freshman dorms and upperclass Houses at very flexible hours and a starting rate of $9.25 per hour. Dorm crew also employs 400 students to clean up dorm rooms for the arrival of first-years in the fall and of alumni or alumnae in the spring. After spring cleanup, Harvard employs 200 students to set up for, serve alcohol to, clean up after, and baby-sit children of alums visiting Harvard during Commencement Week.

Harvard Square businesses employ students for bike repair, street-performance, bartending, stand-up comedy, ice cream scooping, and subway conducting. The federal government gives money to those eligible for work-study to do public service work in Cambridge and Boston. There's also less traditional work available. The New England Cryogenic Center, just a 20-minute T-ride from Harvard, offers male undergraduates $70 a pop for their sperm if they can pass an extensive physical examination and personal interview more selective than Harvard's admissions committee: NECC accepts only one out of every 25 sperm donor candidates.[313] The Boston Phoenix ad posted annually in The Harvard Crimson that reads: "Wanted: Egg Donor, must have 1400+ SAT score, $50,000 compensation" draws no fewer than 30 Harvard undergraduates each year.[314]

RESERVE OFFICERS TRAINING CORPS (ROTC)

About 50 Harvard undergrads are in the ROTC program as Army, Navy, and Air Force cadets training to become military officers. Harvard has long been unwelcoming of ROTC. The college banished ROTC off campus to MIT at the height of the Vietnam War in 1969, and current faculty legislation proscribes official university recognition or funding of ROTC because the military's "don't ask, don't tell" policy against homosexuals violates Harvard's nondiscrimination policy. Cadet training is instead funded by an independent group of Harvard ROTC alums. Harvard neither permits open ROTC recruitment on campus nor recognizes students' military accomplishments in the yearbook or during commencement. Cadets keep a low profile on campus, identified only once a week when they're required to wear their uniforms around campus on Mondays. [315]

Harvard ROTC cadets devote between five and twenty hours per week to military commitments. They attend regular training and drill sessions, take one military class per semester, and commit four years after graduation to military service. In exchange, students in the ROTC program develop leadership skills and receive a government scholarship that pays for tuition, book, and fees—a total of about $20,000 each year. ROTC students say they learn valuable leadership skills during physical and drill training and have fun at Military Excellence Competitions (MECs), where ROTC squads from across the nation battle in athletic events and military procedures. ROTC undergrads have to wake up at 5:30 A.M. at least twice a week in order to make the early morning shuttle to MIT for military classes and laboratories. ROTC cadets say that military courses aren't too difficult and don't take up much time.[316]

President Summers's recent backing of ROTC signals a radical shift in the university's attitude toward the program. Since taking office in 2001, Summers has voiced staunch support for the ROTC program and has called for a re-evaluation of Harvard's long-standing estrangement from ROTC. In a fall 2002 address at the John F. Kennedy School of Government, Summers urged Harvard to show the armed services greater deference, and in spring 2002, he became the first university president in 30 years to attend the commissioning ceremony for the college's ROTC graduates.[317] More significantly, in 2002 the FAS approved a Harvard course (Government 1730: "War and Politics") for military credit for the first time since 1969. "Larry Summers and Dean Lewis have done more for ROTC in the past 12 months than any leader at Harvard in the past 40 years,"[318] says Lieutenant Colonel Brian Baker, professor of military science at MIT and commander of the Army battalion for Harvard cadets. The university's increasingly hospitable attitude toward ROTC dismays undergraduate members of Harvard's Bisexual, Gay, Lesbian, Transgendered, and Supporters Alliance, who oppose institutional support for ROTC as long as the military maintains discriminatory policies toward gay people.[319]

VOLUNTEER WORK

Harvard students log half a million hours each year doing volunteer public service work.[320] More than 65 percent of Harvard undergraduates do volunteer work at some point during college, and 30 percent of all undergraduates, about

2,000 students, volunteer in any given semester. Student volunteers work an average of five hours per week. More women volunteer than men, and more juniors and seniors volunteer than freshmen and sophomores. About 50 percent of volunteers work with children and teens, 12 percent work with the homeless and the poor, 10 percent with handicapped people, 10 percent in adult education, 10 percent in health policy and arts access, and 8 percent with senior citizens.[321] Some students devote their time throughout college to multiple causes within a single low-income Boston-area neighborhood. According to the 2000–2001 Annual Report on Public Service, 19 student groups provide service to Roxbury, 9 provide service to Dorchester, 9 to the South End, 8 to Chinatown, and 7 to Jamaica Plain.

Harvard students volunteer because they enjoy helping others, they want to give something back, they get paid through work study, or they believe that volunteer work will look attractive to employers and graduate school admissions officers. Some put in just two hours of volunteer work per week, and some drop volunteer commitments as soon as personal and academic priorities come into conflict. But a large number of Harvard students make public service an integral part of their lives. Harvard doesn't award credit for volunteer work, but does offer courses on community organizing, childhood development, urban poverty, nonprofit management, and environmental issues. According to Assistant Dean for Public Service Judith Kidd: "Equal access is available to the aspiring leader, the one-shot volunteer, the resume builder, the guilt expiator, the pre-professional, or the faithful weekly volunteer."[322] Ninety-six percent of student volunteers say that they plan to continue volunteering their time after they graduate from college.[323]

Ninety percent of Harvard's student volunteers work through one of the 82 programs in the Phillips Brooks House Association (PBHA), Harvard's student-run/staff-supported social action organization serving over 10,000 people in the Cambridge-Boston area. The PBHA is run by a cabinet of 60 students, a board of student officers, 8 professional staff members, and a Board of Trustees, made up of students, administrators, and faculty members. During the summer, the PBHA provides room and board for undergrads helping to direct one of its 13 intensive summer camps for children living in the same low-income Boston neighborhoods that the PBHA serves during the academic year.

One of the most popular programs through the PBHA is the University Lutheran Homeless Shelter (UNILU), the largest student-run homeless shelter in the country. UNILU, which has washing machines, showers, linens, towels, toiletries, donated clothing, and 24 beds, operates out of the basement of the Lutheran church in Harvard Square and stays open from November until April. About 140 Harvard undergraduates maintain the facility, serving evening, overnight, and morning shifts, and cooking, serving, and cleaning up after breakfast and dinner meals, which are donated from Harvard Square businesses and university dining halls.

POLITICS

A 2000 survey by *The Harvard Crimson* found that 75 percent of undergraduates are registered to vote.[324] The Institute of Politics (IOP), which draws close to 600 students, offers political programs and resources like internships, speakers, study groups, conferences, and visiting and resident fellows. Fellows, who are experienced public servants and political figures, interact with students and participate in weekly forums. Student groups that are run though the IOP include: Pizza and Politics, *Harvard Political Review*, the Harvard AIDS Coalition, CIVICS, and the Women's Leadership Project. The IOP also provides internships, stipends, and research grants for thesis work relating to government and politics.[325]

POLITICAL ACTIVISM

The height of political activism at Harvard College was the 1969 takeover of University Hall by anti-ROTC Students for a Democratic Society (SDS), which ended when university police officers dragged students out of the building against their will.[326] While most current students' Harvard experience is "less a hotbed of political activism than a springboard for comfortable cosmopolitan jobs," in recent years rallies, protests, and marches have once again become routine events in Harvard Yard and Harvard Square.[327] "As campuses go" one student says, "Harvard may rank itself among the more politically active. We may not have a population at colleges like Wesleyan, comprised exclusively of hippie sign-wavers who protest any and everything, [but] the environment [at Harvard] remained politically charged."[328]

In the 1998–1999 academic year, the Coalition Against Sexual Violence condemned the college's insufficient sexual assault policies, the Students Against Sweatshops exposed Harvard's use of factories with poor labor conditions in the production of Harvard-insignia apparel, and the Living Wage Campaign—what University Professor Cornel R. West ('74) called "the most significant wave of student activism since the [1960s]"[329]—protested for higher wages for Harvard employees. In April 2000 members of the Black Students' Association (BSA) staged a "teach-in" at Byerly Hall in protest of Kenan Professor of Government Harvey Mansfield's ('53) unsubstantiated claims that grade inflation at Harvard had been caused by "white guilt" among Harvard professors after the influx of African American students with the adoption of affirmative action policies in the 1970s. In February 2002 the Asian American Association (AAA) led a protest in Harvard Square against Abercrombie and Fitch clothing that was deemed offensive to Asian Americans. In April 2002 members of Harvard Hillel staged several pro-Israel rallies on campus in response to conflicts in the Middle East. And in August 2002, Harvard College and Summer School students organized a protest in Harvard Square urging Coca-Cola to provide HIV and AIDS health care to its employees in Africa.[330]

The Progressive Student Labor Movement (PSLM) has made national media headlines with its living wage and anti-sweatshop campaigns in the last few years. From 2000 to 2002, the PSLM has staged a walkout during commencement, an "anti-sweatshop tour" of Harvard Square, and a 21-day takeover of Massachusetts Hall, accompanied by dozens of camped-out students in tents around Harvard Yard and daily marches and hippie-style chants. Through efforts like these, the PSLM successfully raised student awareness about the difficulties faced by lower-paid Harvard workers like custodians, security guards, parking attendants, and dining-services employees, but managed to persuade few nonmember students to support their cause. Widespread apathy, annoyance, and counter-protests among the student body indicate that twenty-first century political activism on the Harvard campus must scale a mountain of cynicism.[331]

ATHLETICS

Harvard's athletics program was ranked 41st in the country, and first among the Ivy League, by *Sports Illustrated* in its 2002 "America's Best Sports Colleges" issue. The college offers athletic opportunities at the varsity, club, intramural (IM), and recreational levels. Harvard has the country's largest Division I athletic program with 41 varsity teams, more than 1,500 athletes, and top-notch athletic facilities. The Soldiers Field facilities, just across the Charles River from Harvard Square, expands over 90 acres of football, softball, soccer, and lacrosse fields, baseball diamonds, running tracks, outdoor hard surface tennis courts, and 15 athletic buildings with indoor tracks, courts, rinks, pools, spectator seating, and weight rooms. You can check out up-to-date athletic news and schedules online at www.college.harvard.edu/student/athletics. The football team plays at Harvard Stadium, which seats nearly 31,000. Harvard's ice hockey, crew, squash, tennis, and golf teams are consistently among the top in the nation. And in 2002, Harvard football secured first place in the Ivy League with its first undefeated season in almost a century. Varsity athletes, who spend at least 20 hours per week in training, travel, and games, have lower grades than nonathletes, on average, but are also among the happiest students on campus, reporting having many good friends on campus and intimate connections to the college.[332]

Despite Harvard's athletic success, varsity sports fail to generate any sense of Harvard pride, loyalty, or school spirit among undergraduates. Harvard's rich athletic tradition, boasting seven national football titles, and perennial contenders in several other sports, draws only indifference from Harvard's nonathletes. Sporting events typically attract measly student crowds, although they are free to undergraduates and conveniently located just across the Charles River every Saturday afternoon. Tailgating is usually limited to alumni, who congregate in the parking lot behind the football stadium around a table of champagne, pate, and shrimp cocktails. The only exception to the student body's general lack of interest in Harvard varsity athletics is the annual Harvard-Yale football game, known as "The Game." Whether it takes place across the River or across the state border in New Haven, Connecticut, The Game always draws several thousand Harvard students, who scream "God hates Yale" in unison while wearing hats reading "Yuck Fale."

Harvard athletics has its fair share of hazing, defined as involuntary (or socially pressured) participation in intentionally demeaning, humiliating, or dangerous activities. Although many Harvard sports do not engage in hazing at all, forced binge drinking plays a significant role in several Harvard athletic initiations. For example, club sport rugby has one tradition called "shooting the boot," where players are forced to drink beer from game-used cleats, and another called the "goat roast," where players are driven to a deserted park, ordered to eat a goat carcass, and then abandoned. A women's cross-country runner recounts her initiation, where "we ran around in the Quad in our bras and panties before going to a party in Cabot, where we found the guys' team in their boxers. From there, all I can remember is that there was a lot of alcohol and a male stripper." A men's soccer player recalls, "Guys had to go into Victoria's Secret and dress up in lingerie, teddies, etc. and take pictures of it. Also, we had to chug a glass of mayonnaise and drink flaming shots." A women's tennis player says that new members of the team "had to do what the [upperclass] girls told us, such as give lap dances to some of the guys."[333] So despite administrative reproach, there remains a good deal of hazing among Harvard varsity sports teams.

Club, intramural, and recreational sports give students who aren't varsity material a chance to train and compete. The two dozen club sports at Harvard come in flavors like boxing, bowling, cycling, croquet, equestrian, mountaineering, and a variety of martial arts, including the Tai Chi Tiger Crane Kung Fu Club. Club sports, supervised and funded by undergraduates, often require just as much time as varsity athletics. Intramural sports offer 3,000 students each year a dose of low-stress, noncommittal camaraderie. Students may participate in as many intramural sports since they don't play at the varsity level. The intramural sports program includes basketball, football, soccer, crew, squash, fencing, table tennis, ultimate Frisbee®, and the one-time Charles River Run. Participation levels vary greatly from abundant to scant, depending on the popularity of intramural athletics in a particular freshman dorm or upperclass House. Overall, intramural competition and rivalry is in short supply on campus.

The recreational athletic program offers free instruction classes in aerobics, racquetball, ice skating, kick boxing, fencing, yoga, and lifeguarding. Rec classes are held in the recently revitalized Malkin Athletic Center (MAC) and its Quad counterpart, the Radcliffe Quadrangle Recreational Athletic Center (QRAC). Normal hours for the athletic centers are 7:00 A.M. to 11:00 P.M. The MAC, nearby the River Houses, and the QRAC offer fitness-minded students Olympic-size pools; air-conditioned weight rooms fully equipped with a wide range of machine and free weights; cardiovascular exercise rooms with Precor ellipticycles, treadmills, stationary bikes, rowing machines, and stairmasters; and squash, racquetball, tennis, basketball, and volleyball courts. Lots of students lift weights and run/step/row/bike in their perfectionist quest for a flawless body to match their impeccable transcript. Exercise rooms can be crowded, requiring waits of up to half-an-hour for your machine of choice. But you can almost always find a decent pick-up game of basketball, and after passing a 100-yard swimming test, you can get a free one-person skull from one of the boathouses to go rowing on the Charles River. For general fitness and health education, students can go to the Center for Wellness and Health Communication (CWHC), which holds one-time workshops, semester-long classes, and one-on-one consultations with specialists on a variety of issues, including nutrition, exercise, yoga, and massage therapy.

ARTS

During a typical academic year, students mount some 80 dramatic productions and 550 musical events, in addition to 200 dance recitals, film festivals, multimedia events, and exhibitions of their own work. Besides regular week-end inundations of student art on campus, the Arts First Festival, a four-day event organized each spring by the Office for the Arts, engulfs the Harvard college grounds with concerts, exhibitions, performances, and films. Student performances take place in the undergraduate Houses as well as in more formal settings around campus like libraries, museums, the Loeb Drama Center, Rieman Center, Agassiz Theatre, Sanders Theatre, Lowell Hall, and Paine Concert Hall. Information about upcoming events in the arts can be found online at www.college.harvard.edu/student/arts. The Undergraduate Council (UC) occasionally brings professional, albeit mediocre bands, to the Harvard campus like Big Bad Voodoo Daddy, Dispatch, Black-Eyed Peas, and the Roots.

Extracurricular groups in the arts feature awe-inspiring levels of performance talent, ranging in size from the gargantuan Harvard-Radcliffe Orchestra (HRO) to a number of independent three-to-eight-piece student bands. Art activities include a radio station, 9 literary journals, 11 dramatic groups, 12 dance groups, and 28 music organizations (6 choirs, 9 a cappella groups, 7 orchestras, 1 band, 1 wind ensemble, and 4 others). More than one-half of Harvard students participate in at least one of these activities during college.[334] Harvard's underappreciated student-run broadcast radio station WHRB (95.3 FM) airs classical music, jazz, underground rock, news, and Harvard sports 24 hours a day, seven days a week. Harvard-Radcliffe Dramatic Club's (HRDC's) common casting auditions allow over 250 aspiring actors each semester to try out for four months' worth of shows (about 20) during the first week of classes. Between HRDC, Gilbert & Sullivan Players, and improvisational comedy clubs like the Instant Gratification Players and On Thin Ice, Harvard's diverse theater community puts on shows nearly every weekend of the year.

Hasty Pudding Theatricals, the nation's oldest student-run theater group, puts on six all-male drag shows each week for a month between February and March, tours New York and Bermuda each spring break, and hosts the annual Man and Woman of the Year events, which bring big-name celebrities like Mel Gibson, Meryl Streep, and Samuel L. Jackson to the Harvard campus each year. Harvard's a cappella choirs, including the all-male Harvard Krokodiloes and co-ed Harvard Callbacks, tour the world during every winter, spring, and summer break, and consistently rank among the top collegiate a cappella groups in the country.

Despite the success of Harvard's student music groups, the college lacks adequate space for them to rehearse for performance. Undergraduates who want to sing or play an instrument on campus have to contend for the limited practice space available in Paine Music Hall, the basements of Thayer and Holworthy Hall, and common areas of classrooms and residential Houses.[335] "Even where space could be available," former Dean Lewis ('68) aptly notes in his "Report on Harvard College, 1995–2000," "musical practice mixes poorly with other uses of nearby rooms, for sleeping, studying, or teaching, in structures not designed with acoustic isolation in mind." As a result, Lewis remarks, "[W]e hear too many tales of students who have given up their long years of training in piano, percussion, brass instruments, or voice upon arriving at Harvard for no better reason than the lack of any place for them to go to play their instruments or to sing."[336]

Harvard doesn't offer her any performance courses for credit, but the college does sponsor a number of noncredit art classes for students. The Radcliffe Dance Program, Malkin Athletic Center, and Recreational Athletics Office offers free or cheap on-campus dance classes ranging from ballet to ballroom to modern jazz. The Office for the Arts (OFA) in Harvard Square sponsors classes, workshops, and apprenticeships where students can work closely with professional artists in music, dance, drawing, ceramics, and theater. The Freshman Arts Program (FAP), to which incoming students apply in the summer before their first year, provides an expansive range of art workshops in which freshman work alongside upperclassmen before fall semester begins. Students interested in the visual arts can paint, sculpt, take photos, or make films in introductory and mid-level courses in the Department of Visual and Environmental Arts.

Many interested students are not allowed to study creative writing at Harvard. While some are able to take advantage of occasional Radcliffe seminars on creative writing, most are left to apply to highly competitive classes for credit. Harvard's creative writing classes—which get near-perfect *CUE Guide* ratings—receive over 400 applications each semester for about 156 spaces, according to Director of Creative Writing Patricia Powell. Despite the crunch, Chair of the English Department Lawrence Buell reports that the department has no plans to increase the number of faculty positions in creative writing.[337]

STUDENT GOVERNMENT

Although unpopular on campus, Harvard's Undergraduate Council (UC) plays an active role in the lives of undergraduates. The UC distributes over $80,000 each year to student groups, runs annual events like the Springfest and the First-Year Formal, and organizes shuttles to Logan Airport for winter and spring break and to New Haven for The Game. The 50 students of the UC represent each of the freshman dorms and upperclass Houses, but tend to join the Council primarily "for their resumes" according to one former UC member. "Everyone is a former high school president jockeying for position," he says.[338]

PUBLICATIONS

There are more than 30 student publications on campus, ranging from political journals like the *Harvard Political Review*, the *Asian Pacific Review*, and the *Harvard Current* to comedy journals like *The Harvard Lampoon*, *Demon*, and *Satire V* to *GAMUT*, the biannual multilingual poetry magazine, and *Diversity & Distinction*, a quarterly journal focusing on issues of student identity. Student newspapers include *The Harvard Crimson* (the nonpartisan college daily), *The Harvard Independent* (nonpartisan weekly newsmagazine), *The Salient* (conservative bi-monthly magazine), and *Perspective* (liberal monthly magazine).

Although they are open for all students to comp and join, Harvard newspapers lack minority students at both the editorial and writing levels. "[I]t's not that we've been getting a lot of minority compers and somehow made them unwelcome," one *Perspective* editor explains. "It's just that we're not getting any minority compers to begin with." The comp process to join a campus publication usually involves attending a few instructional meetings and writing a few pieces. After which 85–90 percent of compers join the publication staff as an editor in either the news, business, editorial, design, photo, sports, arts, science, online, or graphics sections.[339]

Two Harvard undergraduate publications are consistent feeders to the news and entertainment professions. *The Harvard Crimson* sends several graduates to *The New York Times* every year. And although undergraduates complain that *The Harvard Lampoon* "makes no sense" and "isn't funny," Hollywood agents, producers, and directors disagree. *Lampoon* graduates comprise large numbers of comedy writers for television shows like *Seinfeld*, *Saturday Night Live*, *Late Night with David Letterman*, *The Conan O'Brien Show*, *Beavis and Butthead*, and *The Simpsons*, which frequently drops jokes bashing Princeton and Yale.[340]

"OTHER" EXTRACURRICULARS

Harvard students have attracted national media attention not only as authors, artists, athletes, but also as thugs, delinquents, and felons. In 1989 Jose Luis Razo, Jr., ('90) was sentenced to 10 years in prison for a string of Los Angeles armed robberies he committed while home on spring break from Harvard College. In 1990 Harvard law student Kevin Watkins was convicted of raping his former girlfriend, a Harvard undergraduate, when she attempted to recover videotapes he had made of them having sex. In 1991 undergraduate John Fountain ('01) was indicted for exhorting $10,000 from a Los Angeles physician when he threatened to report the doctor's HIV positive status. In 1995 Charles Lee ('93), was sentenced to one year in prison for stealing $120,000 from Evening With Champions, an annual event sponsored by Eliot House that donates money to the Jimmy Fund charity for children with cancer. That same year, Sinedu Tadesse ('96) hanged herself after stabbing her roommate, Trang Phuong Ho ('96), 45 times while she lay sleeping in her bed. In 1996 Harvard dismissed Stephen V. David ('96) and William A. Blankenship ('96), found guilty on six counts of drug possession and intent to distribute drugs within a school zone. In 1998 and 1999, Joshua Elster ('00) and Drew Douglas ('00) were dismissed from the college for raping Harvard undergraduates. In 2002 Suzanne Pompey ('02) and Randy Gomes ('02) pled guilty to grand larceny for embezzling nearly $100,000 from Harvard's Hasty Pudding Theatricals.[341] In 2003 Harvard graduate student Alexander Pring-Wilson was arrested for murder after allegedly stabbing a teenager five times outside a Cambridge pizza parlor.[342]

CHAPTER SIX
SOCIAL LIFE

HANGING OUT

Undergraduates bewail the lackluster social scene at Harvard. Although students complain about the lack of social venues on campus, the fact is that most Harvard undergrads simply choose to spend their time analyzing principles and formulas rather than having laughs. Those who want to meet people, form relationships, and have fun do. As one student aptly says, "Harvard is academically intense, and sometimes that can be [socially isolating]. But minimal effort will produce legions of similarly lonely yet terrific individuals to hang with."[343]

One of the best places to chill with people is the cafeteria. Annenberg Hall and House dining halls serve enough kids that there are always some people there that you recognize and always some new people to meet. Hard-core socialites spend upward of six hours a day hanging out in the dining hall. Besides socializing over meals, there are also concerts, exhibits, plays, lectures, and forums to go to on campus almost every day.

Still, it's true that Junior Common Rooms (JCRs) in the upperclass Houses and Loker Commons outside of Harvard Yard don't make up for the absence of a 24-hour student center, where students would be able to congregate, play games, eat, drink, and dance. JCRs are always booked for extracurricular rehearsals, so they can't be the social sanctuaries that the college makes them out to be. "These beautiful, frequently wood-paneled rooms are the sort of places Harvard plasters over its brochures," explains one student. "[They are] enticing naïve applicants with dreams of endless intellectual discourse in quaint, posh settings."[344] Loker has a television, ATM, jukebox, two pool tables, and a variety of good food, but hosts few students anytime except during the 11:30–2:15 Fly-by lunch run every afternoon. Undergraduates account for the socializing that doesn't go on at Loker by its study-oriented layout and ugly furnishings: "The wan overhead lights complement the sterile decor, partitions inexplicably blocking off entire sections of tables from one another."[345]

Although there isn't any central place on campus for undergraduates to hang out, the presence of a student center wouldn't solve social problems at the college: "The mistaken premise behind the student center is that Harvard students have the time, or interest, in being social. In reality, we don't want to hang out unless there's a productive sense of accomplishment in doing so. We don't want to party. What we really want is to study—study all the time …Give Harvard a new student center and what will people do? They will bring their sourcebooks there."[346]

PARTYING

Most weekends feature at least one club-organized or House-sponsored dance party. And Houses and student groups host more than 30 formals each year. But strict administrative policies, incommodious architecture, and negligible Greek life render the party scene less than stellar.

College policy requires hosting students to submit a party registration form to residential proctors or tutors and the Dean's Office and to purchase a $55 liquor license from the city of Cambridge. Unregistered parties are shut down immediately. HUPD officers shut down all registered parties at 2:00 A.M., resulting in the "ready, set, go!" phenomena of campus night-life: "Nothing is going on until at least 11:00 P.M., and everything comes to a dead stop by 1:00 A.M., 2:00 A.M. for all city establishments."[347] Campus architecture provides but a few choice suites whose size and layout lend themselves to "the all-too-rare Harvard beerfest."[348] Several open dorm room parties on campus are held every weekend, but partygoers end up drenched in sweat after being packed into small angular common rooms with poor ventilation. And none of Harvard's three on-campus fraternities, two sororities, or three female social clubs has their own houses or contributes much to nonmember social life on campus.

The after-hours scene at Harvard is dominated by the eight "Final Clubs" on campus: the Porcellian, the Fly, the Spee, the AD, the Pheonix SK, the Fox, the Owl, and the Delphic, all of which have their own houses on campus. Rich in tradition and controversy, Final Clubs are social organizations for students to hang out, take meals, and hold parties in their spacious buildings located around Harvard Square. About 300–350 male undergrads among the student body belong to one of the Final Clubs on campus. Club membership is open only to male upperclassmen, who also tend to be rich, white, and Protestant. One Final Club member reports that Club members "become wholeheartedly obsessed with their WASPy traditions, sacrifice individuality in the name of brotherhood, and … make it the be-all and end-all of their Harvard life. They assume the elitist attitudes of the elitist few, support each other's conservative values, talk about I-banking, and celebrate a culture of excess."[349]

Selection for Final Club membership—called the punch process—is Harvard's survival of the coolest. Here's how the punch process works: first, about five percent of male upperclassmen are "punched" when they get a special invitation slid under their door inviting them to a special social event, such as a day outing, cocktail party, or luncheon. Usually the men who are chosen to be punched are those who are friends with members of the Final Club. At the social event, punches try to make a good impression on Club members, and afterward, a number of punches are cut. Whoever makes it to the next round gets another invitation under their door. If one makes it through a series of cuts, then one is invited to join the club. One student who'd gone through the punch process explains, "It's not so much the person you are, but who you know."[350]

Like frats, Final Clubs offer their members a fixed social scene without a work- or performance-related component. Final Clubs serve alcohol at their parties and limit attendance to Club members, females, and close male friends. Final Club members maintain that guest restrictions are necessary due to limited building capacities and legal liability. In the words of one Final Club member, their parties are merely social outlets more appealing than "bars, cramped dorm rooms, and city streets," providing a venue where you "can drink if you like, dance if you like, mingle if you like, or you can do any or none of the above."[351]

However, many students and administrators criticize the 100-year-old Final Clubs as cliquey, elitist, and intimidating. The Final Clubs have no official affiliation with Harvard College because they violate the college's nondiscrimination policy by denying admission to women. A 2000 survey conducted for *The Women's Guide to Harvard* indicates 47 percent of undergraduates feel that Final Clubs have a negative influence on the social scene compared to just 15 percent who feel that they have a positive influence. The Clubs negatively affect nonmember males who are excluded from social events and also women who are excluded from membership as well as those who find themselves in uncomfortable or threatening situations at Final Club parties.

Former Dean Lewis ('68) describes the administration's disapproving stance on Final Clubs: "[t]he unequal status of women at the Clubs—unwelcome, as members, but welcomed for the amusement of the male members at their parties—continues to be of great concern to the college."[352] *The Harvard Crimson* explains, "Encouraging female students to drink in a male-dominated establishment may create a threatening dynamic for a woman who does not know how to handle her alcohol or keep herself out of uncomfortable situations; even those who do may find themselves in trouble regardless of their college social life street smarts."[353] At the Safe Community meeting for freshmen, administrators warn women of the potential for sexual violence at the Clubs, telling students that upperclass male students may try to take advantage of younger females, using alcohol or date rape drugs to lower their inhibitions. According to one female student: "… girls need to be careful when they go to Final Clubs, because call them what you want, they're frats. Just because they're private clubs for Harvard boys doesn't mean they're classy or that the members aren't complete assholes …. A horny frat boy is a horny frat boy. So pour your own drinks." Recent reported incidents of "inappropriate behavior" at Final Clubs include underage drinking, extreme drunkenness, drug-dealing, fighting, public nudity as part of initiation requirements, lewd sexual acts performed by hired women, and many occasions of sexual harassment.[354]

Club members claim that "the myth that Final Clubs are bastions of misogyny is just that … it's a very open atmosphere and most of the girls hanging out are our friends."[355] Many females feel safe at Final Clubs and deem them an important social presence on campus, inasmuch as they provide women with free alcohol and great parties that can't be found elsewhere. "Women who go to final clubs are not being victimized," says one female undergrad. "[T]hey are trying to have fun."[356] Another woman explains, "I really can't say that I've ever felt uncomfortable … in a Final Club—as far as the question of rape or sexual harassment goes. That doesn't mean I think they are amazing, upstanding institutions—I just see them as places where my guy friends hang out."[357] The most realistic evaluation of Final Clubs comes from one undergrad who says, "Because these social spaces are the only ones [on campus], the full gamut of deviant social activity that happens among drunk people at any college happens right in these spaces."[358] So they're not the honors society Phi Beta Kappa, and they're not the corrupt secret society from the movie *Skulls*. Despite administrative efforts to boot them off campus, it looks like Final Clubs are at Harvard to stay.

ALCOHOL

Harvard is not a dry campus. Unlimited alcohol is readily available on campus to undergraduates at dorm room parties and Final Club events. While Harvard students binge drink far less often than most college students, a 2001 survey by *The Harvard Crimson* indicated that undergrads at Harvard feel the secondary effects of alcohol—peer-babysitting, vandalism, sexual assault, and violent fights—just as much as on campuses nationwide.[359]

According to a 2001 study conducted by Henry Wechsler, a professor at Harvard's School of Public Health, 46 percent of Harvard students "binge drink," defined as five drinks in a row for men and four drinks in a row for women. Twenty-three percent of Harvard students who binge drink report having had an alcohol-related episode in which they forgot where they were or what they did. And 26 percent of Harvard binge drinkers do so "frequently," defined as more than twice in a two-week period. While the number of binge drinkers at Harvard is on par with the national average among college students, Wechsler reports, Harvard undergrads binge drink half as frequently as students at other colleges.[360]

Fifteen percent of Harvard students feel a direct negative effect on their lives related to alcohol consumption on campus, according to a 1996 survey conducted by Target Management.[361] More than half of those polled by *The Harvard Crimson* in 2001 reported having found vomit in their dorm hall or bathroom in the past semester. Eleven percent have had their property damaged, nine percent have been hit by a student who'd been drinking, and twenty-two percent have suffered unwanted sexual advances by those under the influence of alcohol. Almost 60 percent of Harvard students say they've had to take care of a drunk friend at least once in the past semester.[362]

Who drinks at Harvard? Harvard men drink a good deal more than Harvard women. Upperclassmen drink slightly more than freshmen. Athletes and Final Club members drink far more often than most students. And undergraduate members of religious organizations drink less than most. Twice as many Harvard men than women get drunk more than twice per month, and three times as many Harvard men than women report drinking more than 10 times every 30 days. Freshmen drink about half as often as upperclassmen, with 40 percent of freshmen abstaining altogether. Seventy percent of male freshmen and 90 percent of female freshmen say that Harvard's ban on underage consumption doesn't deter them from drinking.[363]

Seventy percent of Harvard athletes report binge drinking at least twice every two weeks and 20 percent of athletes report having had more than six drinks the last time they drank, compared to seven percent of Harvard undergraduates overall. Twice as many athletes as nonathletes say their drinking has caused them to forget where they were or what they were doing. Seventy-five percent of Final Club members are binge drinkers, and 20 percent describe themselves as "heavy drinkers," compared to five percent of the Harvard undergrads on the whole. Eleven percent of Final Club members report having had nine or more drinks the last time they drank, compared to less than two percent of all Harvard students, and 25 percent of Final Club members report drinking 10 to 19 times per week, versus 10 percent of the total college population. One Final Club member says that club members drink more than most because Clubs offer easy access to alcohol. "You go down to the Club and grab a beer between classes," he explains. "You don't have to go to a store and it's not a hassle. Drinking is just convenient [at Final Clubs]." Undergraduate members of religious organizations report binge drinking a third less and abstaining twice as much as students overall. Forty percent of religious students abstain, compared to just 20 percent of all Harvard students.[364]

What are the disciplinary consequences for drinking at Harvard? In accordance with state laws, the college prohibits the consumption of alcohol by students under the age of 21 as well as the sale or service of alcohol to student under 21. The standard administrative response to simple underage drinking is a warning, which does not go on a student's record. Repeated incidents of underage drinking or alcohol-related offenses such as physical assaults or irresponsible hosting typically result in disciplinary action, which goes on a student's permanent record and is usually reported by the college in response to employment or grad school inquiries. Repeated offenses also usually incur recommendations by the college to have students seek counsel from professionals at UHS or BSC.

Alcohol policies are enforced inconsistently among underage freshmen and underage upperclassmen. While a few freshman proctors are lax, the majority is extremely strict about enforcing the college's prohibition on underage drinking and will not hesitate to barge into students' rooms, ask questions, and report students acting peculiarly to the Administrative Board for disciplinary review. By contrast, most House tutors don't enforce the prohibition at all. Unless police are attracted to a party in the upperclass Houses, students who drink there will be left alone. One student rightly noted, "Once you get into an [upperclassman] House, they don't care as much about what you do, as long as you keep it quiet."[365]

The main goal of the college's alcohol policy is that students not drink themselves to death. If students go to UHS for alcohol-related incidents, they are usually required to attend counseling or to speak with assistant deans or senior tutors about their drinking in order to see if there if a history of drinking that would cause concern for the student's well-being. The college encourages students who overdrink to seek immediate medical attention at UHS by guaranteeing that they will incur no disciplinary penalty if admitted, so long as the only infraction is the drinking.[366]

The effectiveness of the college's no-fault policy in saving lives depends on student perception, which is compromised at Harvard by poor communication and inconsistent policy application of the policy by administrators. Another 2001 poll conducted by *The Harvard Crimson* indicated that nearly one-third of undergraduates think they are "likely" or "very likely" to be disciplined by the college if they were admitted to UHS for an alcohol-related illness. And almost one-half of undergraduates believe that senior tutors or assistant deans won't find out if they seek medical treatment at UHS, even though it's UHS policy to inform university officials always when a student is admitted to UHS or any other hospital. But Harvard makes little effort to publicize or clarify its alcohol policy. In response to statistics on students' confusion about Harvard's alcohol policy, former Dean Lewis ('68) said he was "impressed" that two-thirds of students "know that a behavior which is clearly illegal under state law and contrary to college rules will ordinarily not result in disciplinary actions." Yet students say that the degree of misunderstanding on campus reduces the frequency with which undergraduates seek medical attention for themselves or others when they suffer from alcohol-related illnesses.[367]

DRUGS

The extent and conspicuousness of drug use at Harvard is less than that at colleges across the country. Five percent of students report feeling a direct negative effect on their lives related to drug use on campus, according to a 1996 survey conducted by Target Management.[368] A 1999 survey by *The Harvard Crimson* indicated that 24 percent of Harvard undergrads have used illegal drugs while at college, compared to 30 percent of undergraduates nationwide. While an equal number of Harvard men and women report using illegal drugs, drug use varies greatly across concentrations and class years. Forty-one percent of humanities concentrators report using drugs at Harvard, compared to just 24 percent of social science concentrators and 18 percent of natural science concentrators. Freshmen report that less than five percent of their friends use illegal drugs, compared to more than 40 percent of seniors.[369] Sixteen percent of the student body reports smoking cigarettes, compared to an average of 25 percent on college nationwide.[370]

Illegal drug use at Harvard goes on behind closed doors. Small pockets of undergrads buy, sell, and do drugs in select dorm rooms on campus. The most popular illegal drug at Harvard is marijuana.[371] Twenty-three percent of Harvard students report using marijuana, but only a handful report using hallucinogens, cocaine, or heroin.[372] "Harvard is conducive to [marijuana use]," one student explains, "[because] people here are pretty affluent and have a lot of access."[373] Diane Bracket of the Boston branch of the Drug Enforcement Agency confirms, "Marijuana is readily available in the Boston area [because] it's traditionally the drug of choice on university campuses throughout the region." The marijuana circulating around the Harvard campus is most often imported from Mexico, Columbia, and Jamaica, but can come from any place that Harvard's geographically diverse student body comes back from while on college breaks. Ecstasy, or "E," has become the "special occasion" drug of choice among undergraduates at Harvard and cocaine, mushrooms, and LSD can be found at several intimate social settings.[374]

The college disciplines undergraduate possession, sale, or distribution of illegal drugs on a case-by-case basis. Depending on the types, quantities, circumstances involved in a particular case of student drug use, distribution, or sale, Ad Board action might include warning, probation, requirement to withdraw, or dismissal.

DATING

Most undergrads express extreme dissatisfaction with the quantity and quality of dating on campus, and they agree that one's chances of dating are significantly diminished by going to college at Harvard. For many, the only dates they attend at Harvard are the semi-annual formal dances on campus. Almost 40 percent of Harvard students say they've never dated someone for more than one week at college, according to a 1999 poll conducted by *The Harvard Crimson*.[375] Even former University President Rudenstine characterized the biggest problem facing Harvard students as loneliness.[376]

Students on campus rarely date. The reason isn't that Harvard undergrads are any worse-looking than your average 16–24 year-olds. In a 2002 Harvard Independent survey on the "attractiveness" of the student body, 54 percent of students gave a rating of "average" to Harvard men and 46 percent gave a rating of "average" to Harvard women. About 20 percent gave men and women a rating of "above average" and another 20 percent gave men and women a rating of "below average." Five percent of men and four percent of women on campus got ratings of "way above average," and five percent of men and seven percent of women got ratings of "way below average."[377]

In fact, the dreary dating scene results mainly from a student body that is both inexperienced with romantic relationships and intensely focused on personal commitments. Typical Harvard students have less dating practice than most incoming college students because many neglected their social lives in high school in favor of academic and extracurricular pursuits. Harvard students' inexperience with love coupled with their success in so many other aspects of their lives make romance disconcerting because it requires, perhaps for the first time, an expression of vulnerability and the potential for failure. Preoccupation with personal objectives also cramps an active dating life on campus. "The self-sufficiency cloak worn by many Harvard students," according to one undergraduate, "follows from the fact that the vast majority of us got here by shielding away distractions in high school that would have siphoned away time and energy from our goals."[378] With so many academic and extracurricular pursuits to prioritize, students often choose not to make time for the generous social interaction required by romantic relationships.[379] Few students are willing to compromise their GPA for the significant time commitment that dating requires. According to one student, "Harvard is a very goal-oriented place, seeing people as a means to an end. Relationships are not conducive to this mindframe."[380]

An alternative to the scarcity of dating at Harvard is off-campus relationships—ranging from high school sweethearts to Harvard Square employees to those who have moved off campus with their significant others. Harvard students who maintain relationships with non-Harvard students say that it can be difficult to balance off-campus romances with on-campus community. If your partner lives far away, you may rarely see him or her, and if your partner lives nearby, you may rarely see other Harvard students.

The romance that does exist at Harvard virtually always entails an all-or-nothing sexual commitment, with informal dating having been replaced by serious relationships and "hooking up," an imprecise term applying to a range of brief sexual encounters. As one student explains, romance at Harvard "works well for serial monogamists (people who like long-term relationships), [but] not well for people who like casual dating."[381] Symptomatic of the "hook-up/marriage" phenomenon is the pervasiveness of "dormcest"—brief sexual encounters between students in the same dorm. And many convey an obsession with finding romantic permanence that leads them to carry any relationship into the realm of matrimony.[382] In fact, 60 percent of Harvard grads eventually marry each other.[383]

Interracial dating at Harvard is fairly common among the dating that happens on campus. Students, who have been involved in relationships with people of another race, report that Harvard students are accepting of, but still slightly taken aback by, interracial dating on campus. "I feel Harvard is very tolerant of mixed-race dating," says a Mexican Catholic undergraduate who has been going out with a white American Jewish woman for four years.[384] There's no prejudice or ill will on campus toward students in interracial relationships, "but they don't go unnoticed."[385]

Homosexual romance is easier to find for guys than for girls on a campus where there are a couple hundred gay undergrads, but only a few dozen lesbian students. The scarcity of homosexual women leads many of them to date students at other Boston area colleges. Some queer students are in long-term

SEX AND PREGNANCY

Harvard students have about half as much sex as undergraduates nationwide, according to 2001 student surveys conducted by *The Harvard Independent* and *Flare* magazine. Approximately 10 percent of Harvard students have some kind of sex on average once a day, 10 percent have sex once a week, another 10 percent once a month, 20 percent have sex once a year, and about 50 percent never have sex. Among Harvard undergrads, approximately 35 percent of males and 45 percent of females are virgins. And among sexually active students at Harvard, more students have oral sex (about 40 percent at least once a month) than vaginal sex (about 30 percent).[386]

Most sex goes on in dorm rooms, although roommates and neighbors are sure to hear even the most gentle of partners getting frisky on the other side of thin firedoors and dorm room walls. The most notorious locale for sex on campus is the "stacks"—the dark, cold, empty underground tunnels of Widener library. According to a 1996 poll conducted by *The Harvard Crimson*, about six percent of undergraduates have had sex in the stacks.[387] Another corporeal tradition at Harvard is "Primal Scream"—the semi-annual ritual where throngs of undergraduates, on the night before final exams, do laps around Harvard Yard totally in the buff. But despite frenzied nudity, Primal Scream is about neither sex nor exhibitionism, but rather about giving stressed-out students an opportunity to step outside the box. Dudley Co-op residents hold their own special version of Primal Scream, called the Lingerie Study Break. While other undergraduates are running naked around Harvard Yard, Dudley Co-op residents strip their clothing piece by piece inside of Lamont Library, amidst hundreds of students cramming for exams the next day.

The silver lining of Harvard's disappointing dating scene? "I may not have had a date in two years," one student says, "but I also don't have burning sensations when I pee."[388] Only one out of every thousand Harvard students polled by University Health Services (UHS) report having had Chlamydia—just one-eighth of the national average. While almost 40 percent abstain from sex altogether, sexually-active Harvard students play it safer than most college students, partially due to promotion and availability of contraceptives on campus. Of those who have had sex, according to a 2001 UHS survey, almost all of them report having only one or two partners in the past year. Fifty-seven percent of sexually active Harvard students reported using a condom for vaginal sex (compared to 45 percent on campuses nationwide), while over 30 percent of Harvard students use a condom for anal sex, and less than one percent use a condom for oral sex. Thirteen percent of sexually active Harvard students use the morning-after pill and only one percent get pregnant.[389]

Of those students that do get pregnant, "Ninety-nine percent of them get abortions," says Gina M. Ocon ('98–'00), a student mother, because "[t]here are so many financial and psychological disincentives to being a parent here." "[T]he initial message…at this school [is that] an abortion is the only really good decision to make," says Anna N. Payanzo ('00), another student who raised a child while earning her undergraduate degree. Harvard does, however, provide a number of resources to help make raising a child and earning a Harvard degree compatible. Harvard adjusts financial aid packages to help provide student parents with off-campus housing, day care, and healthcare. While the housing system is poorly equipped to provide the extra help that student parents need, UHS offers a great deal of services and counseling relating to pregnancy and childbirth, and the college "introduce[s] parents to one another, so they can benefit from each other's shared experiences," according to Associate Dean of the College Thomas Dingman ('67).[390]

CHAPTER SEVEN
LIFE BEYOND CAMPUS

Harvard's location is ideal for life at college. The campus rests along the Charles River, just beside suburban hub Harvard Square, in the center of assorted charming Cambridge neighborhoods, and three miles from the city of Boston.

HARVARD SQUARE

Spilling out from the intersection of Mt. Auburn Street, Massachusetts Avenue, and JFK Avenue just outside of Harvard Yard, Harvard Square is constantly animated. An eclectic mix of students, locals, tourists, shoppers, panhandlers, and entertainers populate the dozen square blocks of red brick sidewalks that encircle one cemetery, one public park, four movie theaters, five performing arts theatres, nine museums, ten music stores, twenty bookstores, one hundred dining establishments, and hundreds of shops of all kinds. But without anywhere for students to eat fast food, drink alcohol, rent videos, go dancing, buy groceries, or get food after 2:00 A.M., the Square caters more to wealthy tourists and yuppie urbanites than to Harvard College students. The recent disappearances of students' favorite bar, hamburger joint, and ice cream shop, The Bow and Arrow, The Tastee, and Baskin Robbins, respectively, all featured in the film *Good Will Hunting*, signaled a palpable shift in the Square's primary constituency. Other notable recent departures include Store 24, good for a late night snack run; Ma Soba, with its student-discounted pad Thai; and the Crimson Sports Grille, the freshman drinking hole whose bouncers never saw an ID they didn't like. In their place, the Square has taken on a chockfull of overpriced chain stores like Abercrombie & Fitch, Urban Outfitters, The Gap, Sunglass Hut, Tower Records, and HMV. The new Harvard Square is, in one students' words, "a melting pot with the heat turned off, the Great Strip Mall of the Ivy League."[391] The official Harvard Square homepage is www.harvardsquare.com/.[392]

The hub of the Square is an area called "the Pit" that surrounds the Harvard Square T-Station across the street from Au Bon Pain and the Harvard Coop. Every afternoon, kids congregate there, adorned with mohawks, piercings, brightly-colored hair, leather clothes, and metal studs. The Pit kids add an unmistakable flair to Harvard Square, but Harvard students rarely interact with them directly. Most of the 100 or so "Pit kids" are local residents who meet there after school, but about 20 are homeless migrants drawn to Harvard Square from around the country. While the Pit attracts Harvard and Cambridge police officers every other weekend or so to deal with fights, gang recruitment, or public intoxication, Harvard students generally feel safe in that area of Harvard Square.[393]

Harvard Square features vendors and performers up and down Massachusetts Avenue and in every corner of the T-station. Vendors sell everything from balloon animals to hemp necklaces to flowers to Mexican pullover sweaters to smoothies to *Spare Change*, the bi-weekly newspaper that's written, produced, and sold by homeless people. Street entertainers—ranging from college students to immigrants to schoolteachers to the homeless—include a staggering breadth of performance. Musicians, singers, dancers, clowns, jugglers, magicians, and living statues perform for the thousands who pass through Harvard Square each day, offering a treat for students on their way to class. The Square's street performers must get one of the Cambridge's 450 $40 permits, and typically make about $10 per hour, with popular entertainers raking in over $1,000 in one afternoon.

Dozens of homeless people live in Harvard Square. A student walking through the Square on a given day can expect to see several people sleeping on the sidewalk and to be asked for money several times. Many undergrads don't know what to do when asked on their way to class to "spare some change," "help a hungry veteran," and "give something for a mother of five." Some students reach into their pockets for a few quarters, some make eye contact and say they're sorry, some look away and keep moving, and others serve in the homeless community through Harvard programs that donate food and clothing, run homeless shelters, build affordable housing, and provide legal aid for the homeless. Dealing with homeless people in some way, however, is an unavoidable part of going to Harvard.

When they've had enough of Harvard University Dining Services' tofu-tomato sizzle and General Wong's chicken, students pick up cheap eats in the Square at Uno's, Chili's, Bertucci's, Real Taco, and The Wrap. There is no fast food in Harvard Square. Ethnic restaurants of varying authenticity include Chinese, Japanese, Vietnamese, Middle Eastern, Italian, Indian, Mexican,

Greek, and Thai. There are a number of top-notch pizza hang-outs, the most popular of which are Tommy's, with its cheap sesame seed-crusted slices, video games, and 2:00 A.M. closing time, and the perennial student favorite, Pinocchio's, with its nonpareil square-cut, thick-doughed Sicilian-style slices. Ice cream in Harvard Square is heavenly. *The Harvard Crimson* aptly reports, "Flavors are divine and mind-rocking. Textures are gooey and velvety. Toppings are endless." Students shell out $5 a pop for a Herrel's "smoosh-in" and flock to Ben and Jerry's for free cone day each spring. A word of advice on Boston-speak: sprinkles are called "jimmies." For coffee and desert, few students escape the chain experience of Starbucks, Au Bon Pain, and Dunkin' Donuts (called "The Eliot Street Café") in place of more unique atmospheres at Café Algiers, Café Pamplona, and Café Paradiso. Harvard's bar scene offers Grendel's, Charlie's, Casablanca, The Cellar, and the recently reopened Grafton Street Pub, and liquor can be bought at Louie's and 7-Eleven. But you have to be over 21 because fake IDs don't work in the Square. Store clerks and bouncers know their stuff and take away fakes on a regular basis. The most popular place to see and be seen on Monday nights is John Harvard's restaurant, which offers half-price appetizers after 10:00 P.M. to the throngs of Harvard students waiting to get in. The Sunday brunch hot spot is the all-you-can-eat Mongolian barbecue Fire and Ice.

For a place to dance outside of Final Clubs and dorm room parties, students have to hop on a train into Boston. But there're several opportunities for less-dynamic fun to be had in Harvard Square. The Harvard Box Office (HBO), located at the Holyoke Center Arcade in Harvard Square and online at www.fas.harvard.edu/~tickets/ sells tickets for well-attended undergraduate performances taking place on campus every weekend, ranging from a cappella concerts to dance performances to fashion shows. The talent, dedication, and "spirit of professionalism"[394] displayed by student performers at these events are truly staggering. Loews movie theater, across the street from the main Johnston Gate entrance to Harvard Yard, shows about five first- and second-run movies at a time, in addition to weekly showings of the cult classic *The Rocky Horror Picture Show*. For cheaper, artsier, and more obscure movies, the Harvard Film Archive shows movies for five bucks at the Carpenter Center just outside Harvard Yard. Students can check out a variety of hot live music in the

Square for cover charges typically under $10 at places like Club Passim, House of Blues, and Sculler's Jazz Club. They can buy every possible type of music at Planet Records, Newbury Comics, Tower Records, Twisted Village, CD Spins, and HMV Music Store. Inexpensive stand-up comedy is available each weekend at The Comedy Studio, on the third floor of The Hong Kong restaurant. Cambridge and Boston are veritable comedy havens, with clubs like Dick Doherty's Comedy Vault, Nick's Comedy Stop, and The Comedy Connection regularly featuring fresh open-mike talent and big-name headliners from Comedy Central and *Saturday Night Live*.

Fairs, cemeteries, and pornography round out Harvard Square entertainment. One-day fairs pack the streets of Harvard Square with tens of thousands of people twice a year. Mayfair and Oktoberfest close the streets of Harvard Square and attract 35,000–50,000 Cambridgites (but not many students) to check out the kiddie playland, tons of ethnic cuisine, dozens of street entertainers, and 200-plus merchants and vendors of artistic crafts, jewelry, and clothing. Harvard Square's least appreciated cultural phenomenon is Mount Auburn Cemetery—among the country's most famous graveyards. The Cemetery features a 170-acre botanical garden, a free guided tour, a comprehensive history of Cambridge, and a public tower that offers one of the best views of Boston, but is rarely visited by undergraduates.

Pedestrians dominate Harvard Square. While students are usually safe jaywalking across the streets of Harvard Square, some crosswalks are poorly marked and may not catch the attention of tourist drivers unfamiliar with the written and unwritten rules of driving in the Square. Newly installed countdown crossing signals improve pedestrian safety in the most congested intersection at the corner of JFK Street and Massachusetts Avenue, but crosswalks on Mt. Auburn Street are located where cars are moving so fast that they may not be able to stop abruptly for pedestrians. In December 2000 Shira Palmer-Sherman ('02) was struck and killed by a car in Harvard Square while walking outside of an Eliot Street crosswalk late at night amidst poor lighting and inclement weather.[395]

Off-Campus Transportation

Having a car with you at Harvard is usually pointless. Not only does Harvard offer one of the best transportation systems in the country—with convenient shuttles, cabs, busses, trains, and planes going anywhere you could want—but *The Unofficial Guide to Life at Harvard* has it right when it says, "Car-owners will quickly learn to curse Boston's narrow, twisting streets plagued by ambiguous one-way designations and death-trap rotaries, as well as its notoriously insane drivers and suicidal pedestrians." Another difficulty for student car-owners is the lack of parking at Harvard. The college's parking lottery provides all students with an available spot according to where they live and their location preference. Students who take a university-assigned parking space pay between $90 and $135 per month, far less than the parking rates for the city of Cambridge. Students with cars rank parking availability at DeWolfe House, Peabody Terrace, 29 Garden Street, or the Business School parking lot across the Charles River—where almost all students are assigned in the end.[396]

Getting out of Harvard Square and into Cambridge, Boston, and beyond is remarkably safe, clean, cheap, and convenient. Harvard students reap the advantages of the oldest and most extensive public transportation system in the country, which keeps traffic down and pollution low. Numerous bus routes running throughout Boston for a one-dollar fare leave from either Johnston Gate or the underground T-station in Harvard Square. And the Massachusetts Bay Transportation Authority (MBTA), known to students as the "T," has a subway stop right in Harvard Square, with two entrances just outside the gates of Harvard Yard. Trains come every five minutes or so, running to and from anywhere in Boston and surrounding cities. At one dollar per ride, the T offers one of the lowest fares in the country. Like any public transportation systems, the T gets crowded at times, making it necessary to stand. The T has four color-coded routes—red, green, blue, and orange. "Inbound" trains on each route run toward downtown Boston and "outbound" trains run away from Boston. There are subway staffers at each T-stop to help out the direction-management-impaired. Vendors and musicians spice up nearly every subway station along the way.

Unfortunately, normal bus routes stop running early in the evening and the T shuts down every night at 12:30 A.M., cutting short many a nighttime excursion into Boston. *The Harvard Crimson* quips "Boston should be proud of its Puritan heritage, but John Winthrop must not be allowed to dictate its transportation policy in the twenty-first century." For those whose plans would defy Beantown's conservative origins, there is the little known late-night bus service on Friday and Saturday called the "Night Owl," which offers 10 bus routes that stop at the same stations that the T does. Buses leave from downtown Boston every half-hour beginning at 1:00 A.M. and ending at 2:30 A.M. The fare is one-dollar per ride—same as the T—with free transfers between buses. After 2:30, students have to wait and pay up for shady private taxis. Cab fare from downtown Boston to Harvard costs $10–$15.

To get anywhere in the northeast outside of Boston, you can take trains and buses out of Boston's South Station, a 20-minute T-ride from Harvard. Or you can take Amtrak and planes out of Boston's Logan Airport, a $1, 45-minute T-ride or $25, 30-minute cab ride from Harvard. Harvard students from New York and Washington, DC, use US Airways and Delta shuttles, which offer exchangeable $80 tickets to and from Boston that you can buy in the airport the day of departure. Planes leaving all day long take one hour to travel between Boston and New York and two hours between Boston and Washington.

CAMBRIDGE

Harvard is located in Cambridge, Massachusetts' seventh-largest city, with a population of roughly 100,000 people. The official Town of Cambridge homepage is www.townonline.com/cambridge/. A 10–20 minute walk in any direction from Harvard Square will take you to one of Cambridge's many diverse regions. Dozens of miles of paved paths along the Charles River provide scenic and ideal routes for jogging, rollerblading, and biking just blocks from Harvard Yard. Although transportation is easy and destinations are enticing, Harvard students rarely leave campus. "Undergraduates tend to be insular," one student aptly remarks, "staying in our rooms and studying, not exploring and interacting with the city."[397] Candid, comprehensive, and comical descriptions of all of Cambridge and Boston attractions—sorted by T-stop, cost, and favorite student picks—can be found in *The Unofficial Guide to Life at Harvard*, published annually by Harvard Student Agencies (HSA), distributed to all Harvard students, and available online at www.unofficialharvard.com.

Tufts' Davis Square, "[o]verflowing with hip cafes, public art installations, and funky music joints," raves *The Unofficial Guide*, "is a welcome change from the franchise-filled, tourist-trodden enclave of Harvard Square." Walkers, joggers, and bicyclists flock to Old Cambridge's Fresh Pond Reservoir and serene tree-filled environs off of Brattle Street and Huron Avenue by the Quad. You'll find some of the best Latino and Asian food among the ethnic restaurants in quiet Inman Square and less quiet Porter Square, where students also go to rent videos at City Video and shop for groceries at Star Market, services conspicuously absent from Harvard Square. Central Square, in between Harvard and MIT, has blocks of chain stores, discount stores, and sex shops amidst an utterly miscellaneous atmosphere—"melodious Italian accents mingle with the drunken ravings ravings of homeless," according to *The Unofficial Guide*, while "acerbic guitar riffs, drown out the mellow croonings of Billie Holiday, Indian curry is dashed into the McDonalds deep-fry, and hip-hoppers wearing garish name-brand gear vie for attention with punk rockers sporting black leather and chains." Kendall Square, next to the MIT campus, features the Boston-area's best cinema (Kendall Square Cinema), bargain shopping (The Garment District), and pool hall (Flat Top Johnny's). Other quality gaming spots in Boston are Jillian's and the Good Time Emporium, which offer massive televisions, arcades, a variety of virtual reality games, and 50–70 pool tables.

BOSTON

Harvard is in Cambridge, not Boston, which is three miles from campus. There are innumerable Boston attractions—parks, restaurants, malls, museums, clubs, games, historical sites—within a 15-minute T-ride from Harvard. The official City of Boston homepage is www.cityofboston.gov/. Most students who choose Harvard over other elite schools factor into their decision Boston's safe and dynamic urban life compared to the dull or dangerous surroundings of some of their other choices. "Between 60 to 65 percent [of students]," estimates Dean of Admissions and Financial Aid William R. Fitzsimmons ('67), "say that … the Boston/Cambridge area … was important or very important in their decision…to visit, apply, and attend." A 1996 Target Management study found that 18 percent of undergrads identified geographical location as an "extremely important" reason for choosing Harvard.[398]

Despite Boston's proximity, excitement, and allure, undergraduates rarely get into the city more than once or twice per semester. Students cite lack of time and local amenities as reasons for not taking advantage of what Boston has to offer. They say that their busy academic and extracurricular schedules just don't permit enough time to make the T-ride into the city. "You get busy," reports one undergraduate, "and then you just kind of stay here."[399] Others note that provisions and attractions on-campus and in Harvard Square frequently make the trip into Boston unnecessary and inconvenient. One student explains, "Anything I'd want to go into Boston for is in Cambridge."[400]

If you make the time to check out Boston, there're countless possibilities. You can taste delectable dim sum in Chinatown and mouth-watering cannolis in the North End, Boston's version of Little Italy. Newbury Street—where beautiful people cruise past beautiful restaurants in their beautiful cars—is very nice to look at, but most everything there is prohibitively expensive. The glaring exceptions are the ice cream, vintage clothing, and off-beat music shops. Just a 10–15 minute subway ride from Harvard Square, extending from Park Street to Downtown Crossing, is the oldest public park in the country, Boston Common: a 48-acre green oasis of landscaped ponds, fountains, monuments, tourists, and relaxed Bostonians. In the fall and springtime, Boston Common is the ideal place to people-watch, feed the Canadian geese, play Frisbee®, take a ride on the swan boats, get a tan, or study in the delicious sunshine. Very few students ever get out to the handsome beaches on the North Shore of Massachusetts Bay. The closest beach is Manchester by the Sea, the most visited by tourists is Salem, and most popular among Boston-area undergraduates is Revere Beach, America's oldest public beach.

At the Boston Common kiosk, students can pick up a guide to the two to five mile Freedom Trail, a tour of Beantown's most prominent historical landmarks. The most visited site along the Freedom Trail, just outside the Downtown Crossing subway entrance, is Faneuil Hall marketplace, where handfuls of diverse street performers entertain crowds lining cobblestone paths amidst a variety of restaurants and outlet stores. Adjacent to Faneuil Hall are pricey gift and craft shops; the Bostix kiosk, where half-price tickets are often available to Boston theater shows on the day of performance; and the Quincy Market building, a colossal food court featuring a little bit of everything, with free samples along the way. The Haymarket outdoor food market sells fresh in-season fruits and vegetables every weekend at extremely low prices.

Students can shop for designer clothes at lower-priced department stores like Macy's and Filene's Basement at Downtown Crossing and at higher-priced stores like Nieman Marcus, Lord and Taylor, and Saks Fifth Avenue at Copley Square. Decent malls are located within a 20-minute T-ride at Copley Plaza and the Cambridgeside Galleria. Copley Plaza offers upscale fashions and jewelry, quaint sweetshops, and the ever-popular California Pizza Kitchen. The Cambridgeside Galleria features fair shopping, a quality food court, and the 20-page menu at The Cheesecake Factory.

You want culture? The Museum of Fine Arts (MFA), which offers free admission with a Harvard ID, has a vast collection of international art and a particularly impressive exhibit of impressionist paintings. The interactive Children's Museum, Museum of Science, Boston Tea Party Ship, Franklin Park Zoo, and New England Aquarium are a little too mediocre and cheesy to hold the attention of college students, but are ideal spots to take younger siblings visiting you at Harvard. Students can even check out Broadway shows at the Wang Center on Tremont Street, which runs along the Park Street T-stop, the first subway station in America.

In 2002 Boston was named the greatest sports city in North America. Baseball, basketball, hockey, and football fans can go see the Red Sox at Fenway Park, just a 15-minute T-ride from Harvard Square, the Celtics and Bruins at the Fleet Center, just 20 minutes from Harvard, and the Patriots at Foxboro Stadium, a 50-minute commuter train ride out of South Station in Boston. Plus undergrads can check out annual racing events like the Boston Marathon and the Head of the Charles Regatta, which bring hundreds of thousands of participants and spectators to Cambridge and Boston each spring. Or students can bet on dog-racing at the Wonderland Race Track, about 45 minutes from Harvard by T, just like Matt Damon ('92) and Minnie Driver in *Good Will Hunting*.

In addition to spectator sports, students have ample opportunities to bowl, roller skate, or ice skate within 20 minutes of Harvard by T. Golfers will be disappointed with the conspicuous lack of courses in the area. But outdoorsy students can go canoeing, fishing, hiking, or backpacking at lakes, rivers, and national parks just outside of Cambridge. And thrill-seekers can go scuba-diving, mountain-climbing, hang-gliding, skydiving, or hot air ballooning for under $200 and less than a two-hour trip from Boston.

For nightlife, hot little music clubs wail live folk, rock, salsa, merengue, jazz, funk, and R&B every night of the week. And the Boston Blues Festival brings free live music to the Charles River shore every September. Boston's comprehensive bar scene caters to international, collegiate, queer, chic, and broke crowds. The dance clubs reach out especially to the European, Latin, and gay scenes. Each weekend, 20,000 people come to party at Boston nightclubs, most of which keep their doors open to students under 21. The most popular nightclub scene in Boston is a one-block strip along Landsdowne Street, in the shadows of Fenway Park, while other dance clubs are scattered around nearby Tremont and Boylston Streets.

Nightclub owners hire several Harvard student-promoters each year to get the word out about upcoming events, DJs, and parties by posting flyers around Harvard and compiling student lists that offer reduced admissions fees and a separate club entrance, which cuts down on otherwise oppressive lines. The biggest complaints about Boston clubs is that some card heavily and all close by 2:00 A.M. Boston clubs aren't too popular among college students, but run cover charges of only $10–$20, and often bring in big-name DJs such as Paul Oakenfold, Armand van Helden, and Paul van Dyke. Like any nightclub scene, Boston is grounds for a potential sketchfest. *Flare* warns that girls ought to "bring guy friends with you if you don't want to be groped by drunk guys."

NEARBY COLLEGES

Boston is a college city. Whatever deficiencies students complain about at Harvard can be found at other colleges just a few minutes away. Although 50 square miles of Boston is home to 50 colleges and hundreds of thousands of their students, Harvard students rarely take advantage of peer-group social scenes in Cambridge and Boston. Few students ever visit other schools or make any effort to meet the tremendous variety of campus social scenes in Boston.

Tufts and the Massachusetts Institute of Technology (MIT) are just a ten-minute T-ride from Harvard. MIT party life, one of the wildest in Boston, is rooted in the fraternity system, which is physically removed from and independent of the school. MIT frat houses offer the nicest amenities among Boston colleges, with lounges, kitchens, cable television, video games, foosball, and ping-pong tables, but in recent years they've experienced numerous incidents of drug abuse, bomb-threat pranks, and binge drinking, including the death of MIT first-year Scott Kreuger of alcohol intoxication in 1997. Since then, the college has banned keg parties, prohibited the service of hard liquor, and closed two major fraternities. As a result, most MIT frats now limit weekend parties to brothers and their friends, so that Harvard students can get in only when frats hold their well-publicized and well-worthwhile open parties twice each term. Like at MIT, the social scene at Tufts revolves around Greek life. With their own houses, live music, and lots of beer, the 10 fraternities and four sororities at Tufts—most on "Professor's Row"—typically outperform Harvard alternatives. Getting into Tufts frats is easy for Harvard girls, but very difficult for Harvard guys who don't have friends that are members.

Emerson College and Boston University (BU) have inner-city campuses in downtown Cambridge and Boston and a decent frat party scene. A 20-minute walk across the Charles River will get you to BU. Emerson College is 15 minutes from Harvard by T. Frat-less Boston College, an hour away by T, holds restricted parties at unsupervised junior apartments and the backyards of senior "mod" houses. Harvard students can't get in unless they know someone on the inside. Within a two-hour bus ride out of South Station in Boston, Harvard students can head to three other Ivy League Colleges—Brown, Dartmouth, and Yale—or upstate to Amherst College, University of Massachusetts (UMASS)—Amherst, Hampshire College, and two all-girls schools—Mount Holyoke and Smith.

CHAPTER EIGHT
CAMPUS DISCIPLINE

Undergraduates lament Harvard's reluctance to seriously consider students' input when making disciplinary decisions and administrative appointments. Unlike at Princeton, Yale, Stanford, Duke, Williams, Swarthmore, Dartmouth, Cornell, and the University of Pennsylvania, Harvard has no students on its disciplinary boards or administrative search committees.[401] While former Dean of the College Harry R. Lewis ('68) maintains that it's "very hard for students to have enough distance and enough perspective to make judgments" on administrative issues,[402] undergraduates at Harvard "feel disconnected from the centers of power," longing for a greater voice in the management of the college and the larger university.[403]

THE AD BOARD

The Administrative Board (the Ad Board) metes out all punishments at Harvard College. The Ad Board, whose procedures are outlined online at www.college.harvard.edu/academic/adboard/, is headed by the dean of the College and consists mostly of Allston Burr senior tutors and the assistant deans of freshmen. The Ad Board reviews unsatisfactory undergraduate records, hears all undergraduate petitions for exceptions to academic rules, and decides on all reported disciplinary matters. You would go to the Ad Board for petitions or academic records if, for instance, you want to take six classes in a single term. The Ad Board votes yes or no on academic petitions and responds to unsatisfactory academic records with action ranging from placing students on academic probation to requiring them to withdraw temporarily from the college.

The Ad Board's disciplinary review—ruling on issues like plagiarism, underage drinking, and sexual assault—is more controversial. The Ad Board's reputation as the secret society of the Harvard bureaucracy follows from its broad impact on student life and strict policy of confidentiality regarding the substance of cases and decisions. The Ad Board's disciplinary review also doesn't look anything like the U.S. justice system. For example, witnesses communicate information to the Ad Board only indirectly through a fact-finder or subcommittee, and no students serve on the Ad Board to hear their peers' cases.

Once a complaint or allegation of wrongdoing has been brought to the attention of university officials, the accused student's freshman dean or Allston Burr senior tutor will meet with the student to discuss the facts of the case from the student's perspective, the relevant college rules, and the possible courses of action. Each situation is evaluated on a case-by-case basis, under the consideration of a range of factors like previous behavior and mitigating circumstances. Sometimes the questionable action merits merely an off-the-record discussion, but more often the Ad Board will issue formal punishment.

The Ad Board formally disciplined 151 undergraduates in the 2001–2002 academic year. Thirteen students were required to withdraw for academic dishonesty. One was permanently dismissed for a second offense of academic dishonesty. Four students were required to withdraw for alcohol related offenses. One was required to withdraw for the second time for sexual misconduct. Seventy-seven students were admonished for liquor law violations, fifty-two were admonished for violations of academic procedures, and three were admonished for weapons violations.[404] Admonishments go in students' permanent files and are noted in any internship, fellowship, grad school, or job recommendations written on behalf of admonished students by anyone at Harvard. Students who are required to withdraw mid-semester for disciplinary reasons lose all course credit and money invested for that semester. They must not be present on the Harvard campus for at least two semesters and will be readmitted to the college only if they hold at least six months of full-time employment while away from Harvard and get a satisfactory performance report from a job supervisor. Any Harvard letters of recommendation will note the reason for disciplinary withdrawal. Permanent expulsion occurs only in the case of a student who has falsified admissions materials to a degree that he or she is not who he or she has claimed. A student has the right to appeal any disciplinary decision of the Ad Board in the Faculty Council and may have any decision of the Ad Board reconsidered when there is additional information available, according to the *Handbook for Students*.

PLAGIARISM

Harvard's Expository Writing Program distributes a booklet to all freshmen that explains how to properly document academic sources in order to avoid academic dishonesty or plagiarism. The Expos Program defines plagiarism as "passing off a source's information, ideas, or words as your own by omitting to acknowledge that source." The Expos Program explains that students who plagiarize usually don't set out to rip off another's work, but rather panic in the face of an impending deadline, and then combine noncited ideas from one or more sources with their own, "hoping to get away with it just this one time." Other instances of plagiarism occur when students misrepresent evidence to better support their argument, when they submit the same work for more than one course without the written permission of instructors in all courses involved, or when two students "submit more or less identical work for an assignment on which they have worked together." If an instructor suspects a student has committed academic dishonesty, the student will face disciplinary proceedings before the Ad Board. If the Ad Board determines that the student misused sources out of "genuine confusion," the student will be required to take a class on the proper use of sources and may be temporarily placed on probation, which goes on the student's permanent record. If the Ad Board finds, even after the student's received a grade in the course, that a student misused sources and knew what he or she was doing, then the student will likely be required to withdraw from the college.[405]

Assuming that the Ad Board actually finds out about only a fraction of the academic dishonesty that happens on campus, how much do Harvard students actually cheat? Almost half of Harvard undergraduates can readily cite instances of cheating among classmates, but they note that it doesn't happen frequently and that it doesn't have much of an impact of grades or class standing.[406]

SEXUAL MISCONDUCT

Sexual assault happens less frequently at Harvard than on most college campuses.[407] The figures at Harvard are startling nonetheless. A 2001 survey conducted by University Health Services and the American College Health Association found that 0.8 percent of Harvard females had experienced sexual penetration against their will in the past year, compared to a national average of 1.8 percent. A 2000 UHS survey indicated that over four percent of Harvard women experienced attempted sexual penetration against their will in the past year.[408] More than eight percent of Harvard females reported involvement in abusive relationships, compared to a national average of 13 percent. [409] And just under 15 percent of Harvard students in a 1998 Target Management survey reported feeling a direct negative impact from sexual harassment on campus.[410]

Two nationally publicized Harvard date rape cases in 1998–1999 resulted in the dismissal from Harvard College of Joshua Elster ('00) and Drew Douglas ('00) and increased community awareness of rape at Harvard. Since the Elster and Douglas cases, students have created the Coalition Against Sexual Violence (CASV), which runs a week of awareness-raising events each spring that includes a clothesline project, where Harvard undergraduate victims of sexual assault write about their experiences on T-shirts that are put on display in Harvard Yard.[411] Since the Elster and Douglas cases, too, the Harvard University Police Department (HUPD) no longer leaves sexual assault reports out of the daily public police log. Harvard police now sponsor Rape Aggression Defense courses, which aim to give women the knowledge and confidence to help prevent sexual assault from occurring. But sexual assault victims on campus still report receiving deficient immediate support from UHS nurses who have little or no experience with sexual trauma cases.[412] And the college hasn't met student demands for a Women's Center, a legal representative for victims seeking disciplinary action or full-time, 24-hour on-call rape counselors.[413]

If a Harvard student is sexually assaulted, he or she can prosecute through both the Ad Board and the criminal justice system. The college recommends that the victim go through the criminal justice system first, so that the Ad Board can make use of evidence uncovered by the courts' more thorough investigative mechanisms. If the accuser chooses to go through the Ad Board first and then decides to go through the criminal justice system before the Ad Board hearing is complete, the Ad Board will temporarily stop its proceedings until a court verdict has been reached. While criminal charges are pending, the Ad Board may ask the accused student to take an involuntary leave of absence, so that the accuser need not confront the accused while on campus.[414]

Harvard defines rape as "any sexual intercourse that takes place against a person's will or that is accompanied by physical coercion or the threat of bodily injury." Harvard defines sexual assault as "any unwanted contact where no consent is given and which includes the threat or actual use of force." Sexual harassment is defined as "unwanted sexual behavior, such as physical contact or verbal comments, jokes, questions, or suggestions, which adversely affect the working or learning environment of the individual." Harassment also includes stalking, continuous unwanted following, communicating, or watching.

The Ad Board doesn't disclose any concrete burden of proof that it uses to evaluate sexual assault cases. Seventy percent of undergrads polled by *The Harvard Crimson* in 2002 said they have a "poor understanding of how the Ad Board handles sexual assault cases," and 56 percent of students believe the Ad Board "handles sexual assault cases poorly."[415] Under the Ad Board's sexual assault policy, a person under the influence of alcohol cannot consent to sex. Because most rape cases involve alcohol, the accused's guilt or innocence oftentimes hinges on the Ad Board's determination of the accuser's level of drunkenness. The college's policy stipulates that consensual sex between a man and woman who are both drunk is defined as rape by the man against the woman. Some students on campus say the Ad Board's policy of noncoercive rape discriminates against men, but others respond that the double standard is necessary to encourage overwhelmingly female victims of rape to take action. In the words of one student: "If the policy stops someone from engaging in something that his partner hasn't consented to, then it's not an unfair or inappropriate burden for men to bear."[416]

The Ad Board punishes students found guilty of sexual violence with disciplinary action ranging from probation to dismissal. Students found guilty of rape are forced to withdraw from Harvard for at least one semester, with a recommendation for permanent dismissal, subject to a majority vote by the Faculty of Arts and Sciences (FAS). Students found guilty of sexual assault are forced to withdraw. Those found guilty of sexual misconduct are placed on probation. A range of administrative actions can result from a stalking case. In 2002 the Ad Board heard seven sexual assault cases and in all but one decided that there wasn't enough evidence or that no offense had occurred.[417]

The Ad Board adopted a new evidentiary standard stating that the college won't investigate, hear, or rule on any complaints by one student against another unless there is "supporting evidence," such as physical evidence or emails or letters acknowledging the incident.[418] This policy applies to peer disputes involving theft, assault, and sexual misconduct, but most notably means that the Ad Board will disregard "he-said/she-said" accusations of date-rape. Robert W. Iuliano, Harvard's deputy general counsel, says that the policy was instituted in order to prevent student accusers from getting "traumatized by a process that we can predict, based on our experience, isn't going to be successful."[419] The College Dean's Office explains "the level of evidence needed to successfully resolve sexual misconduct cases is ... difficult to achieve, even after a protracted, often emotionally painful investigation for all the students involved."[420]

Undergraduates complain that the Ad Board's evidentiary standard "enable[s] the college to turn a blind eye to sexual violence." Because the Ad Board "lacks specialized training ... to ask the right questions or render responsible decisions,"[421] students argue, "Harvard should establish a separate board to hear these painful and complex cases ... [i]nstead of throwing up its hands when victims of sexual assault seek help."[422] In fact, one undergraduate filed a formal complaint in June 2002 with the U.S. Department of Education Office for Civil Rights (OCR), claiming that the corroboration requirement prevents inadequate grievance procedures for Harvard women, in violation of Title IX's prohibition against discrimination on the basis of sex in educational programs.[423] The OCR ruled that Harvard's sexual assault policy did not "deprive students of access to a process providing a prompt and equitable resolution of their complaints."[424]

CHAPTER NINE
CAMPUS HEALTH CARE

UNIVERSITY HEALTH SERVICES

All Harvard undergraduates pay a mandatory Health Services Fee that gives them access to confidential, on-campus medical care at University Health Services (UHS), whose online webpage can be accessed at uhs.harvard.edu. All students are also required to carry personal health insurance, either through the Blue Cross/Blue Shield Plan offered by Harvard or through a private carrier. Located in the Harvard Square, UHS maintains an infirmary, pharmacy, urgent care clinic, immunization clinic, mental health clinic, birth control and pregnancy clinic, and specialty services such as dermatology, gastroenterology, neurology, ophthalmology, orthopedic surgery, physical therapy, urology, obstetrics, gynecology, and anonymous HIV testing. The standard health services fee covers most services like physical examinations and X-rays, but students have to pay extra for dental care, eyewear, long-term psychiatric care, substance abuse treatment, and medication.[425]

When you arrive to Cambridge your first year, Harvard assigns you to a primary-care physician (PCP), who you typically won't see unless you make an appointment to meet with him or her weeks in advance. The UHS inpatient facility is Stillman Infirmary, which provides physician and nursing services, medicines, laboratory tests, X-rays, and overnight care. Students requiring emergency care or major surgical procedures are transferred to one of the affiliated Harvard teaching hospitals. The UHS Pharmacy accepts insurance through PCS, PAID, and EXPRESS prescription cards and lists nothing specific about purchases for term-billed pharmacy charges. The After Hours Urgent Care Clinic is open nights, weekends, and holidays for 24-hour urgent care throughout the calendar year.

About 83 percent of undergraduates make at least one visit to UHS annually, and 64 percent make two or more visits each year, mostly because of minor health problems like colds, infections, and routine check-ups. A survey conducted by Harvard University in 1999 indicated that students weren't satisfied with health care at UHS. Only 58 percent of students rated UHS health care as "good or better," and a full 41 percent said that it was either "fair" or "poor." Just three percent called university health care "excellent," and merely six percent said they would "definitely" recommend UHS to others in the Harvard community. Student dissatisfaction with UHS, according to the survey, stems mostly from fear of misdiagnosis and poor, incomplete, rushed, or delayed care. Students are frustrated with the delays they experience at UHS while trying to get through to a receptionist to make an appointment and while waiting for care once they arrive for a scheduled appointment. Although UHS care could stand improvement in several areas, over 80 percent of students gave favorable ratings to UHS' convenient location, specialty services, and its staff, including PCPs, nurse practitioners, and health assistants.[426]

MENTAL HEALTH SERVICES

Most students at Harvard achieved success in high school with high spirits and fond memories. But their level of accomplishments is indication of neither happiness nor mental health. Most Harvard students were motivated to work hard before college in order to fulfill the pre-packaged, all-purpose goal of getting into a top college. Some were motivated simply by the affirmation that comes from within. Others were motivated by the admiration of parents and peers. A few were driven by social isolation—a need to expend energies not spent interacting with others. Or by "depression—a need to make oneself feel better." Or "insecurity—a need to prove oneself better than everyone else."

Although students at Harvard are generally no less happy, well-adjusted, or mentally balanced than students at other colleges, "[t]he forces that lead a young person to unusual achievements are, of course, not the same forces that constitute psychological well-being."[427] So Harvard students aren't any happier than other college students by virtue of their high test scores and long lists of extracurricular leadership positions.

In fact, a 2001 survey conducted by UHS and the American College Health Association indicated that many more Harvard students suffer from depression than do students on campuses nationwide. Thirty-four percent of Harvard undergraduates reported being diagnosed with depression within the past year, compared to an average of 23 percent at colleges across the country.[428]

Harvard students, more than most, have internalized the pressures of a meritocratic society, leading them to apply excessive gravity to the pursuit and distribution of academic, extracurricular, and personal prizes and advantages. Paper grades, exam scores, summer internship opportunities, grad school admissions, extracurricular leadership positions, blocking group votes, Final

Club punches, romantic interests—all intimate that sense of personal failure that seems particularly crushing for Harvard students who have reaped early successes and who have internally inflated the meaning of the substantive advantages and disadvantages to be had in society.

For students who were always the best before coming to Harvard, being in an environment where they're no longer the cream of the crop can be disconcerting. Many suffer from a sense of disappointment and inadequacy that comes from no longer maintaining the all-star persona they developed at high school as Varsity Tri-Captain/All-State Jazz Band/Class President and Vale-dictorian. "It's hard to feel extraordinary," says one student, "when you're surrounded by extraordinary people."[429] UHS Chief of Mental Health Services Dr. Catlin asserts that "Harvard students may be somewhat more at risk because of the perceived need to live up to extraordinarily high expectations and the difficulty in meeting these expectations at a highly competitive and intellectually demanding academic environment."[430] No matter how talented you are and no matter how hard you work, you're guaranteed to encounter people who blow you away, in and out of the classroom. Having just failed the first exam of your life, the anxiety you feel might range from the passing insecurity that you were an undeserving admissions mistake to the horror of awaiting the phone call you'll get when your transcript arrives home and your parents see that you bombed worse than Ted Kaczynski ('62).

Harvard students face sharp competition beyond just final exam curves and grade point averages. The "gauntlet of inevitable rejections" facing undergrads includes first-year orientation programs, freshman seminars, honors-only concentrations, seminars and conference courses, and extracurricular admissions processes like publication comps, athletic tryouts, public service applications, and a cappella auditions. One student goes so far as to call rejection "the definitive Harvard experience." Having arrived at Harvard by winning the admissions contest, undergraduates often "confuse selectivity with value because that's always been what makes us—and Harvard—what we are."[431] In addition to the special brand of insecurity found within the gates of Harvard Yard, Harvard students display the whole slew of difficulties commonly associated with college-age students—depression, eating disorders, drug addictions, and relationship problems.[432]

Compared to those diagnosed with depression at other colleges, almost twice as many Harvard students access psychotherapy. Still, 68 percent of those suffering from depression at Harvard don't get any kind of mental health counseling.[433] High academic expectations and pervasive independence among Harvard undergrads often makes it difficult for those with problems to get the help they need. One Harvard counselor observed a pattern of students "repressing personal needs and problems while concentrating on coping with academic requirements and expectations."[434] Students at Harvard believe they should be able to get everything done on their own without any outside assistance. "What any potential Harvard undergraduate needs to understand," one student says, "is that Harvard prides itself on being Spartan."[435] Fiercely self-reliant students emphasize strength and control and shun displays of frailty and vulnerability. According to one student: "Harvard students see going for help as giving up or as a sign of weakness, not as a sign of resourcefulness or courage."[436] So while Harvard offers students loads of resources for academic and personal concerns of every nature, many don't get the help they need because students always have to make the first move to get any assistance. "At Harvard, they're always telling you how many resources there are and that all you have to do is seek them out," says one student. "But when you're ill, you can't always fight for what you need."[437]

When Harvard students face mental health problems, they can tap on-campus resources for either profession counseling at UHS and the Bureau of Study Counsel (BSC) or peer counseling at one of five student-run organizations. The vast majority of those seeking mental health counseling choose professional help over peer help. Most of the students who walk into UHS or BSC to make an appointment with a counselor don't know exactly what it is that is bothering them or what kind of help they are looking for. UHS and BSC therapists provide free, confidential one-on-one and group mental health therapy on issues including: classes, concentrations, and careers; intimacy, sexuality, and reproduction; anxiety, anger, or depression; mood, sleep, and trauma; eating or substance abuse; motivation, learning approaches, and college adjustment; and relationships with family, teachers, roommates, friends, or significant others.[438] UHS also has urgent and walk-in care for four hours each day, Monday through Friday, as well as an on-call mental health clinician available to see students on evenings and weekends.[439]

Mental health records are kept confidential, like all health services at Harvard. The only person with access to a student's medical files is the student. If you're admitted to Stillman Infirmary, your parents aren't notified. Your freshman dean or senior tutor will be informed of your admittance to the infirmary, but not of the diagnosis. If university officials ask you for what reason you were admitted, you don't have to tell them.[440]

The five undergraduate counseling groups on campus are trained and supervised by professionals at UHS and BSC and offer confidential hotline and drop-in counseling throughout the academic year. Not many students go to these groups for help, however; they typically field only a few phone calls or drop-in visits each week.[441] Harvard's oldest peer counseling group, Room 13, promises "cookies, condoms, and conversation," and provides peer counseling on a broad scope of issues, ranging from Harvard procedures, roommate difficulties, alcohol, and sexuality.[442] Room 13's Harvard Yard office is staffed by one male and one female student every night from 7:00 P.M. to 7:00 A.M. The Peer Contraceptive Counselors (PCC) are trained to provide information about sexuality, pregnancy, sexually transmitted diseases, and the efficacy and use of the major types of contraceptives. Response is a peer counseling organization staffed by women undergraduates to respond to issues of abuse, incest, rape, sexual harassment, and relationship violence. Contact provides support, counseling, and education on issues of sexual orientation. InCommon takes up relationship concerns, academic difficulties, and stress. Life Raft offers support to students dealing with issues relating to life-threatening illness and death. And Eating Concerns Hotline and Outreach (ECHO) addresses issues related to eating disorders at Harvard.

About 20 percent of female undergrads at Harvard suffer from eating disorders, according to a 1992 survey by Assistant Professor of Psychology Todd F. Heatherton. Dr. Margaret S. McKenna, former head of the UHS eating disorders program, reports that UHS sees hundreds of students each year for eating disorders and that hundreds more probably suffer from eating disorders, but don't seek help. Professor Heatherton's survey indicated that five percent of Harvard women have clinically diagnosable eating disorders like bulimia and anorexia, compared to two percent of undergraduates nationwide. Thirty-two percent of Harvard women believe that they are overweight, and 80 percent want to lose weight. Eighteen percent of female students at Harvard binge eat, five percent have vomited to get rid of unwanted calories, and 24 percent have used starvation fasting as a method of weight control at some point during college. Thirteen percent of women are compulsive over-exercisers, and 46 percent of women report that they diet sometimes, usually, or always. "[T]he profile of someone with an eating disorder," explains Sheila M. Reindel ('80–'81), a counselor at the Bureau of Study Counsel, "very much matches the profile ... of the [prospective student] Harvard values: high-achieving, perfectionist, people-pleasing, and driven." Heatherton's survey indicated that only one percent of men on campus suffer from eating disorders.[443]

On average, one Harvard undergraduate has taken his or her own life per year on average from 1990 to 2004. According to a 2003 survey conducted by the American College Health Association, Harvard's suicide rate is slightly less the national average for college students over that period. In a 2004 survey by *The Harvard Crimson*, 80 percent of undergraduates polled reported that they had felt depressed in the past year, 47 percent said that they had felt so depressed it was difficult to function, 10 percent reported having seriously considered suicide at least once in the past year, and 1 percent reported having attempted suicide.[444] Harvard University Police Department (HUPD) spokesperson Steven G. Catalano reports that HUPD has responded to 14 attempted suicides between 2000 and 2003.[445] In a 1995 UHS survey, 6 percent of undergraduates had made a plan to kill themselves, and 0.4 percent had made an attempt that required medical attention.[446] One recent tragedy brought particular attention to the problem of suicide on the Harvard campus. In 1995 Sinedu Tadesse, a junior Dunster House resident from Ethiopia, hanged herself after killing her roommate, Trang Phuong Ho, an immigrant from Vietnam. Tadesse stabbed Ho 45 times while she lay sleeping in her bed.[447] After the 1995 Dunster House murder-suicide, UHS psychologists and psychiatrists maintained that it is impossible to know which students will act out violently on their depressive episodes and mental illnesses. Former Dean Lewis ('68) assured students and parents that Tadesse and Ho, like all Harvard undergraduates, had been assimilated into the college's "carefully woven advising system."

But what some call Harvard's "incompetence at dealing with students suffering from psychiatric disorders" may contribute to the suicides that happen on campus.[448] Deficiencies in the college's student services range from fragmented support networks to the lack of long-term mental health care.[449] Students unwilling or unable to actively seek out the help they need often go unnoticed. Busy resident dorm proctors and House tutors rarely interact with students enough to detect the signs of depression like social isolation and loss of sleep, appetite, motivation, concentration, or self esteem. There are no college guidelines stipulating the amount of time proctors or tutors must spend with students, and few make an extra effort to get to know students.

While a 1999 undergraduate survey showed that two-thirds of students gave favorable ratings to UHS Mental Health Services, a 2000 report submitted by a provost-appointed committee found that mental health services were understaffed and provided inadequate extended and immediate care. The report found that it was especially difficult to get emergency help within 24 hours.[450] UHS resources do not meet the recent demand for mental health support. UHS Mental Health Services' staff of 12 psychiatrists, 9 psychologists, 6 nurse practitioners, and 13 social workers saw almost 2,000 students in the 2003-2004 academic year.[451] The lack of coordination among University Health Services, the Bureau of Study Counsel, and the resident proctor/tutor system may also keep university mental health officials in the dark and keep mentally ill students from getting the help they need. Unlike mental health services at most colleges, where students receive care from a single psychiatrist, under UHS's "split care" system, students are typically assigned to different care providers for medical and therapy. Even if ill students are noticed and properly supported, Harvard might not be able to provide them with the treatment they need. UHS's system restricts university provided mental health support to four months. Because Harvard offers psychotherapy only a limited basis, long-term patients are forced either to manage the expense and logistics of mental health care outside of Harvard or to withdraw from the college for at least one full semester.[452]

CONCLUSION

I asked 3,000 Harvard undergraduates in 2002 what they liked most and least about going to Harvard from among 40 different elements of college life. The 10 things that students like most about going to Harvard are

(1) other students
(2) prestige/reputation of the Harvard name
(3) financial aid
(4) scope of curricular offerings
(5) extracurricular, cultural, political, and artistic opportunities on campus
(6) Harvard Square, Cambridge, and Boston
(7) housing conditions/accommodations
(8) faculty expertise and teaching quality
(9) career counseling
(10) library, laboratory, and computer resources

The 10 things that students like least about going to Harvard are

(1) accessibility to and interaction with faculty
(2) social life/dating scene
(3) weather
(4) intense academic atmosphere
(5) core requirements
(6) cost of college/financial responsibilities
(7) university health care
(8) academic advising
(9) influence of Final Clubs
(10) lack of student voice in administrative decision-making

So what's the low-down? Although 19 percent of Harvard undergraduates said they have seriously considered transferring at one time or another,[453] 91 percent said they would choose Harvard again, a higher proportion than at any other Ivy League school except for Princeton.[454] Students rate their overall happiness at Harvard a 3.9 on a scale of 1 (low) to 5 (high).[455] They rate Harvard's academic life at 3.9, extracurricular life at 3.9, and social life at 3.5.[456] But sweeping figures like these aren't particularly illuminating for the prospective student.

For "the difference between happiness and unhappiness at Harvard," one student rightly points out, "is a matter of individual fit, of whether one's personal values match up with those held by Harvard." Most prospective students take into account Harvard's urban surroundings, fickle weather, institutional resources, and its distance from their home. But your personal level of individual independence is perhaps the most important element to consider before making a decision about whether or not to attend the college. Harvard's self-directive approach to the various opportunities and support services on campus means that students who are capable of independently seeking out whatever personal, social, academic, financial, and medical help they need will generally have a more favorable college experience at Harvard. "[P]eople who are self-confident, and individualistically goal-oriented in all aspects of their lives will flourish," one graduating senior reflects, "whereas those who are less sure of themselves … may have been better off elsewhere."[457]

Whether or not Harvard is right for you also depends on the specific goals you have for your undergraduate education. Those whose objectives lie in strong community-building, relaxed academic atmosphere, intense social partying, and immediate personal gratification may be less suited to Harvard's general campus ethos than those who are motivated most substantially by long-range professional ambition. But how do you go about evaluating your own goals?

The word "goal" calls out to you, the prospective Harvard student, in an audible proclamation of "Go Al." "Go," it says. "Go, Al, go." You may ask, "What do I do if my name is not Al?" Then you must look deep inside yourself, search the far reaches of your innermost desires, and change your name to Al. Seriously, just give a little thought to what sort of things are most important to you—community, family, scholarship, wealth, leisure, friendship, music—and think about how Harvard fits in with those short- and long-term aspirations.

For those whose personalities and expectations mesh with the character of the student body and of the larger institution, Harvard certainly has the resources and opportunities to make for a meaningful and valuable college experience. But like anything else, life at Harvard is whatever you make of it: the product of academic, extracurricular, social, and personal choices among innumerable possibilities. Not profound, but a worthy disclaimer.

A graduating senior tells her classmates, "[E]ach of our Harvards is different from the other Harvards we could have experienced …. There are plenty of open houses that I skipped because they didn't have free pizza, plenty of students I never met because the Quad seems so far away, plenty of courses I never took because they met too early."[458] Instead of sleeping in, she could have met her soulmate at 9:00 A.M. in "History 1653: Baseball and American Society on the first Tuesday of Shopping Period." Or instead of hanging out in her Quincy House suite, she could have trekked out to the Quad on Monday night for the undercooked kielbasa at the Folklore and Mythology open house and gotten sick on her soulmate the next morning, never to realize true love again. Point is, what Harvard will be for you depends foremost on the decisions you make as a future undergraduate: what you choose to study, whom you choose to hang out with, and how you choose to spend your time.

Whether or not you apply to Harvard, whether or not you get accepted at Harvard, whether or not you attend Harvard, whether or not you graduate from Harvard— understand that Harvard is not the be-all and end-all of anything. Going to Harvard tangibly advances your chances of cracking the market for high-profile professionalism, but the Harvard name neither guarantees lifelong fame and fortune nor stands crucial to future success and happiness. If you're thinking about applying to Harvard, chances are you've got a number of attractive opportunities available to you. Any or many of them may open just as many doors and, more importantly, may more suitably meet the particular needs and aims you have for your undergraduate education. The mystique will always lie at the core of Harvard's allure. But it's the Harvard experience that most meaningfully informs the prospective student about whether or not he or she should come to Harvard. For you, that experience may be good and it may be bad. It's up to you to decide whether or not you want to make that experience your own.

INTERNET RESOURCES

University homepage .... www.harvard.edu/

University President .... .www.president.harvard.edu/

University Factbook ....
.... http://vpf-web.harvard.edu/factbook/current_facts/mktvalue_endow_38a.html

College homepage .... www.college.harvard.edu/

Report on Harvard College, 1995–2000 www.college.harvard.edu/dean/annualreport2000/

Dean of Undergraduate Education ... www.fas.harvard.edu/undergraduate_education/

FAS Courses of Instruction .... www.registrar.fas.harvard.edu

Student Handbook .... www.registrar.fas.harvard.edu/handbooks/student/

Fields of Concentration .. www.registrar.fas.harvard.edu/handbooks/student/chapter3/

Concentration departments .... www.fas.harvard.edu/academics/departments/

Core curriculum .... www.courses.fas.harvard.edu/~core/

CUE Guide .... www.fas.harvard.edu/~cueguide

Old final exams .... www.fas.harvard.edu/~exams/

Campus map .... http://map.harvard.edu/

Virtual campus tour .... www.news.harvard.edu/tour/

College viewbook .... www.college.harvard.edu/admissions/viewbook.html

Residential House System .... www.fas.harvarrd.edu/~phyres/houses.html

Harvard University Dining Services .... www.dining.harvard.edu

Harvard Online Library Information System .... http://lib.harvard.edu/

Harvard University Health Services .... http://uhs.harvard.edu

Office of Career Services .... www.ocs.fas.harvard.edu/

Administrative Board .... www.college.harvard.edu/academic/adboard/

Harvard University Police Department .... www.hupd.harvard.edu

Student Organizations .... www.college.harvard.edu/student/organizations/

Arts .... www.college.harvard.edu/student/arts

Athletics .... www.college.harvard.edu/student/athletics

Cultural and Racial Initiatives .... www.fas.harvard.edu/~harvfoun/

Institute of Politics .... www.iop.harvard.edu/

Philips Brooks House Association .... www.pbha.org/pbha/index.html

Harvard Square homepage .... www.harvardsquare.com/

Town of Cambridge homepage .... www.townonline.com/cambridge/

City of Boston homepage .... www.cityofboston.gov/

Boston weather information .... www.erh.noaa.gov/er/box/

Customized Harvard student webpage .... http://my.harvard.edu

Harvard Webmail .... http://webmail.fas.harvard.edu

The Unofficial Guide to Life at Harvard .... www.unofficialharvard.com/

The Harvard Crimson .... www.thecrimson.com/

The Harvard University Gazette .... www.hno.harvard.edu/gazette/index.html/

The Harvard Independent .... www.harvardindependent.com/

Harvard Magazine .... www.harvardmagazine.com/

Harvard Box Office .... www.fas.harvard.edu/~tickets/

Harvard COOP Bookstore .... www.bkstore.com/harvard/

Undergraduate admissions .... www.college.harvard.edu/admissions

Admissions Office E-mail .... http://college@fas.harvard.edu

Harvard College Financial Aid Office ...... http://adm-is.fas.harvard.edu/FAO/index.htm

Request application .... http://web.fas.harvard.edu/ha/Inquiry/InquiryFrame.html

Submit application .... www.college.harvard.edu/admissions/online_app.html

Pay application fee .... www.fas.harvard.edu/~appfee/payment_form.cgi

Download transfer application supplement .... www.college.harvard.edu/admissions

Register for the SATs .... www.collegeboard.com

Submit Profile Form .... http://profileonline.collegeboard.com/index.jsp

Submit Free Application for Federal Student Aid .... www.fafsa-online.org

APPENDIX

MY HARVARD COLLEGE ADMISSIONS ESSAYS

Essay Prompt: Evaluate a significant experience, achievement, risk you have taken, or ethical dilemma you have faced and its impact on you.

Magic

He reeked.

My brother Ari sat beside me nervously on the way to the New Haven tournament in late October. Rolling down the car window, I took in the autumn trees whizzing by like pages in a golden flip book. The Beach Boys blared on the radio. The music energized me. I burned to compete. Lifting myself halfway out of myself, I gyrated with the pulse, contorting my face to achieve an impassioned falsetto until I realized that Ari in horror was staring at me, at which point I feigned violent coughing fits. Distracted from the wheel, my mom swerved toward a U-Haul truck, prompting the driver to make thoughtful gestures at us and shout helpful suggestions that muffled the music and shattered my moment at Rocky.

I have to inspire myself before each "Magic" card tournament, and now, fifteen minutes from the biggest competition of my life, I felt nothing.

Since I've never had a TV in my house, I've devoted many Saturdays to dueling at the local gaming hangout. Meanwhile, my friends marvel at the number of "Bar Mitzvahs" that prevent me from going to a weekend movie or pick-up basketball game. I couldn't tell them I spent my time playing a strategic card game. They'd think I played with Barbies, too. They just wouldn't understand the thrill of creating a deck from endless possibilities and engaging in a cutthroat battle of wit. My brothers would never tell either.

Ari, Jacob, and I pool our snow-shoveling money to buy Magic cards, brainstorming deck concepts on our walk home from school. Often two of us play-test tournament decks late into the night, while the third looks out for our mom coming home form teaching nights after a day of repairing diesel pumps. When the Watcher spots the car lights gleaming around the street corner, we scurry into bed and pretend to be asleep, giggling loudly enough for our mom to hear us, but softly enough for us to think that she doesn't. After a week of practice, we win every local Saturday tournament. Compared to the New Haven Regional Tournament though, winning local tournaments is like being crowned Miss Latvia. Even worse, as we arrived at the tournament hall, I became painfully aware that we were the youngest participants among over three hundred of the cream of New England's Magic-playing crop, all competing for a prize of one thousand dollars.

My first opponent was a tall man.

"This your first time playing in a real tournament?" he asked.

"Nah," I responded in my deepest twelve-year-old timber. "I've been to a dozen of these. I won two or three in the Midwest and figured I'd hit a few up North." I hoped my voice didn't quaver.

Lacking the powerful, expensive cards, I had learned other ways to win: I blended lesser cards in creative, carefully calculated combinations; I crafted an entirely original deck; and I read my opponent's hand through each idiosyncrasy. These tactics were too much for the tall man. I shook his hand after the match and wished him luck in the rest of the tournament. As I pushed in the chair and left to report the outcome, he looked as if he had eaten a bad fish taco. Rocky was going strong.

Seven victories later, I found myself in the Final Four. After eleven hours of intense gaming, the other three finalists wanted to divvy up the prize and go home. Rocky disagreed. Outnumbered however, he and I were content with $250. I split the money with my brothers and decided to call up a friend when I got home to ask if he wanted to learn how to play a game I enjoyed. Then my family and I poured into the car and with "California Girls" reverberating in my ear and hands clasped behind my head, I smelled the sweet aroma of success.

And Ari.

Essay Prompt: Indicate a person who has had a significant influence on you, and describe that influence.

Mr. Hoyt

I come in early to AP Physics each day, waiting for the man whose passion I absorb. Then Daniel Hoyt canters into class, puffs out his belly and wheezes, "Did the bell ring?" Scurrying about his desk though a disheveled heap of papers, he snatches a broken piece of chalk and begins scrawling at all angles across the blackboard. His hand races excitedly in an array of vector diagrams and stick figures depicting Madonna and Humpty Dumpty. Never slowing, he finally reaches the bottom of the board. Then he squats to the floor, hopelessly shrouded behind his desk, and continues to scratch out his lesson on the wall, announcing, "I hope you all understand this—it's important."

There's a lot of child in him. All through class he fidgets in his rumpled jacket like an adolescent at a wedding. He is incessantly hitching up his belt, which does little to harness his stubborn shirttails, set free as he contorts his body to instill within us his intensity for physics. We do not doze while a sixty-year-old man vaults around the room, flailing his arms to illustrate the operation of the Turkish longbow. No notes are passed as he blows into oversized spitball-shooters to demonstrate the relationship between distance and velocity. Then, even when he stands still and empty-handed, lecturing on magnetic flux, 23 pairs of eyes converge on the man at the head of the class who would rather be nowhere else.

Intrigued with his verve, we coincidentally grasp applications of kinetic molecular theory and the uncertainty principle. When he pronounces, "A unitless number is like a motherless child," we affix a mph. ppi, or m/s^2 symbol to each of our solutions. When he remarks, "Greater love hath no student than to inquire of his professor at the risk of being taunted by his classmates," we ask questions. And when he pleads, "Derive the formulas, don't just memorize," we take the extra time to understand the object of his affection a little bit better.

Mr. Hoyt is as willing to talk with us about family as about thermodynamics. He teaches me about life with a genuine compassion that I admire. When a student answers his question during a discussion on quantum relativity, Mr. Hoyt scrunches his face and grunts conspicuously. In response to the same question, each student offers a different reply and gets a similar reaction from Mr. Hoyt. Finally, we learn that the first student was correct after all. "Have confidence in yourselves," he declares.

When I struggle while evaluating data from our motion laboratory, Mr. Hoyt squeezes into a desk beside me. He tells me, "You can't appreciate the lab's implication until you ignore what your common sense tells you is true. Be creative. Dov, answer me this: What is the result when a pursuing hawk with an initial velocity of 20 feet/second and an acceleration of 5 feet/second^2

overtakes a robin traveling at a constant velocity of 35 feet/second?" I don't know. "Shredded tweet," he replies. I laugh. And I try to pursue the imagination, motivation, and excitement that Mr. Hoyt demands of me.

After a jazz rehearsal extends late one night, I step upstairs to grab a book from my locker. Puncturing the somber lull come Beethoven and a single light emanating from the physics classroom. I peer in and see Mr. Hoyt, tie loosened and crimson felt-tip in hand, nodding to the classical cadence with a hefty stack of lab reports still to be graded. Like every other evening, he has given of himself to students who need his assistance less than they wish to be in his company. I stay there longer than I should, watching the man who inspires me always.

END NOTES

70 Floyd, Margaret Henderson, ed. *Harvard: An Architectural History*. (Cambridge: Belknap Press, 1985), Forward.

71 Hsu, Nelson. "Stormy Weather and Stormy Moods." *The Harvard Crimson*. January 31, 1996.

72 Greene, Howard R. and Greene, Matthew. *Inside the Top Colleges*, 11.

73 Tambar, Uttam. "Group I and Only." *The Harvard Independent*. April 17, 1997.

74 Ralston, Olivia. "Class Reflects on College Experience." *The Harvard Crimson*. June 5, 1996.

75 No writer attributed. "Talk Alone Is Not Sufficient." *The Harvard Crimson*. March 13, 1998.

76 Light, Richard. *Making the Most of College*. (Cambridge, Massachusetts: Harvard University Press, 2001).

77 McPherson, F. Reynolds. "Students' View of Campus Health Skewed." *The Harvard Crimson*. May 4, 2001.

78 Flood, Joseph and Mani, Divya. "Harvard Student Just Can't 'Slow Down.'" *The Harvard Crimson*. September 17, 2002.

79 Wasserstein, Ben. "Getting In." *The Harvard Crimson*. September 27, 2001.

80 Freinberg, Anthony. "Harvard Grads, Four Years Early." *The Harvard Crimson*. October 4, 2002.

81 Arronjo, David, quoted in Nwandu, Antoinette, Weaver, Kenyon. "Ambition" *Fifteen Minutes*. November 2, 2000.

82 Light, Richard. *Making the Most of College*, 87.

83 Stephanopouolos, Nick. "Harvard in a Nutshell." *The Harvard Independent*. Freshman Issue.

84 Fitzsimmons, William; McGrath Lewis, Marlyn; and Ducey, Charles. "Time Out or Burn Out for the Next Generation." July 17, 2002. <www.college.harvard.edu/admissions/time_out.html>.

85 Horn, Dara. "O, Fair Career." *The Harvard Crimson*. November 7, 1997.

86 Greene, Howard R. and Greene, Matthew. *Inside the Top* Colleges, 270.

87 Horn, Dara. "O, Fair Career." *The Harvard Crimson*. November 7, 1997.

88 Yglesias, Matthew. "Grade Inflation Is Real." *The Harvard Independent.* February 21, 2002.

89 The Staff of *The Harvard Crimson* and Office of Career Services. "Should I Look at the Student Employment Office or OCS for a Summer Job?" *The Guide to Summer.* April 11, 2003.

90 Myers, Kevin. "Lazy Days Are No More." *The Harvard Crimson.* July 2, 1999.

91 Doyle, A.C. "Letters: Advice to the (Briefly) Young." *Harvard Magazine.* July-August 2002.

92 Greene, Howard R. and Greene, Matthew. *Inside the Top Colleges*, 39.

93 Meng, Sue. "Our Better Selves." *The Harvard Crimson.* April 21, 2003.

94 Derman, Joshua. "Put on Something Sexy and Hit the Stacks." *The Harvard Crimson.* March 12, 1999.

95 Light, Richard. *Making the Most of College*, 112.

96 Harvard College Cultural and Racial Initiatives online. August 24, 2002. <www.fas.harvard.edu/~harvfoun/>.

97 Dorgan, Lauren. "Panel Held To Highlight Issues Facing Harvard College Women." *The Harvard Crimson.* December 11, 2000.

98 Seltzer, Sarah. "This Is Not Your Mother's Feminism." *Fifteen Minutes.* April 17, 2003.

99 No writer attributed. "Class of '06 Chosen From Record Pool of 19,605." *The Harvard Gazette.* "August 2002.

100 Barr, Eric and Ganeshananthan, Vasugi. "Worlds Apart: Why Harvard and the South Don't Get Along." *The Harvard Crimson.* February 2, 2000.

101 Schoenberger, Chana. "Far From Home." *The Harvard Crimson.* January 5, 1996.

102 Milzoff, Rebecca. "Homeschooled Harvardians." *Fifteen Minutes.* May 3, 2001.

103 Schaefer, Naomi. "Transfer Kinks." *The Harvard Crimson.* October 1, 1997.

104 Yuen, Nina. "Outsiders Within: The Cult and Culture of Harvard's Transfers." *Fifteen Minutes.* February 10, 2000.

105 No author attributed. "Why Diversity at Harvard is Only Skin-Deep." *Fifteen Minutes*. November 13, 2003.

106 The FAO provides statistics on family income levels for only the 70 percent of Harvard undergraduates who have applied for aid. Information is unavailable for the 30 percent of students who haven't applied for financial aid. But given that all students from lower and middle class families apply for aid "unless they've just won the lottery," according to Robert S. Clagett, Associate Director of Harvard College Financial Aid, and that even some students whose families make more than $180,000 a year get scholarship grants from the college, it is safe to say that the FAO statistics accurately reflect the income levels of all undergraduates whose families have annual incomes of less than $100,000.

107 These percentages were calculated by dividing the number of students from various family income levels in 2001–2002, provided on the Harvard College Office Financial Aid website at <adm-is.fas.harvard.edu/FAO/index.htm> on August 4, 2002, by 6,600, the total number of undergraduates at Harvard College in the 2001-02 academic year. The accuracy of the methodology and income levels for the overall student body were confirmed by Robert S. Clagett, Associate Director of Harvard College Financial Aid, in a phone conversation on August 6, 2002.

108 Alter, Jonathan. "What Merit Really Means." *Newsweek*. January, 27, 2003.

109 Lee, Jennifer. "Glossy Brochure Diversity." *The Harvard Crimson*. April 3, 1996.

110 Hefty, Adam. "Commentary." *The Harvard Independent*. May 2, 1996.

111 Conrad, Parker and Studlien, Kirsten. "What We Truly Believe." *The Harvard Crimson*. February 2, 2000.

112 Ferrick, Tom, Harvard United Ministry Chaplain, cited by Corliss, Cody. "Holy Harvard!" *The Harvard Independent*. April 4, 2002.

113 Conrad, Parker and Studlien, Kirsten. "What We Truly Believe." *The Harvard Crimson*. February 2, 2000.

114 Light, Richard. *Making the Most of College*, 163–169.

115 Jacoby, Tobias. "Keeping the Faith." *The Harvard Independent*. March 18, 1999.

116 Grizzle, Ben. Undergraduate Campus-wide Christian Unity Coordinator. Email letter. September 1, 2002.

117 Hayes, Brian, Undergraduate President of the Catholic Student Association. Email letter. August 29, 2002.

118 Harvard undergraduates associated with the group call joining Opus Dei "the most valuable decision of [their] li[ves]," but others criticize the group as an all-consuming, mind-controlling organization. (Green, Elizabeth. "Opening the Doors of Opus Dei." *Fifteen Minutes.* April 10, 2003.)

119 Green, Elizabeth. "Opening the Doors of Opus Dei." *Fifteen Minutes.* April 10, 2003.

120 Harvard-Radcliffe Hillel website. July 29, 2002. <hillel.harvard.edu>, and Solomon-Schwartz, Ben, Undergraduate President of Harvard-Radcliffe Hillel. Email letter. August 15, 2002.

121 Dharma website. August 14, 2002. www.hcs.harvard.edu/~dharma/, and Kulkarni, Sandeep Chidambar, Undergraduate Board Member of Dharma. Email letter. September 12, 2002.

122 Harvard Buddhist Community website. August 15, 2002. www.hcs.harvard.edu/~zen/, and Blair, Tom, Undergraduate President of the Harvard Buddhist Community. E-mail letter. August 11, 2002.

123 Hashmi, Sara. "Inside Islam." *The Harvard Independent.* March 18, 1999.

124 Yasin, Tariq. Undergraduate Board Member of the Harvard Islamic Society. Email letter. August 7, 2002.

125 No writer attributed. "The Indy Survey." *The Harvard Independent.* May 2, 2002.

126 No speaker attributed, quoted in Flare Staff. "Coming Out at Harvard." *Flare.* February 21, 2001.

127 Anonymous undergraduate BGLTSA board member. Email letter. August 26, 2002.

128 No speaker attributed, quoted in Flare Staff. "Coming Out at Harvard." *Flare.* February 21, 2001.

129 Persilly, Seth, quoted in Murphy, Maureen. "Happy to be Gay." *The Harvard Independent.* October 23, 1997.

130 Myers, Alex, quoted in Frank, Ariel. "College Counseling Service Helps Gays." *The Harvard Crimson.* October 9, 1997.

131 Delawala, Imtiyaz. "Mather House Tutor Resigns After Vandalism." *The Harvard Crimson.* December 14, 1999.

132 Castillo, Thomas. "Tough to Handicap." *The Harvard Independent.* October 16, 1997.

133 Resnick, Scott. "Harvard's Deaf Students Reject 'Culture of Deafness.'" *The Harvard Crimson.* February 2, 1998.

134 Conrad, Parker and Studlien, Kirsten. "What We Truly Believe." *The Harvard Crimson.* February 2, 2000.

135 Keller, Morton and Keller, Phyllis. *Making Harvard Modern*, 469.

136 Barr, Eric and Ganeshananthan, Vasugi. "Worlds Apart: Why Harvard and the South Don't Get Along." *The Harvard Crimson.* February 2, 2000.

137 Seton, Noah. "The Right Place to Learn." *The Harvard Independent.* September 24, 1998.

138 Shapiro, Kevin, quoted in Tassel, Janet. "The 30 Years' War." *Harvard Magazine.* September-October 1999.

139 Rudenstine, Neil L. *Pointing Our Thoughts: Reflections on Harvard and Higher Education 1999–2001.* (Cambridge, MA: President and Fellows of Harvard University, 2001), 39.

140 Greene, Howard R. and Greene, Matthew. *Inside the Top Colleges*, 270.

141 Asian American Association website. August 18, 2002. <www.hcs.harvard.edu/~hraaa/>.

142 Rakoczy, Kate. "College Enrolls Fewer Blacks." *The Harvard Crimson.* October 21, 2002.

143 Black Student Association website. August 16, 2002. <www.hcs.harvard.edu/~bsa/>.

144 Myers, Kevin. "Black Enterprise Ranks Harvard In Its Top 50 List." *The Harvard Crimson.* December 10, 1998.

145 Fuentes, Jonathan and Pais, Stephanie. Undergraduate Board Members of RAZA. E-mail letters. August 4-6, 2002.

146 Bitsoi, Lee, chair of Harvard University Native American Program. Email letter. August 22, 2002, and Harvard University Native American Program website. August 16,2002. www.gse.harvard.edu/~nap/index.html.

147 Greene, Howard R. and Greene, Matthew. *Inside the Top* Colleges, 140.

148 No writer attributed. "Talking Race." *The Harvard Crimson.* March 11, 1998.

149 Zerhouni, William. "Race Relations at Harvard: Full of Rhetoric Instead of Action." *The Harvard Crimson.* February 11, 1997.

150 Wilde, Anna. "Student Discuss Race Relations." *The Harvard Crimson.* May 4, 1992.

151 Ganeshananthan, Vasugi. "The Comfort Zone." *The Harvard Crimson.* April 25, 2002.

152 Keller, Morton and Keller, Phyllis. *Making Harvard Modern,* 479.

153 Sneider, Mark. "Only Students Can Solve Racial Problems." *The Harvard Crimson.* December 11, 1992.

154 Lim, Peggy, ed. *The Women's Guide to Harvard.* (Cambridge, MA: The Harvard-Radcliffe Women's Leadership Project, 2002), 101.

155 Jackson, Judith, included in Sollors, Werner, et al, ed. *Blacks at Harvard.* (New York: New York University Press, 1993), 482.

156 The Crimson Staff. "Harvard Unfairly Criticized on Hiring." *The Harvard Crimson.* April 14, 1994.

157 Ganeshananthan, Vasugi and Levy, Erica. "Positions At Top Still Have Few Minorities" *The Harvard Crimson.* November 16, 1999.

158 Rakoczy, Kate. "Crashing the Club." *The Harvard Crimson.* June 6, 2002.

159 Helderman, Rosalind. "Diversity Among Faculty Increases." *The Harvard Crimson.* April 8, 1999.

160 Ganeshananthan, Vasugi and Levy, Erica. "Positions At Top Still Have Few Minorities" *The Harvard Crimson.* November 16, 1999. and Harvard University Fact Book online. September 4, 2002.

161 The Crimson Staff. "Widening the Circle." *The Harvard Crimson.* March 14, 2002.

162 Ethnic Studies at Harvard College 2002/03 website. August 24, 2002. <www.fas.harvard.edu/~cesh/>.

163 Vascellaro, Jessica. "West Friend Cites Disputes in Departure." *The Harvard Crimson.* April 15, 2002.

164 Seltzer, Sarah. "Pushing for Identity Studies." *The Harvard Crimson.* June 6, 2002.

165 Seltzer, Sarah. "Foundation Releases Report On Diversity." *The Harvard Crimson.* April 29, 2002.

166 Quoted from Gomes, Peter J. *One Teacher's Life,* published in *More Sundays at Harvard.* (Cambridge: Harvard University Memorial Church, 1996), 190.

167 Lewis, Harry. "Report on Harvard College, 1995–2000." August 20, 2002. www.college.harvard.edu/dean/annualreport2000/>, January 2, 2001.

168 Ginsberg, Alex. "Getting the Last Laugh." *Fifteen Minutes.* April 17, 2003.

169 Heller, Jenny. "Establishment and Revolution." *The Harvard Crimson.* June 5, 2001.

170 No writer attributed. "100 Reasons Why Harvard Sucks." *The Harvard Crimson.* April 22, 1999.

171 Bangs, Elizabeth and Lewin, Jonathan. "Shopping Period: Looking For a Bargain." *The Harvard Crimson.* September 25, 1995.

172 Quoted in Nyren, Alex. "The Never-Ending Term." *The Harvard Independent.* December 10, 1998.

173 Gest, Justin. "Comedian Will Ferrell To Speak On Class Day." *The Harvard Crimson.* April 16, 2003.

174 Wollinsky, Robert, quoted in Walthall, Marna. "Class Consciousness." *The Harvard Independent.* October 3, 1996.

175 Hallett, Vicky and Van Der Zee, Avra. "Beasts: Taming Harvard's Largest Classes." *Fifteen Minutes.* February 11, 1999.

176 Quoted in Walthall, Marna. "Class Consciousness." *The Harvard Independent.* October 3, 1996.

177 Walthall, Marna. "Class Consciousness." *The Harvard Independent.* October 3, 1996.

178 The Crimson Staff. "Taking Our Profs Out to Dinner." *The Harvard Crimson.* June 6, 2000.

179 Suleiman, Daniel. "Hiring the Blind to Lead the Blind." *The Harvard Crimson*. October 13, 1998.

180 Crick, Camberly. "Student TFs Balance Friendship, Fairness." *The Harvard Crimson*. May 3, 2001.

181 Quoted in Crick, Camberly. "Student TFs Balance Friendship, Fairness." *The Harvard Crimson*. May 3, 2001.

182 No author attributed. "John Harvard's Journal: Amending Advising." *Harvard Magazine*. March-April, 2002.

183 Derek Bok Center for Teaching and Learning website. August 22, 2002.

184 The CUE Guide online. September 4, 2002.

185 Gillman, Andrew, quoted in Older, Malka. "The Good, the Bad, and the Fluent." *The Harvard Crimson*. February 10, 1997.

186 Bangs, Elizabeth and Lewin, Jonathan. "Shopping Period: Looking For a Bargain." *The Harvard Crimson*. September 25, 1995.

187 Tobin, Susannah. "Learning a Little of Everything." *The Harvard Crimson*. March 9, 2000.

188 Vascellaro, Jessica. "Kirby Pushes Preregistration For Courses." *The Harvard Crimson*. September 26, 2002.

189 Serkin, Tova A. "When TFs Don't Make the Grade." *The Harvard Crimson*. April 8, 1999.

190 Quoted in Brown, Jermaine. "TF Q&A." *The Harvard Independent*. February 8, 2001.

191 Derek Bok Center for Teaching and Learning website. August 28, 2002.

192 Quoted in Vascellaro, Jessica. "CUE Considers Importance of Sections." *The Harvard Crimson*. April 25, 2002.

193 Lim, Peggy, ed. *The Women's Guide to Harvard*, 102.

194 Smallwood, Chris. "The Ten-ure Itch." *The Harvard Independent*. April 18, 2002.

195 The Crimson Staff. "Fighting For a Chance at Tenure." *The Harvard Crimson*. February 21, 2002.

196 Greene, Howard and Greene, Matthew. *Making It Into a Top College*, 41.

197 The FAS does not conduct peer evaluations wherein professors sit in on each other's classes assess each other's teaching effectiveness.

198 2000 Faculty of Arts and Sciences Tenure Statement. "A View From the Top." Reprinted in *The Harvard Independent.* "May 9, 2000."

199 Tompkins, Vincent, Assistant Dean of the Faculty. E-mail letter. August 26, 2002.

200 Derek Bok Center for Teaching and Learning website. August 29, 2002.

201 Quoted in Brown, Jermaine. "TF Q&A." *The Harvard Independent.* February 8, 2001.

202 Wolcowitz, Jeffrey, Associate Dean for Undergraduate Education. Email letter. August 22, 2002.

203 Freinberg, Anthony. "Harvard Grads, Four Years Early." *The Harvard Crimson.* October 4, 2002.

204 Light, Richard. *Making the Most of College*, 51.

205 Greene, Howard R. and Greene, Matthew. *Inside the Top* Colleges, 58.

206 Debartolo, David. "Where to Learn." *The Harvard Crimson.* September 4, 2001.

207 Mosteller, Daniel. "Four-Year Writing Study Concludes." *The Harvard Crimson.* May 25, 2001, and Light, Richard. *Making the Most of College*, 57–58.

208 Studlien, Kirsten. "Teaching to the Chairs." *The Harvard Crimson.* April 13, 2000.

209 Horn, Dara. "Beware the 200-Level Course." *The Harvard Crimson.* February 25, 1998.

210 Lewis, Jordanna. "The Procrastinators Among Us." *The Harvard Crimson.* May 10, 2002.

211 Greene, Howard R. and Greene, Matthew. *Inside the Top Colleges*, 49.

212 FAS Office of the Registrar online. July 28, 2002.

213 Balliet, Douglas, quoted in Vascellaro, Jessica. "Teaching Fellows Under Fire." *The Harvard Crimson.* November 16, 2001.

214 Walthall, Marna. "More Bureaucracy: Grade Complaints." *The Harvard Independent.* January 29, 1997.

215 Rakoczy, Kate. "Faculty Alters Grading, Honors." *The Harvard Crimson.* May 22, 2002.

216 The Crimson Staff. "A Vicious Spiral." February 12, 2002.

217 The Crimson Staff. "A Collapse of Critical Judgment." *The Harvard Crimson.* February 11, 2002.

218 Rakoczy, Kate. "Academy Report Reveals Grade Inflation Nationwide." *The Harvard Crimson.* February 1, 2002.

219 Rakoczy, Kate. "Faculty Alters Grading, Honors." *The Harvard Crimson.* May 22, 2002.

220 Rakoczy, Kate. "Faculty Agrees Grade Inflation Troubling," *The Harvard Crimson.* November 21, 2001.

221 Quirk, Matthew. "Hope Springs Eternal: General Studies Debunked." *The Harvard Crimson.* April 6, 2000.

222 Cambell, David. "Under the Gun: Choosing A Field." *The Harvard Crimson.* April 13, 1998.

223 FAS Office of the Registrar online. August 11, 2002.

224 The *Fifteen Minutes* Staff. "The Chart." *Fifteen Minutes.* April 25, 2002.

225 Marek, Angie. "Special Education." *Fifteen Minutes.* April 25, 2002.

226 Murphy, Carlye. "Not So Special?" *The Harvard Independent.* February 5, 1998.

227 Gibbon, Brendan. "Students Criticize Theory Emphasis." *The Harvard Crimson.* March 11, 1996.

228 Funke, Jeremy, quoted in Dolgonos, Sarah and Pasternack, Claire. "In a Liberal Arts College, Students Find Their Own Pre-professional Tracks." *The Harvard Crimson.* June 6, 2002.

229 Darling, Sarah, quoted in Studlien, Kirsten. "A Different Tone." *The Harvard Crimson.* December 7, 2000.

230 Anderson, Emily. "Distinction Popular But Underpublicized." *The Harvard Crimson.* May 6, 2002, and FAS Office of the Registrar online. August 18, 2002. <www.registrar.fas.harvard.edu/>.

231 Core Program Guide. March 28, 2003.

232 The Crimson Staff. "The Core Must Go." *The Harvard Crimson.* June 4, 2001.

233 Murg, Stephanie and Moura, Andre. "In Defense of the Core." *The Harvard Crimson.* February 13, 2001.

234 The Crimson Staff. "Petition Process Flawed." *The Harvard Crimson.* February 5, 2001.

235 Light, Richard. *Making the Most of College*, 78–80.

236 FAS Office of the Registrar online. August 11, 2002.

237 Conrad, Parker. "Course 'Unaccounted' for at Harvard College." *The Harvard Crimson.* September 30, 1999.

238 Ruder, Debra Bradley. "Study Abroad: Broadening Students' Horizons." *The Harvard Gazette.* September 25, 1997.

239 Boguchwal, Audrey. "Abroad View." *Fifteen Minutes.* March 14, 2002.

240 No author attributed. "John Harvard's Journal: Study Abroad, Honors at Home." *Harvard Magazine.* July-August 2002.

241 Rakoczy, Kate. "College to Revamp Study Abroad." *The Harvard Crimson.* November 2, 2001.

242 No author attributed. "John Harvard's Journal: Study Abroad, Honors at Home." *Harvard Magazine.* July-August 2002.

243 Homsey, Margaretta. "Reforms Spur Students to Pursue Study Abroad." *The Harvard Crimson.* November 25, 2002.

244 Diamond, Lori. "Taking Time Off." *The Harvard Crimson.* February 22, 1997.

245 Jaffe, Lonne. "Take It and Enjoy It." *The Harvard Crimson.* February 9, 1998.

246 Maytal, Anat. "Thesis Writers Find Unexpected Rewards." *The Harvard Crimson.* May 17, 2002.

247 McGrath, Sarah. "Write, Don't Write: Should You Write a Thesis?" *The Harvard Independent.* September 28, 1995.

248 Wexler, Stephanie. "Harvard Lacks Training for Artists." *The Harvard Crimson.* June 9, 1994.

249 No author attributed. "John Harvard's Journal: Amending Advising." *Harvard Magazine.* March-April, 2002.

250 Lewis, Harry. "Report on Harvard College, 1995–2000." August 20, 2002. www.college.harvard.edu/dean/annualreport2000/>, January 2, 2001.

251 No author attributed. "John Harvard's Journal: Amending Advising." *Harvard Magazine.* March-April, 2002.

252 Huang, Jessica, quoted in Adams, William and Ganguli, Ishani. "The Proctor Gamble." *The Harvard Crimson.* November 29, 2001.

253 Samuels, Susan, ed. *The Crimson Key Guidebook to Harvard University.* (Cambridge, MA: President and the Fellows of Harvard University, 1998), 215–216.

254 Michelstein, Erica. "Sidebar Rating the Recruiting Process." *The Harvard Crimson.* October 29, 1999.

255 Paley, Amit. "Kick-Off Recruiting Meeting Attracts Hundreds of Students." *The Harvard Crimson.* September 27, 2000.

256 Skier, Stephanie. "Career Fair Disappoints Many." *The Harvard Crimson.* October 19, 2001.

257 Pierson, Hunter, quoted in McPherson, F. Reynolds. "A+ for Effort." *The Harvard Crimson.* November 17, 2000.

258 Mehta, Jal. "Deconstructing Harvard" *The Harvard Crimson.* June 9, 1999.

259 Trowbridge-Cooney, Nicola, quoted in Arenson, Adam. "What Are House Libraries For?" *The Harvard Crimson.* December 8, 2000.

260 Carter, Alex. "Mission Impossible: Finding Library Books." *The Harvard Crimson.* December 3, 1996.

261 Graham, Cary, quoted in Nyren, Alex. "More Fun in the Stacks." *The Harvard Independent.* November 19, 1998.

262 No writer attributed. "Let Us Into Langdell." *The Harvard Crimson.* April 28, 1999.

263 Ungar, Jonathan. "Harvard E-Mail Debuts on Web." *The Harvard Crimson.* April 10, 2002.

264 The Staff of *The Harvard Gazette.* "Queen Latifah Crowned Artist of the Year by Harvard Foundation." *The Harvard Gazette.* February 20, 2003

265 Fahrenthold, David. "Get on the Bus." *The Harvard Crimson.* November 20, 1997.

266 Rosenbaum, Laura. "Six Guys Named J." *The Harvard Crimson.* April 21, 1997.

267 Shen, Andrea, Harvard College Office of Communications. Email letter. September 18, 2002.

338 Pineiro, Mike, quoted in Petrosino, Frankie. "Out of Holworthy." *The Harvard Independent.* March 25, 1999.

339 Santini, Marina, quoted in Stone, Kaya. "Covering the Spectrum?" *The Harvard Independent.* February 27, 1997.

340 Keller, Morton and Keller, Phyllis. *Making Harvard Modern*, 474.

341 Paley, Amit. "Two Students Accused of Theft." *The Harvard Crimson.* June 6, 2002.

342 Alberts, Hana. "Grad Student Arrested for Murder." *The Harvard Crimson.* April 11, 2003.

343 No speaker attributed, quoted in Greene, Howard R. and Greene, Matthew. *Inside the Top Colleges*, 94.

344 Fenster, Robert. "Space To Slow Down." *The Harvard Crimson.* October 3, 2001.

345 Hicks, George. "Livin' La Vida Loker." *The Harvard Crimson.* October 15, 1999.

346 Derman, Joshua. "Put on Something Sexy and Hit the Stacks." *The Harvard Crimson.* March 12, 1999.

347 No writer attributed. 100 Reasons Why Harvard Sucks. *The Harvard Crimson.* April 22, 1999.

348 Hallett, Victoria. "From Barbeque to Kegerator: Harvard's Party Suites." *The Harvard Crimson.* April 16, 1999.

349 Grossman, Nicholas and de Charette, Valerie, ed. *The Unofficial Guide to Life at Harvard 2001–2002*. (Cambridge: Unofficial Publications, 2002).

350 Corliss, Cody. "Just punch Me." *The Harvard Independent.* November 2, 2000.

351 Unattributed Final Club member. "Final Clubs Stereotyped." *The Harvard Crimson.* February 23, 1999.

352 Lewis, Harry. "From the Top." *The Harvard Independent.* October 29, 1998.

353 Franken, Thomasin D. et al. "Rape Happens at Harvard." *The Harvard Crimson.* November 8, 2001.

354 Koster, R. Lane, quoted in Franken, Thomasin D. et al. "Rape Happens at Harvard." *The Harvard Crimson.* November 8, 2001.

355 Unattributed Final Club member, quoted in Franken, Thomasin D. et al. "Rape Happens at Harvard." *The Harvard Crimson*. November 8, 2001.

356 Melendez, Vanessa. "No Shame in Having Fun." The Harvard Crimson. November 9, 1998.

357 Estabrook, Helen, quoted in Franken, Thomasin D. et al. "Rape Happens at Harvard." *The Harvard Crimson*. November 8, 2001.

358 Matthew, Chiqui, quoted in Nyren, Alex. "A Final Approach." *The Harvard Independent*. April 13, 2000.

359 Flood, Joseph and McPherson, F. Reynolds. "Students Binge Less, But Hurt More By Others' Drinking." *The Harvard Crimson*. February 9, 2001.

360 Wechsler, Henry. "A Hard Look at Binge Drinking." *The Harvard Crimson*. February 15, 2001.

361 Greene, Howard R. and Greene, Matthew. *Inside the Top* Colleges. (New York: HarperCollins, 1999), 153.

362 Flood, Joseph and McPherson, F. Reynolds. "Students Binge Less, But Hurt More By Others' Drinking." *The Harvard Crimson*. February 9, 2001.

363 *The Harvard Independent* Staff. "IndyPolls . . . Freshman Drinking." *The Harvard Independent*. November 11, 1999.

364 Dry, Rachel and Usher, Nicole. "Survey Confirms Alcohol Stereotypes." *The Harvard Crimson*. February 12, 2001.

365 No speaker attributed, quoted in Buchanan, Catherine. "A View From the Old World." *The Harvard Independent*. November 11, 1999.

366 Lewis, Harry. "Dean Lewis Speaks Out." *The Harvard Independent*. November 11, 1999.

367 Lamas, Daniela. "Inconsistently Applied: UHS and Alcohol Policy." *The Harvard Crimson*. February 8, 2001.

368 Greene, Howard R. and Greene, Matthew. *Inside the Top Colleges,* 154.

369 Zuckerman, Elizabeth. "Harvard's High Achievers." *The Harvard Crimson*. January 25, 1999.

370 Cohen, Adrianne. "Students' Health at Harvard Favorable." *The Harvard Crimson*. October 1, 2001.

371 Winkler, Lauren. "Welcome to the Jungle." *The Harvard Independent.* October 21, 1999.

372 Zuckerman, Elizabeth. "Harvard's High Achievers." *The Harvard Crimson.* January 25, 1999.

373 Paley, Amit. "Study Finds Marijuana Use Up on Campuses." *The Harvard Crimson.* November 1, 2000.

374 Lester, Amelia. "How Harvard Gets High." *Fifteen Minutes.* March 14, 2002.

375 Conrad, Parker. "Students Forced to Find Love in Greeks or On-line." *The Harvard Crimson.* June 10, 1999.

376 Cohen, Adrianne. "Where Are We to Flirt." *The Harvard Crimson.* October 30, 2001.

377 Carlson, Drew, editor in chief, *The Harvard Independent.* Email letter. September 15, 2002, and No writer attributed. "The Indy Survey." *The Harvard Independent.* May 2, 2002.

378 Stevenson, Jason. "Love Seasonings." *The Harvard Independent.* April 24, 1997.

379 Stellato, Jesse and Kwok, Judy. "A 'Date' is not a Fruit." *The Harvard Independent.* April 13, 2000.

380 Andras T. Forgacs, quoted in Schacter, Erica. "The Singles." *The Harvard Crimson.* February 14, 1996.

381 Mehta, Jal. "Deconstructing Harvard." *The Harvard Crimson.* June 9, 1999.

382 Taxin, Adam. "Whining and Dining Your Date." *The Harvard Crimson.* February 20, 1993.

383 Carlin, Tova, "Four Semesters and a Wedding: Did you know..." *The Harvard Independent.* February 26, 1998.

384 Cuellar, A. Maximo, quoted in Colby, Edward. "Interracial Dating." *The Harvard Crimson.* November 12, 1999.

385 Rhodes, Christopher. "Driving In." *The Harvard Independent.* May 2, 2002.

386 No writer attributed. "The Indy Survey." *The Harvard Independent.* May 3, 2001.

387 Laskey, Alexander. "Harvard Sex Life Endures." *The Harvard Crimson.* March 19, 1996.

388 The Flare Staff. "Sex at Harvard." *Flare*. October 11, 2001.

389 Cohen, Adrianne. "Students' Health at Harvard Favorable." *The Harvard Crimson*. October 1, 2001.

390 Alexakis, Georgia and Diamond, Lori. Harvard Assists Student Mothers." *The Harvard Crimson*. December 15, 1997.

391 Meng, Sue. "Our Town." *The Harvard Crimson*. October 11, 2001.

392 Rubalcava, Alex. "The Real Purpose of the Square." *The Harvard Square*. May 14, 2001.

393 Graff, Garrett. "Harvard Crime Surge Connected to Cambridge Increase." *The Harvard Crimson*. November 29, 2000.

394 Kinen, Glenn. "Little Fish in a Big Pond." *The Harvard Independent*. April 22, 1999.

395 Flood, Joseph. "Police Reports Released in Palmer-Sherman Accident." *The Harvard Crimson*. March 14, 2001.

396 Ashkey, Susan. "At a Standstill." *The Harvard Crimson*. September 28, 2000.

397 Colby, Edward, quoted in Grizzle, Benjamin. "Stereotypes of Students Prevail Among Locals." *The Harvard Crimson*. November 3, 2000.

398 Greene, Howard R. and Greene, Matthew. *Inside the Top Colleges,* 270.

399 Grigsby, J. Elisenda, quoted in Chen, Susan. "Students Ignore Boston's Allure." *The Harvard Crimson*. December 9, 1994.

400 Hanlon, Seth, quoted in Chen, Susan. "Students Ignore Boston's Allure." *The Harvard Crimson*. December 9, 1994.

401 Alexakis, Georgia. "Five Minutes of Your Time." The Harvard Crimson. June 8, 2000.

402 Plants, Todd. "The President's Priorities." *The Harvard Crimson*. March 12, 2001.

403 Seltzer, Sarah. "Seen and Not Heard." *The Harvard Crimson*. June 6, 2002.

404 Sattar, Madhita. "The Facts." *The Harvard Independent*. February 21, 2002.

405 Harvey, Gordon. *Writing with Sources*. (Cambridge: Hackett Publishing Co., 1998), 22–23, 25–27, 30.

406 Greene, Howard R. and Greene, Matthew. *Inside the Top* Colleges, 63.

407 The Crimson Staff. "Rape Happens at Harvard." *The Harvard Crimson.* October 25, 2000.

408 Smith, Stephen. "Surviving Sexual Assault." *The Harvard Crimson.* October 24, 2000.

409 Cohen, Adrianne. "Students' Health at Harvard Favorable." *The Harvard Crimson.* October 1, 2001.

410 Greene, Howard R. and Greene, Matthew. *Inside the Top* Colleges, 169.

411 McIntyre, Joyce. "Clothesline Insufficient." *The Harvard Crimson.* April 16, 2002.

412 Kofol, Anne. "Rally Protests Sexual Assault Policy Change." *The Harvard Crimson.* May 17, 2002.

413 Vanier, Lexy. "One Small Step for Harvard, One Giant Tiptoe for Women." *The Harvard Independent.* October 3, 2002.

414 Franken, Thomasin D. et al. "Rape Happens at Harvard." *The Harvard Crimson.* November 8, 2001.

415 Kofol, Anne. "Coalition Seeks Grant To Combat Sexual Violence." *The Harvard Crimson.* April 11, 2002.

416 Franken, Thomasin D. et al. "Rape Happens at Harvard." *The Harvard Crimson.* November 8, 2001.

417 Zernike, Kate. "Campus Court at Harvard Alters Policy on Evidence." *The New York Times.* May 9, 2002.

418 Seltzer, Sarah. "Revised Sexual Assault Policy Affirmed." *The Harvard Crimson.* April 2, 2003.

419 Quoted in Zernike, Kate. "Campus Court at Harvard Alters Policy on Evidence." *The New York Times.* May 9, 2002.

420 Cited in Honig, Ellenor and Murphy, Wendy. "Skirting Campus Rape." *The Harvard Crimson.* September 9, 2002.

421 Honig, Ellenor and Murphy, Wendy. "Skirting Campus Rape." *The Harvard Crimson.* September 9, 2002.

422 The Crimson Staff. "Title IX Complaint Questionable." *The Harvard Crimson.* September 18, 2002.

423 Sombuntham, Nalina. "Complaint Filed on Sexual Assault Change." *The Harvard Crimson.* June 5, 2002.

424 Seltzer, Sarah. "Revised Sexual Assault Policy Affirmed." *The Harvard Crimson.* April 2, 2003.

425 McIntyre, Joyce. UHS Patients: Results Unsurprising." *The Harvard Crimson.* September 23, 2001.

426 Kovner, Rachel. "Student Survey Blasts UHS Care." *The Harvard Crimson.* September 23, 1999.

427 Thernstrom, Melanie. *Halfway Heaven.* (New York: Plume, 1997), 158.

428 Cohen, Adrianne. "Students' Health at Harvard Favorable." *The Harvard Crimson.* October 1, 2001.

429 Anonymous student, quoted in Adams, William. "When Success Encounters Failure." *Fifteen Minutes.* April 8, 2004.

430 Catlin, Randolph. "Confronting Suicide." *The Harvard Crimson.* December 10, 1993.

431 Wasserstein, Ben. "Getting In." *The Harvard Crimson.* September 27, 2001.

432 Wand, Rebecca. "At Harvard, Eating Disorders Common." *The Harvard Crimson.* November 4, 1994.

433 Cohen, Adrianne. "Students' Health at Harvard Favorable." *The Harvard Crimson.* October 1, 2001.

434 Greene, Howard R. and Greene, Matthew. *Inside the Top Colleges,* 207.

435 No speaker attributed quoted in Greene, Howard R. and Greene, Matthew. *Inside the Top Colleges.* (New York: HarperCollins, 1999), 206.

436 Friedman, Rachel, quoted in "Are You Quite Well?" *Fifteen Minutes.* November 30, 2000.

437 Schloming, Damian, quoted in Thernstrom, Melanie. *Halfway Heaven.* (New York: Plume, 1997), 167.

438 Nguyen, Alexander. "Ordinary People." *The Harvard Crimson.* April 5, 1999.

439 Lim, Peggy, ed. *The Women's Guide to Harvard*, 218.

440 Jacoby, Sarah. "Help Is Just a Phone Call Away." *The Harvard Crimson.* October 26, 1998.

441 Ibid.

442 Bohlen, William. "A Visit to Room 13: A Friendly Late Night Ear." *The Harvard Crimson.* February 26, 1999.

443 Wand, Rebecca. "At Harvard, Eating Disorders Common." *The Harvard Crimson.* November 4, 1994.

444 Kaplan, Katharine. "College Faces Mental Health Crisis." *The Harvard Crimson.* January 12, 2004.

445 Ibid.

446 Kadison, Richard. "Facts and Figures" *The Harvard Independent.* March 25, 1999.

447 Nguyen, Alexander. "Ordinary People." *The Harvard Crimson.* April 5, 1999.

448 Thernstrom, Melanie. *Halfway Heaven*, 162.

449 Rao, Sandhya. "Falling Through the Safety Net." *The Harvard Crimson.* February 8, 1994.

450 Kovner, Rachel. "Student Survey Blasts UHS Care." *The Harvard Crimson.* September 23, 1999.

451 Kaplan, Katherine. "College Faces Mental Health Crisis." *The Harvard Crimson.* January 12, 2004.

452 Thernstrom, Melanie. *Halfway Heaven*, 157.

453 Lewis, Harry. "Romance and Love at Harvard." *The Harvard Crimson.* February 12, 1999.

454 Greene, Howard R. and Greene, Matthew. *Inside the Top Colleges,* 248-250.

455 Lewis, Harry. "Report on Harvard College, 1995–2000." August 20, 2002. www.college.harvard.edu/dean/annualreport2000/>, January 2, 2001.

456 Lewis, Harry. "Romance and Love at Harvard." *The Harvard Crimson.* February 12, 1999.

457 Mehta, Jal. "Deconstructing Harvard." *The Harvard Crimson.* June 9, 1999.

458 Kovner, Rachel. "A Hundred Different Harvards." *The Harvard Crimson.* June 7, 2001.

ABOUT THE AUTHOR

Dov Fox was born in Rehovot, Israel, and attended William H. Hall Public High School in West Hartford, Connecticut, where he was a member of the Math Club, Latin Team, and *Magic* Card Society. Curiously, the ability to recite digits of Pi, conjugate the verb "to squat," and wage pixie gnomes against goblin trolls did not score him the babes. Currently a junior living on campus in Cambridge, Massachusetts, he volunteers at a student-run homeless shelter in Harvard Square, does legal aid work for low-income tenants in Boston, and performs stand-up comedy at clubs around New England. He is planning to write a senior thesis on the ethics of biotechnological enhancement and to graduate from Harvard College in 2004 with an honors degree in government.

NOTES

NOTES

NOTES

www.PrincetonReview.com

The Princeton Review Admissions Services

At The Princeton Review, we care about your ability to get accepted to the best sch[o] for you. But, we all know getting accepted involves much more than just doing well standardized tests. That's why, in addition to our test preparation services, we also offer fr admissions services to students looking to enter college or graduate school. You can find the services on our website, *www.PrincetonReview.com*, the best online resource for researchir applying to, and learning about how to pay for college.

No matter what type of program you're applying to—undergraduate, graduate, la business, or medical—**www.PrincetonReview.com has the free tools, services, a advice you need to navigate the admissions process.**

Read on to learn more about the services we offer.

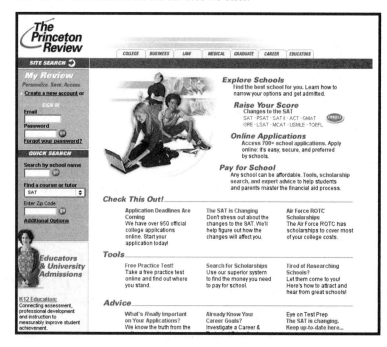

Research Schools
www.PrincetonReview.com/Research

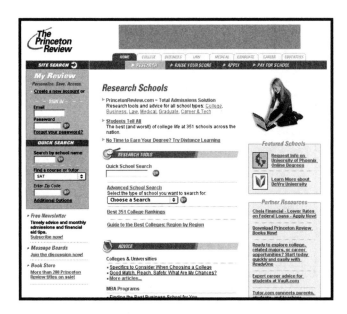

www.PrincetonReview.com features interactive searches. **Counselor-O-Matic** allows you to enter stats and information about yourself to find a list of your best match, reach, and safety colleges. From there you can read statistical and editorial information about thousands of colleges and universities. In addition, you can find out what currently enrolled college students say about their schools. When you use the **Advanced School Search** in any of the grad school centers, you can also find a list of schools that match your qualifications and preferences..

Our **College Majors Search** is one of the most popular features we offer. Here you can read profiles on hundreds of majors to find information on curriculum, salaries, careers, and the appropriate high school preparation, as well as colleges that offer it. From the Majors Search, you can investigate corresponding careers, read **Career Profiles**, and learn what career is the best match for you by taking our **Career Quiz**. The **Graduate School Program Search** allows you to read about hundreds of grad school programs and find which schools offer them.

No matter what type of school or specialized program you are considering, **www.PrincetonReview.com has free articles and advice, in addition to our tools, to help you make the right choice.**

Apply to School
www.PrincetonReview.com/Apply

For most students, completing the school application is the most stressful part of t admissions process. www.PrincetonReview.com's powerful **Online School Applicati Engine** makes it easy to apply.

Paper applications are mostly a thing of the past. And, our hundreds of partner schoc tell us they prefer to receive your applications online.

Using our online application service is simple:

- Enter information once and the common data automatically transfers onto each application.
- Save your applications and access them at any time to edit and perfect.
- Submit electronically or print and mail in.
- Pay your application fee online, using an e-check, or mail the school a check.

Our powerful application engine is built to accommodate all your needs.

Pay for School
www.PrincetonReview.com/Finance

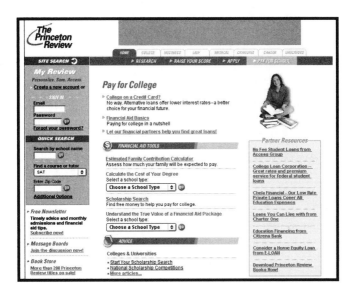

The financial aid process is confusing for everyone. But don't worry. Our free online tools, services, and advice can help you plan for the future and get the money you need to pay for school.

Our **Scholarship Search** engine will help you find free money, although often scholarships alone won't cover the cost of high tuitions. So, we offer other tools and resources to help you navigate the entire process.

Filling out the FAFSA and CSS PROFILE can be a daunting process, use our **strategies for both forms** to make sure you answer the questions correctly the first time.

If scholarships and government aid aren't enough to swing the cost of tuition, we'll help you secure student loans. The Princeton Review has partnered with a select group of reputable financial institutions who will help **explore all your loans options**.

If you know how to work the financial aid process, you'll learn you don't have to **eliminate a school based on tuition.**

Be a Part of the
www.PrincetonReview.com Community

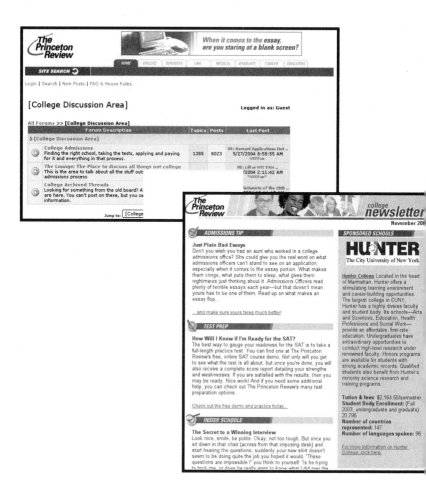

PrincetonReview.com's **Discussion Boards** and **Free Newsletters** are additional services to help you get information about the admissions process from your peers and from The Princeton Review experts.

Book Store

www.PrincetonReview.com/college/Bookstore.asp

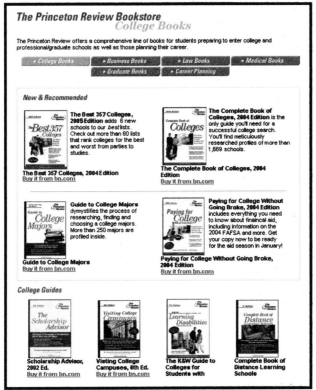

In addition to this book, we publish hundreds of other titles, including guidebooks that highlight life on campus, student opinion, and all the statistical data you need to know about any school you are considering. Just a few of the titles we offer are:

- Marching to College: Turning Military Experience into College Admissions
- The Truth About Harvard: A Behind the Scenes Look at admissions and Life on Campus
- How to Save for College
- The Best 357 Colleges
- The K&W Guide to Colleges for Students with Learning Disabilities or Attention Deficit Disorder
- Paying for College Without Going Broke

For a complete listing of all of our titles, visit our **online bookstore**:

www.princetonreview.com/college/bookstore.asp